# EUROPE BETWEEN EAST AND WEST

# EUROPE BETWEEN EAST AND WEST

## IN COSMIC AND HUMAN HISTORY

Twelve lectures for members of the Anthroposophical Society held in Munich between 13 September 1914 and 4 May 1918

TRANSLATED BY CHRISTIANA BRYAN
INTRODUCTION BY TERRY M. BOARDMAN

RUDOLF STEINER

RUDOLF STEINER PRESS

CW 174a

*The publishers gratefully acknowledge the generous funding of the translation of these lectures by the Anthroposophical Society of Great Britain*

Rudolf Steiner Press
Hillside House, The Square
Forest Row, RH18 5ES

www.rudolfsteinerpress.com

Published by Rudolf Steiner Press 2024

Originally published in German under the title *Mitteleuropa Zwischen Ost und West. Kosmische und Menschliche Geschichte Band VI* (volume 174a in the *Rudolf Steiner Gesamtausgabe* or Collected Works) by Rudolf Steiner Verlag, Dornach. Based on shorthand notes that were not reviewed or revised by the speaker. This authorized translation is based on the second German edition (1982), edited by Helmut von Wartburg and Robert Friedenthal

Published by permission of the Rudolf Steiner Nachlassverwaltung, Dornach



A catalogue record for this book is available from the British Library

ISBN 978 1 85584 662 3

Cover by Morgan Creative
Typeset by Symbiosys Technologies, Visakhapatnam, India
Printed and bound by 4Edge Ltd., Essex

# Contents

# Publisher's Note

This volume contains lectures given to members of the Anthroposophical Society in Munich during the First World War, 1914–1918. Collected Works volume 174b combines the lectures held in Stuttgart during the same period (*The Spiritual Background to the First World War*, Rudolf Steiner Press 2024).

# Introduction

It is not only military men who know and say that the best-laid plans do not survive contact with the enemy—that war is unpredictable and one never knows where it will lead and what will come out of it. Many people in the two decades before the outbreak of what was soon called the 'Great War' in 1914 never imagined that Europe, in the 'progressive', new twentieth century would fall into a terrible, pan-European war catastrophe as had been the case in the Napoleonic era. Europe was now far too advanced for that, they said; its economies were too interdependent, its values no longer so primitive. The shock was therefore all the greater when the assassin's bullets fired in an obscure Balkan town in June 1914 resulted not only in just such a European war catastrophe only 34 days later, but a conflict that spanned the world. A few, more insightful people had seen the disaster looming, however. Rudolf Steiner had been one of them, although he had still hoped that it might yet be avoided. In Vienna in the spring of 1914, he had given lectures[1] in which he spoke about 'the cultural carcinoma' that had developed in European society over recent centuries, a disease rooted in materialism, and which had resulted, amongst other things, from overproduction in capitalist economies, their consequent need for cheap labour, and hence the poisonous class conflicts that were so violent and tense throughout Europe on the eve of the Great War.

A major factor in these class conflicts was the bourgeois comfort in which the middle classes lived, insulated from the suffering of the workers and farmers. This lack of interest and concern for the lives

[1] *The Inner Nature of Man and the Life Between Death and Rebirth* (Collected Works GA 153), Vienna, 14 April 1914.

of others is a major feature of the lectures in the present volume. A terrible result of this 'cultural carcinoma' was the Communism which, in the crisis of the war, seized upon Russia from late 1917 and then overshadowed Europe and the world for the next 72 years. In 1910 in Oslo (then Christiania), Steiner had given a cycle of lectures in which he had spoken about the urgent need for Europeans to understand the archangelic spiritual forces (Folk Spirits) that guided, shaped and informed their cultures, and to see how these mighty beings were related to each other in the ways that tribes, nations and races emerged, flourished and faded in history. War, then and now, has been one of the worst consequences when such understanding has been absent. Fascism and Nazism were both consequences of the Great War of 1914-1918.

Many people were also shocked by the conflict that broke out—or rather, suddenly expanded—in February 2022. As in 1914, they too had not seen it coming or else had felt that such a conflict was not possible in our advanced European civilization of the twenty-first century, interlinked by all its telecoms and AI technology, its smart-phone-connected younger generation. The mass media have tended not to show pictures of the old red Soviet flags flying on some Russian tanks fighting in the Donbass or the swastikas and other Third Reich imagery openly displayed on some tanks and uniforms of the soldiers of the Armed Forces of Ukraine. As we have seen so many times since 'the end of the Cold War' in 1989-1991, the shadows of the consequences of the Great War of 1914-1918 have been long indeed. Today, we are being told by European politicians that we are no longer in a postwar era (i.e. post-World War II or post-Cold War) but have entered a 'pre-war' era (analogous to the 1930s) and must prepare accordingly for war with nuclear-armed Russia.[2] The propaganda of 1914 and 1939 is being reheated. The only thing that can stem another catastrophe, says Rudolf Steiner in these twelve lectures, is consciousness, awareness, real insight into what is going on in our world, and that must include insight into the forces of the spiritual world which are reflected in and by current events.

[2] Grant Shapps, UK Defence Minister, in a speech on 15 January 2024.

To develop this insight, Steiner urges, we must expand our active interest in contemporary events along with our understanding of spiritual-scientific principles.

*

The twelve lectures in this book were originally all given by Rudolf Steiner to members of the Anthroposophical Society in the city of Munich, the capital of Bavaria, southern Germany, on eight visits to that city during the First World War, 1914-1918. The overall German title given to the lectures was *Mitteleuropa Zwischen Ost und West, Kosmische und Menschliche Geschichte, Band VI* (Central Europe Between East and West. Cosmic and Human History Volume VI, which is GA 174a of Steiner's *Gesamtausgabe*, or Collected Works).

The first four lectures were given on four separate visits, two in late 1914 and two in the spring and autumn of 1915. During this period Steiner gave many lectures about the Folk Souls and Folk Spirits of the European peoples in relation to Christ and also about experiences on crossing the threshold of death.[3] The next two lectures are from a visit in March 1916, in the first of which Steiner addresses recent criticism of himself by Annie Besant, president of the Theosophical Society. The immediate background to this is the separation of Steiner's pupils from the Theosophical Society in 1912-1913 and the founding of the Anthroposophical Society in 1913. The deeper background lies in the aims of Western occult groups and the differences between the East, West and Central European approaches to spirituality, all of which are discussed in the lectures in this book.

The two lectures from March 1916 are followed by two lectures from a visit to Munich in May 1917. In these, Steiner took up certain problems that had recently been emerging in the Anthroposophical Society, and also spoke about the principle of humanity's 'decreasing age' in contrast with the *increasing* age of human individuals. This was

---

[3] See, for example, the lectures contained *The Destinies of Individuals and of Nations* (GA 157), Rudolf Steiner Press 1986.

something he had researched the previous winter. He also addressed the threefold nature of the human being and the Eighth Council of Constantinople in the year 869. The last four lectures were given in 1918, two in February and two in May. Amongst other things, the February lectures address communication with the dead, a subject on the hearts of countless bereaved family members who had lost loved ones in the war, and also the struggle between the Archangel Michael and his spiritual opponent Ahriman since the 1840s. The final pair of lectures, from May 1918, deal with growing opposition to anthroposophy, with the effects of the Folk Spirits, and with certain growing contemporary phenomena: bigotry in thinking, a mean-spirited pedantry in feeling, and clumsy ineptitude in willing, and how to overcome them.

*

From August 1914 Germany was fighting on two fronts, against Britain and France in the West and against Russia in the East. The well-equipped Russian armies invaded German East Prussia on 17 August, some two weeks before the main German armies in the West entered northern France from Belgium. The day before the first lecture in this book, the German strategy for the invasion of France had failed at the Battle of the Marne (5-12 Sept.). Later that autumn, mobile warfare in the West would cease and a fixed system of trenches would stretch from the Channel to Switzerland. This remained basically static, despite massive assaults to breach it by both sides, until the summer of 1918 when, after the German Spring Offensive had failed, a war of mobility finally resumed, and the Allies, reinforced now by large numbers of American troops, began to push the Germans back towards their own borders. For four long years, Germany and its ally Austria-Hungary—which was itself engaged against Russia in the East and against Serbia and Italy in the South—faced enemies all around them (except Scandinavia), a strategic situation of encirclement that had resulted from carefully constructed Anglo-French-Russian diplomacy over the period 1887-1907 as well as by the Germans' own errors.

Looking at Europe's spiritual crisis in the war from his vantage point in German-speaking Central Europe (Germany, Austria and German-speaking Switzerland), Rudolf Steiner saw that the Western Powers of Britain and France were actually led from *behind the scenes* of their much-vaunted 'democracies' by the ancient, desiccated forces of Freemasonry—much stronger then than they are today—while to the East, Russia was guided by the semi-mystical rituals of the even more ancient forces of Orthodox monarchy and religion, which reached back to Byzantium and the late Roman Empire. Steiner himself had sought to unite the achievements of modern natural science with a new, esoteric Christian understanding that was not Protestant, Roman Catholic or Orthodox. He recognized that our modern age—which began in the fifteenth century and has the task of developing what he called the Consciousness Soul (and sometimes the Spiritual Soul), the individual understanding of oneself as a *spiritual* being in this material world—is led in a sense by the *economic* motivations of the English-speaking peoples of northwest Europe and their North American offshoot, just as the previous epoch had been led by the *political* motivations of the peoples of southern Europe, the Greeks and the Romans.

In our current epoch, which will last until the mid-fourth millennium, the leadership by the English-speaking peoples will in its first part be of an external and material nature. But the role of the English-speaking peoples in *natural* science, politics and economic life needs to be complemented by what Central Europe can contribute in the cultural and spiritual sphere. This is where Steiner saw the task of *spiritual* science, or anthroposophy. In order to lead development in a healthy way in this present epoch, the English-speaking peoples need to collaborate with the peoples of Central Europe and not seek to dominate or ignore them. Moreover, in these lectures Steiner emphasizes that it is a vital need *for the future* that Central and Eastern Europe also collaborate and not fight or hate each other. In the epoch after ours, which will begin in the fourth millennium, it will be the Slavic peoples of Eastern Europe and Russia that will have the 'vanguard' role to help humanity create a new form of genuine community life based not on the ancient forces of blood and heredity but on inspired feeling and spiritual insight. This has to be *prepared* today and not *undermined*, which it was in the twentieth century in the two huge wars *between* Central and Eastern Europe and the subsequent *division* of Europe between those two regions—a disastrous process that was very much steered from the West.[4] In February 2015, in a speech in Chicago titled 'Europe: Destined for Conflict?' the American geostrategic analyst George Friedman revealed something that no Western politician had ever dared mention in public but which, he said, had actually driven the policy of the USA for over 100 years: 'The primordial interest of the United States over which, for a century, we have fought wars, the First, Second and Cold War, has been the relationship between Germany and Russia, because united, they are the only force that could threaten us—and to make sure that that doesn't happen.'

Because of the restrictions of wartime conditions, Rudolf Steiner could not travel abroad widely and had to hold his lectures in German-speaking regions. All the combatant populations in the first two years of the war, driven on by the propaganda of the state or the media, were largely possessed by a fiercely nationalistic or chauvinist mood. Until 1916, Steiner at first tried to deal with this mood not by condemning it outright but by encouraging his German-speaking listeners to re-evaluate and re-esteem those great achievements of German culture of the period 1750-1840 which were *not* of a nationalistic but of a universally human and individual nature. These had been much forgotten in Germany since the reunification in 1871. In the febrile nationalistic atmosphere of 1914 and 1915, Steiner sought to elevate the feelings of German-speakers away from chauvinistic attitudes of superiority and antipathy towards other peoples and towards the highest and essentially *human* faculties and achievements of German-speaking culture. He had, after all, sensibly chosen to relocate the centre of his activities from Berlin, Stuttgart and Munich to Dornach, near Basel, in the neutral country of Switzerland, and during the war, people from some seventeen countries, including many from

---

[4] See R. Steiner, *The Karma of Untruthfulness, Vols. I and II* (GA 173, 174), Rudolf Steiner Press 2005.

opposite sides in the war, collaborated in Dornach in the construction and decoration of the Goetheanum building, which was intended to be the new centre of the anthroposophical movement and was designed by Steiner himself.

This multinational effort could itself be seen as an example of the future collaboration of European impulses: the new spiritual impulse coming from Central Europe, the new social (and non-Bolshevik!) impulse coming from Eastern Europe, and a physical impulse coming from the West. Steiner himself said, after the destruction of the Goetheanum by arson on the last night of 1922, that it was most regrettable that the people of the West would no longer be able to *see* the Goetheanum and the living wisdom that it visibly represented, for it is, he said, especially the English-speaking people of the West who feel the need to see the spirit realized in the physical world. Through those ten years of the construction of the Goetheanum, there were a few people from English-speaking countries working on it and one in particular, the sculptress Edith Maryon, had moved to Dornach in 1914. There she worked closely with Rudolf Steiner on the nine-metre-high wooden sculpture titled 'The Representative of Humanity', which was to be the artistic centrepiece of the building, and on one occasion, in the autumn of 1916, she saved him from serious injury and possibly even from death when he nearly fell from scaffolding.[5]

*

After the great defeats for both sides on the Western Front in the second half of 1916 at the battles of Verdun and the Somme, the enormous losses of the Russian armies in the East, and then the refusal of the Allies at Christmas and New Year to engage with German proposals for peace talks, there was a great change in the mood of the war. The enthusiastic, even exalted patriotism and nationalism of the first two years had by the end of 1916 given way to a resigned, grim

---

[5] Christoph Lindenberg, *Rudolf Steiner—Eine Chronik 1861-1925*, Verlag Freies Geistesleben 1988, p. 370.

determination to fight on until total victory, and the war became even more savage, ruthless and machine-like, increasingly driven by technological developments and the imperatives of state bureaucracies.

In June 1916, the commander-in-chief who had led Germany's armies in the first months of the war, Colonel-General Helmuth von Moltke (the Younger) died. His wife was one of Rudolf Steiner's earliest pupils, and Moltke himself became close to Steiner in the last two years before his death. After he died, a remarkable, indeed unique, series of conversations began between his soul and Rudolf Steiner which continued for seven years until July 1924.[6] After his death, Moltke's soul reflected deeply on his past life and continued to observe events on earth closely. He communicated these reflections and observations to Steiner, who passed them on to Moltke's widow, Eliza.

We can see a certain change in Steiner's view of the war after Moltke's death, most likely as a result of these communications with the late general. Steiner's earlier appeals to the higher nature of German-speakers and their cultural achievements in the age of Goethe and Schiller *et al.* receded and instead he focused more and more on the threefold nature of the human being and the threefold nature of European civilization and on the consequences for that civilization of the fateful decisions of the Eighth Ecumenical Council of Constantinople in the year 869, where, as Steiner explains it, the human *triad* of body, soul and spirit was effectively reduced through a new dogma to a *dyad* of body and soul only. The effects of this dogma (Canon XI of the Council) rumbled on through the centuries and had culminated in the Great War. They would go on into the future, creating more disasters, unless Europeans reawakened to the reality of the human triad and the threefold nature of human society (culture-politics-economy) and of Europe itself (East-Middle-West).

This new focus of his activities in the last two years of the war led Steiner eventually to launch the threefold movement for social renewal

---

[6] See T. H. Meyer, Ed., *Light for the new Millennium—Rudolf Steiner, Helmuth von Moltke, Eliza von Moltke: Letters, Documents and After-Death Communications*, Rudolf Steiner Press 1997.

amidst the social and political turmoil of the immediate postwar years 1919-1922, and also to a whole series of practically-oriented social initiatives in the fields of education, agriculture, health and medicine, curative work and finance and banking, alongside his earlier initiatives in the arts, which had begun in Munich in 1907. While one can certainly see connections between this later threefold focus and Steiner's earlier activities going back some 30 years, it is no exaggeration to say that his unique communications over the period 1916-1924 with the soul of Helmuth von Moltke, especially given the karmic destiny of that soul,[7] are likely to have played a significant part in Steiner's new focus after 1916. The question of the relations between East, Middle and West and their ramifications in numerous aspects of culture now urgently took centre stage in his thought, as the influence of America and Russia grew to cast overwhelming shadows from the West with Wilsonism[8] and from the East in Leninism.

The twelve lectures in this book can be seen in the context of this change in Rudolf Steiner's focus after 1916. Those from 1914 and 1915 addressed the cultural issues of the German-speaking world that reached back to the time of Kant, Goethe, Schiller, Fichte *et al.*, as well as aspects of the issues surrounding the parting of the ways between the Theosophical and the Anthroposophical Societies in 1912-1913, and how this was connected to the issues of the subsequent world war. The enormous death toll of the battles of 1914 and 1915 deeply shocked many Europeans. It had been a long time,

---

[7] Steiner's research revealed that the late General von Moltke had previously incarnated as the very significant mid-ninth century Pope Nicholas I (858-867), who had, for profound reasons, striven *at that time* to separate Roman Catholic and Orthodox Christianity. See note 6 above.

[8] Woodrow Wilson, 28th President of the USA, 1913-1921. His administration created the Federal Reserve system, invaded Mexico, took the USA into the First World War despite having promised to keep out of it, and in his 14 Points (Jan. 1918) programme, Wilson championed the League of Nations. At the Versailles Peace Conference of 1919, Wilson and his close adviser Col. Edward M. House played a key part in reconstructing the map of Europe, a continent which neither man knew well.

a hundred years, since there had been such massive death in warfare in Europe—and the shock of this directed people's attention to their loved ones who had suddenly crossed or might, at any time, suddenly cross the threshold of death, most of them young conscripts. Providing a compassionate understanding of the nature of the spiritual world on the other side of that threshold was thus one of Steiner's constant endeavours in the first two years of the war, and the lectures in 1914 and 1915 reflect this.

However, one feels that after 1916, while he continues to enlighten his listeners with important information about the spiritual world and about the nature of the human organism and relations between East, West and Middle, his own attitude, after the middle lecture of 20 March 1916, which is of a kind of transitional nature within this group of twelve lectures, changed to become firmer and grimmer, stricter even, as he had to witness the failures of many of those in the anthroposophical movement to overcome their inclinations towards comfort and sectarianism, despite the worsening situation of the war, and their reluctance to engage actively with the needs of people in the wider world.

The later lectures in this collection therefore have more of an urgent mood, encouraging and sometimes critically admonishing his listeners to make radical changes in their thinking. In the last lecture, for example, he notes a question asked by the young Austrian philosopher Otto Weininger (1880-1903): 'How do I become the continuer of the impulses of my soul and spirit that I had between my last death and my recent birth?' Steiner comments that many answer this question in the wrong way—through focusing on the nerves, blood, skin colour, muscles, i.e. through sex, genetics, racism. (This particular material focus would lead on to Fascism and Nazism after the war.) Weininger also asked: 'Why do we have no memories... of the time that flowed past before birth?' Such questions, says Steiner, can be answered by those who occupy themselves with spiritual science (anthroposophy) but only if all narrow-minded philistinism is removed:

> All bourgeois pettiness—all philistinism—has to recede. People sealing themselves off in narrow interest groups has to be systematically

> combatted. Certain questions have to be framed quite differently than has so far been the case. How did the religious evolution of the past millennia itself frame the question through which a few people are still able to relate to the spiritual?

That question was: 'What happens in my soul and spirit when I have gone through the gate of death?' Steiner's answer was that many people's motives here are egotistical, but if they were informed by spiritual science, they would ask: 'To what extent is life here on earth a continuation of the life I spent earlier in worlds of soul and spirit?' In his book *The Education of the Child from the Perspective of Spiritual Science* (1906), Steiner showed how children in the first seven years of their lives are primarily imitators:

> ...imitating—transposing yourself into others—is a continuation of the Intuitive world of the last third of existence between death and a new birth. You can still see—streaming into and illuminating their lives—that existence between death and rebirth if you observe children's lives in a meaningful way.

This, he says, will lead to a feeling of *responsibility*, not egotism, and people will come to feel that: 'I have to continue here what I was enjoined to do, in that I have brought with me a legacy from worlds of soul and spirit.' And furthermore:

> ...wanting to understand this 'Beyond' [the threefold spiritual world of Imagination, Inspiration and Intuition]—wanting to revere and recognize it—will become part of the newly-framed question about immortality, which will occur in spiritual evolution in a less egotistical way than the question of immortality did so widely throughout the evolution of religions in past millennia.

In relation to thinking, feeling and willing, he says that *it is vital that petty narrow-mindedness be overcome and that mobility in finding one's way into the circumstances of the world gains ground; that philistinism is overcome and open-hearted interest takes hold of human hearts; that clumsy ineptitude is overcome and people once more become skilled, educated to dexterity in the most varied areas of life. Learning to understand the world in the most varied areas of life! A skilful understanding, so as to be capable of dealing with the most diverse situations in life—this is what matters.*

All these are questions that are still of very great moment today when we struggle with issues of education in an age increasingly pervaded by technology, which threatens to draw children into virtual fantasy worlds away from the practical world of the five senses. Issues of war and peace, of political freedom and economic totalitarianism, of the decline and rebirth of religion, China's rise and the decline of the West, the so-called 'Clash of Civilizations', pseudo-empires versus the nation state, spiritualism and materialism, and in the middle of it all, the ongoing question as to the nature of the human being itself, when much-vaunted voices allied to global elites tell us 'the time of soul, spirit and free will is over'[9]—in all these issues spiritual forces of various kinds are moving.

*

In the later lectures in this book Steiner calls on his listeners to have the courage to face what is going on in the wider world. We certainly need such courage today. In this age when people intuitively rebel against the 'extinction' of nature but ignore the *spiritual* forces working through the world, we seem to be pushed—or are we pushing?—towards yet another great world conflict that might even prove terminal for humanity. Clearly, despite the hard lessons of two world wars and a Cold War, humanity did not sufficiently awaken to the truth of the human condition. Today, is such terrible pain and suffering, close to actual extinction, the only way that (what will be left of) humanity can awaken? In these twelve Munich lectures by Rudolf Steiner from the Great War of a century ago, there is much for us to learn about the spiritual impulses that will help us avoid a far worse catastrophe and plant the seeds of a better future.

*Terry M. Boardman*
*April 2024*

---

[9] The Israeli historian Yuval Noah Harari, interview Oct. 2020: https://www.youtube.com/watch?v=NV0CtZga7qM

# Lecture 1

## 13 SEPTEMBER 1914, MUNICH

IT is to my deep satisfaction that karma has enabled us to meet this evening and for me to say a few words in these solemn times. Above all, at this moment we would like to think of those who are out in the field, sacrificing their courage, their lives, their blood for the tasks set for humanity by these extraordinary times. First and foremost, we wish to direct our loving, help-imploring thoughts to those who have often sat among us in our communal contemplations and who are now abroad, having to take direct part in those great events that are bringing national and human karma into evolution—initially to those connected with us and then, more widely, to all those involved. Then we want to nurture an onward perspective—looking ahead in a specific way, both in an immediate and in the widest possible sense—such as we also seek in the course of our spiritual stream, which binds each soul with every other soul in being challenged by these colossal events. Let us direct our loving, beseeching thoughts to those out in the fields and, in token of our bond with them, let us stand up and dedicate the following words to them: [1]

Spirits ever watchful, guardians of your souls,
May your wings bear
The beseeching love of our souls
To those earthly beings entrusted to your care
So that, united with your power,
Our prayers may radiate help
To the souls whom they lovingly seek!

We wish to send out our loving thoughts to you, that Christ the helper may be with you, whom we seek, Christ who calls upon our souls, challenging them, seeking out harmony amidst disharmony, that He will lead those souls to whom He has to apportion suffering, in certainty to the redemption they need so that the purpose mapped out for human- and folk karma is fulfilled: With you, O souls, do we wish to be united in the sign that connects us with the sole true Spirit of the Earth, with Christ.

What has apparently so suddenly engulfed what we have to call all earthly humanity could long have been foreseen. It erupted so surprisingly because, it has to be said, occult sources have also had a hand in these events,[2] influences that have only since 28 June[3] gradually been revealing themselves. During these times it has been possible to acknowledge ever new aspects of spiritual worlds. I can only allude to what I mean here in a few words. When I returned in July from Sweden, from the Norrköping lecture cycle[4], I had to alert someone, who is in a certain sense connected with current events, as to how that event in Sarajevo had some remarkable consequences for occultists; how it had been an outer symbol and how curiously differently this deceased person behaved from all the others who could hitherto be observed in death in occult fields. It was in this way that in the occult background there also broke out what—in such terribly rapid steps—played out as events on the physical plane during the last days of July and the first days of August. However, those disposed to keeping their distance from spiritual life must lately have had certain premonitions and inklings of a spiritual world, have been occasioned to become aware of the presence of a spiritual world. It can indeed be said that the experiences earthly humanity is undergoing are unprecedented and daunting.

Dear friends, wishing as I do to address a few words to you, let them be connected with remarks that have often over the years been reiterated within our spiritual-scientific considerations. What should we seek as our deepest soul connection with the spiritual world? That it should grant us certainty and inner strength; certainty that, amid all the vicissitudes of the times, all the vagaries of events, there is something firm onto which we can hold fast. In times such as these, more than a belief in the unconquerable nature of spirit life and its tasks can imbue our souls: we need to learn to connect this faith in the victory and indomitability of the spirit with outer events.

In early August, as the first squalls of war declarations were mustering from the most varied directions in the world, I had to recall words recently spoken, which may engrave themselves deeply upon each of us, words just reiterated that affect us very directly. An important figure[5] said the following in a prominent place a few weeks before the outbreak of hostilities: We and all our forces are in complete and amicable agreement. We fell out this spring after the machinations of the press started up in Russia and were echoed in the German and Viennese papers. Let us take no notice of press issues, let's stick to the neighbourly friendships of old. Another thought-provoking statement was issued in June: The general easing of tensions is making progress. A further phrase in that same statement claimed: Talks with England are not yet concluded but are being conducted in the same spirit of friendship that characterizes all relations with Great Britain. Just think about now! Just think how changeable is what human beings believe at the moment in the physical world, and what they will be obliged to see over the course of events even in the coming weeks. Do reflect on the surging, storming, havering, hectoring events of this physical world, do remind yourselves how necessary all this surging and storming is. I'd like to say: What can be believed today will prove to be untrue tomorrow. How essential it is, amid this turbulence, to have something solid and certain onto which to hold, something which will remain true tomorrow, the day after tomorrow and for all eternity! What is true in those terms is truth from spirit sources, truth of the spirit's mission pervading all human evolution.

I would like to mention something because it is quite symptomatic—and is not personal—really symptomatic and symbolic, speaking to the soul. You know that the first volume of *The Riddle of Philosophy* came out in July. Volume 2 was printed as far as page 206[6] when war broke out. It was just at the point of transition from the thoughts of the French philosophers Boutroux and Bergson to the German philosopher Preuss and was referring to the way in which Bergson renders a thought in a slightly frivolous, superficial way, skimming over it where he previously approached with robust thoroughness the unknown and solitary Preuss as he prefigured our theosophical world view in the last third of the nineteenth century. I was trying to portray that solitary thinker correctly. It then turned out that the print run had to be interrupted and continued later, just at that transition from France to Germany. War broke out. I had to see those two-thirds-printed pages as a symbol of what was taking place between Western and Central Europe by way of the transition in my description.

Other issues might appear symbolic. Here I am remembering our building in Dornach,[7] which was also able to thrive to a certain point, albeit not as far as we would so dearly have wished. Perhaps some of our friends know how fervently it was desired—in face of salient facts and as long as this made sense—that this building could be finished by the first of August this year: not only as my heart's wish but as a necessity for all to see. One might now reflect whether it would have been good had the building been finished by 1 August. In face of the facts, something such as a wish could not be combated and, among several construction issues that needed solving—about which I will not speak today—was the problem of the acoustics for a larger space and its solution through greater resonance. It was in July, when the building was already timber-shuttered, that a few words, spoken at a particular spot in it, confirmed an inkling that this acoustic problem could be solved once the building was finished. At certain points it could be heard—through the emergent resonance and the occult calculations for its location—how words and music could be expected to sound, how they could really be expected to resound as they should. It was a kind of ideal—even in those first days of August—to hear the word spoken there that was to sound from out of the spirit ... and yet what our friends first heard in our building was the reverberation of cannon fire as it thundered on the nearby Alsace fields of slaughter. Thus did the space we had in a sense dedicated to the resounding of spirit words first become witness to cannon fire rumbling in its close vicinity. Other friends of ours saw, as it were symbolically, the great ideal we were awaiting. We were awaiting the annunciation of spirit light—sounding forth from spiritual worlds—that this light of spirit worlds would come into being. Yet what transpired was that the lights of Istein Fort could be seen on several nights, stretching across, piercing and lighting up our building for four minutes at a time; the sound and light of present events!

Other thoughts and feelings were also able to pass through our souls, however. On 26 July I was speaking with several of our friends,[8] amongst other things about our building, and had referred to the gravity of the times piercing our windows. I must say: I could only read through tears the letter which one of our younger friends, who had been with us on 26 July, subsequently wrote to his mother. Immediately afterwards, he was called up[9] and returned to his home country of Austria. From the spiritual strength he had gained through our spiritual striving, this relatively young member found the strength—in the most beautiful and, I must say, pure and holy way—to take up the lot assigned him by his karma.

And again it was another of those who had been with us on 26 July who himself wrote to me en route to the Serbian theatre of combat, full of feelings flowing from certainty in the spirit and faith in its triumphant victory, on the one hand, and nourished, on the other, by enthusiasm for his participation in the events of our time and his place within them.

Truly, my dear friends, one feels souls growing at this time—souls maturing—and it spoke to our hearts both beautifully and magnificently when observing that all the feelings and sensations that had suffused and passed through the souls of our friends also turned out to be suited to leading people to the right place, in the right way, amid today's gruelling situation.

When speaking of the certitude that ought to be gained from considering the spirit and spiritual being, this certitude is intimately linked with our chosen motto,[10] based on Goethe's words. It is rendered like this: *Wisdom lies in truth alone* or *Wisdom exists only in truth.* Among the deep hopes one is justified in cherishing out of these times is that everything connected with *Wisdom lies only in truth* will be imprinted upon humanity, precisely through the great pain and deeply affecting tests of these times. Everything contained in the words *Wisdom is in truth alone* needs to impress itself ever more deeply upon people—and now much has already been brought about by the great teacher in overcoming materialism.

Shortly before the outbreak of war I read what a respected journalist[11] had written. He says the following:

> Despite the reproval of Mr Liebknecht, I remain convinced that responsible agents of Government are not only justified but are obliged to repudiate truth and to affirm untruth. This right, this duty of collective morality in what is conveyed by those under their leadership, is restricted by two preconditions: Untruth must be neither provable nor counter to state interests.

Just compare this declaration with the axiom we decided upon when we founded the Anthroposophical Society: *Wisdom lies only in truth!* Much will collapse because quite a different sentient ethos has come to inhabit the souls of those who sense the seriousness of the present situation.

How often, my dear friends, have the words spoken in this place elicited what sounds like this: Reality is not constituted only by all that takes place on this physical plane, but human thoughts have even greater reality, strength and power of agency. Let us admit, for it is true: such things have only been said on the basis of foundations bearing a spiritual imprint. Just now, on the very complex journey I had to make, a document[12] came my way bearing the date 1 September 1914. It contains a very nice essay by a soldier, Robert Michel, who jots down his battlefield thoughts. His essay details how the mobilization came about and how he and his comrades set off into the unknown. His last words are important for us: 'But every single remnant of the monarchy has a duty to galvanize to its utmost their supportive forces until decisive victory has been achieved. All the fine words, heartfelt acclamations, good wishes and blessings accompanying our exodus increased our confidence. They were slivers that have not been lost. This bounty of psychic strength needs to accompany our army continuously and the will for victory needs to vibrate, to shimmer, from every single individual to the fighters on the Front. This is why nobody fled the decisions being prepared in the North. Those obliged to passively watch the immense deployment of armed forces and nations from the sidelines also need to contribute their sliver, their shard, sending forces to souls on their way. Those who have God's ear should pray; those who cannot pray should gather all their thoughts and will power in aid of a fervent longing for victory, and those with nothing else to offer should cross their fingers and repeat: We must be victorious, we must be victorious. In this way even the weakest will have contributed to victory.'

A soldier leaving for battle writes from the field words that sound like an echo of what has often been said on a basis of spiritual life: Whoever cannot pray, let them gather their thoughts and will forces in a fervent wish for victory. Now we see belief in the spirit, at the start of momentous events.

We need subscribe to no illusions. Some things may look different in the near future, but the time will come when what has been implied in these few words will become reality. World progress has to take place and what must happen will happen. Sometimes this occurs in a remarkable way; people's wills are led in gradual stages, so that one can see how, step by step—no differently from the way a teacher would do it—directions they will later take are poured into souls. In truth, one need only watch briefly to see how—above human powers—spiritual powers are spreading out, working pedagogically for the greater progress of humanity.

It is now timely to nurture a thought, which may affect one but is seldom considered. 1866: German brother stood against German brother—German against German. No more than a decade passed: 1870–71. A portion of Germany had to take part in an enormous event, one in which the other part could not participate. One of my teachers at Vienna High School[13] often said something that struck my heart deeply at the time. 'We Germans in Austria must be aware that what happened is our fate and not our fault: that we were not allowed to take part in an exceptional event. Now, this time, both parties are as if welded together by an iron force, where once they were opponents, when each stood separately without the other.'

This is no coincidence but important and momentous, and this major insight has taken less than a century to affect all subsequent times: human progress and what the spiritual hierarchies will for humanity has to take place. But it can come about in the most varied ways. By a certain point in time something quite specific has to have been achieved. Let's say—not that this necessarily tallies with what I was wanting to say—that by the year 1950 a certain amount of willingness for sacrifice, capacity for love and selfless conquest over egotism has to have been expended across humanity. Let's say that by 1950 what has to happen will have happened in accordance with the demands of the time. On the one hand, this will come about by speaking to human hearts that the power of the word is to be trusted, that what holds the fate of humanity in its hands will approach human individuals spiritually, seeking to advance them to a point where the spirit can work upon them. But the other taskmaster, that second teacher who speaks through living proof, often has to step in. And haven't we seen his successes! What immeasurable sacrifice, human love and selflessness have been engendered in an amazingly short time in this materialistic age since the great instructor stepped forward and the war, on the one hand so terrible yet which has, on the other, enabled what occultism terms iron necessities to be achieved: the goals essential to this particular moment in human evolution. Streams of blood are being shed, precious lives wilt and fade away, others are ripped from physical life in an instant when the hostile bullet strikes. All this is happening on such a vast scale today. What does it signify? It is a great sacrifice, my dear friends, an enormous sacrifice on the altar of pan-human evolution. On the one hand is something that has to transfuse humanity—something to which humanity has to be surrendered in order to progress—and on the other is the necessity for sacrifice.

It has been infinitely telling for me to watch how deeply bound—beyond death—are those souls who are directly involved in these momentous events. It could often be seen how those who had been laid out by an enemy bullet would be taken up into spiritual worlds, not yet having awoken into their greater individuality but still bound up with all that was transpiring below. I am not sure whether you can empathize with the extent to which one is affected by seeing, behind those fighting on the battlefield, their psychic personality, which has already encountered death, protecting and abiding with the one below still fighting and bound to the physical plane. They belong to those occult experiences of mine which I could not compare with any others. Un-awakened fighters who, having gone through death, are still connected with events below and are simultaneously like doubles to those still fighting in the physical. In spiritual worlds, too, realities exist that can pour confidence into our hearts, even if such confidence is not easily won.

Who would have thought what percentage of humanity is fighting each other? Who would have thought—we are just at the start; this war has only been raging for a few weeks—what losses of human souls these few weeks would have cost? They might be inclined to waver, wondering what might ensue were this to continue for a long time. Though it often dismays me—it can really take one aback—the thought revives me that what is right will happen and what is presaged by spiritual worlds will take place. If one can muster the certainty that not only are the living engaged in fighting, but that the dead remain bound to their destinies, then sufficient strength will be available to us.

Something else occurred to me recently. Our Society unites in a single spiritual stream those from the most varied peoples: nations who are presently fighting each other. This can be something of a comfort to us! We look back on times when we were quite dissimilar and had little in common, back to the age which the Bhagavad Gita describes for us, the oft-depicted human conditions and times when people lived in small, blood-related circles. The transition from blood-relatedness to a time when blood fights blood is described in the Bhagavad Gita,[14] when Arjuna is directed by the great spirit: Truly, over there are your brothers, and here are you; you will fight each other though the same blood flows in their veins as in yours. Yet in the spirit there is the potential to find a compensatory equality. What fights each other evolves from out of what ought not to be at war—another iron necessity essential to human evolution! The spirit bridges the gap that causes brother to fight brother in enmity, so that the other develops the means to bridge the disharmony existing between them. Those times are unlike our own. We take the opposite path within our spiritual movement. We seek to gather up what was strewn across the Earth. Those belonging to the most diverse nations connect with each other in community, becoming brothers within our ranks. Now we are seeing how here someone comes from France, having left friends there, how they have had to face the massed Germans and have to expect to face their anthroposophical friends in battle. It is the opposite situation here: scattered members of humanity are seeking each other in spirit, and we will find one another rightly once we understand the spirit of truth in all seriousness and can take hold of it in all earnestness—we just need to find ways to do this.

I must say that we Germans have a hard time in making our way, possibly the hardest! It may sound strange to you that I say this, but it is difficult for us because—without wishing to boast—it is always hard to justify ourselves; it is easier to justify someone else's entitlement than one's own. It is also difficult because it will not be easy for present humanity to see things with what I'd like to call the requisite objectivity, with a sufficiently unbiased overview, amidst the perspectives often put forward in our spiritual science and which are also found in the lectures on Folk Souls.[15] It is going to be necessary for anyone seeking to grasp spiritual life in the true and genuine spirit of our times to learn how these Folk Souls—those true and genuine Folk Souls—form a kind of choir, in which they already live together in harmony. But one has to find one's way to their being, and this can only be done in spirit.

Actually, this is not the right moment to draw attention to the feelings and sensations being voiced in the background of souls at present, so I would like to divert your attention towards a way of communicating that is open to us, a way of holding a dialogue—a closely discrete inner dialogue—with the spirit of the nation to which we belong and finding the right path for our souls to follow. I can only advise you: if you allocate a few minutes, especially at this time, you can use the following words to orientate yourself in the present world situation:[16]

You, Spirit of my earthly realm!
Reveal the light of your age.

Why 'your *age*'? With spiritual beings, one says 'your *age*' where on Earth one would say 'The light of your *being*.' Age is for the spirit what being is for earthly existence.

> You, Spirit of my earthly realm!
> Reveal the light of your age
> To the Christ-endowed soul,
> So that, striving, I may find you
> In the choirs of the spheres of peace
> Resounding in the praise and power
> Of human hearts devoted to the Christ.

Here we find a way to the Folk Spirit to whom we belong and the way from this Folk Spirit to the dialogue between that Folk Spirit and Christ, teacher of all Folk Spirits. When they come together in the Christ, they will be duly foregathered, because for all these Folk Spirits, leading nations as they do, Christ is to be regarded as their teacher, as can be learnt from the book *The Spiritual Guidance of Humankind.*

I often have cause to hope that what is being communicated is not true: in an Eastern national assembly—in their Duma—in which the ruler[17] had rallied his people to join the war, the ultimate cry was: The God of Russia is great! What a dreadful invocation, were it so! Thoughtlessly, they call upon a Spirit whose character is imagined as acting within their own limited context instead of invoking a Spirit so connected with the destiny of humanity that also those opposing them in enmity place themselves in its service, seeking the salvation of all humanity as well as their own. When the Christ leads a people, He leads them such that in seeking their salvation they seek the salvation of all humanity. We are justified in calling upon the Folk Spirit with whom we are inwardly connected, so that we look aloft to the way in which it, in turn, communes with Christ; via our Folk Spirit do we commune with Christ. Many thoughts are prepared in this way, thoughts which remain in the spiritual atmosphere of humankind until such time as a meaningful war is followed by a significant peace.

A sacrifice, as I say, is one that is brought on the altar of humanity; and it is sacred blood that flows onto our Earth, blood which is witness to those who are now fighting a war between peoples, whose souls are rising up out of the physical into spiritual worlds, and who will return in future incarnations to be important members of humanity's spiritual advancement—a sacrifice indeed, a great sacrifice! What is now happening has to take place in this way. Whoever wants to look back to times long passed, seeking first causes, needs to look back to the Punic Wars of the third century BCE, to the time when the Roman military leader[18]—you can read this up in historical records—used boarding ramps and ladders to achieve their initial decisive victories. It is debatable as to what the original event[19] of this present war was; future history will tell—it is difficult to go into these things.

Many things lead us back to the times when the Romans were warring with Germanic peoples, when human fate was being determined for many millennia. Then we come to the third great event—that is, our present situation—which will have as significant an effect as did the Punic Wars. Despite their albeit long extent, they were minor by comparison with today's world affairs, yet the *qualitative* effects of the Punic Wars still project into our times. Just as the great determining events of humanity recur in a certain sense, connected as they are with migration periods—a whole human cycle is encapsulated in the term—just as then, in Rome, what needed to be resolved had to take place: that the form of the human I, as it was in the third century BCE before the event on Golgotha, transformed into its later state, so that this form of I would find its way, via the Romans, into all that has happened since then; in just such a way must today's form of I—pivotal for the next cycle of human existence—be similarly placed within a war between peoples. This goes to the deepest impulses of humanity.

Once we have connected with what we have together been pursuing spiritually for years, we can believe in victory, in the victorious nature of the spirit. Then we will face all that comes towards us armed with that belief, knowing that whatever takes place under the leadership of the higher hierarchies is justified and will take its course. It just depends on us following this course faithfully. We will be doing this if we find the right way to observe our karma, if we do not shrink from the great tasks set by these momentous times—and when we can thank spiritual science for all that it can impart. Of prime importance is this: that spiritual science sharpens our gaze and our spirit to see that we do whatever our personality allows and that we are in the right place to do what is required. The more factually and impersonally we do this—without focusing on anything else—the more will spiritual science have sharpened our gaze, the more will it have made our hearts receptive and the more will we have understood the language in which these grave times are speaking to us.

One of the spirit-given tenets of the present, shared here among friends, brings to mind the countenance of suffering which we so often, so very often, encounter. The pain engendered in souls is so enormous—the sacrifice demanded so great—that the willingness for sacrifice and our receptivity to the pain of others must be equally great. Christ is only resurrected for many people once they understand that no pain can exist for another that is not also our pain; for wherever He appears, it becomes our pain, too. For as long as it is possible for us to see the pain of another without sympathizing with it, the Christ cannot fully inhabit the world. We should not be able to evade another's pain! This ideal is hard, exalted and wide. Yet Christ's ideal is also hard, exalted and wide. It is only fulfilled when our own wounds do not burn more fearfully than those borne by the other. It is therefore good to make ourselves fit to offer help through the following words, which we can direct towards a community or those suffering pain:

As long as you feel the pain
Which I am spared
Does Christ, unrecognized,
Work in world existence.
For weak remains the spirit
In one who suffers
Only through their own body.

Try to really immerse yourself in these words. If in the first phrase we can especially feel a connection with the Folk Spirit, then with these lines we can penetrate to a sense in which humanity's pain—the pain of a human community—resonates in our own souls, allowing us, in a truly Christian sense, to do everything we are allotted to do. May we do this in present times, imbued, particularly, with a sense of the Spirit!

My dear anthroposophical friends, the wound caused by the bullet would not heal were there no healing forces in the wonderful microcosm of the human body. It is good that an approach to treating and binding wounds, as practised by our dear friend, Dr Peipers,[20] is being carried out in some of our branches. It is beneficial because we can all get into situations requiring its application. But we also need to be aware, in such situations, that spirit is a reality and that whatever we do during the treatment of wounds, whatever the injury sustained, will be all the more efficacious if we act with spirit-presence-of-mind than without. So that we have the right thoughts when tending a wound in the human organism, we may think:

Well up, O blood,
In welling be active,
Lively muscle
Enliven cells,
Loving care
Of warming hearts
Be healing breath.

For in the blood, welling from a wound, are the signs that behind it lie forces, lie healing powers for wounds.

Well up, O blood,
In welling be active,
Lively muscle
Enliven cells,

... the cells that die off when a bullet has passed through them. You send the right feelings to those applying dressings and helping their fellow human beings:

Well up, O blood,
In welling be active,
Lively muscle
Enliven cells,
Loving care

Of warming hearts
Be healing breath.

Let us allow this attitude to infuse our souls, let us fill our entire being with its ethos when helping our fellow human beings and then, my dear friends, the spirit will in turn aid whatever efforts we can physically muster as physical human beings. And let us individually think of those individuals out there in exposed places, let us think of them at the start of our meetings, they who are outside our circles and labouring on battlefields. A verse for this purpose—which I dedicated to those on the battlegrounds at the start of today's meeting—can be used by each one of you and directed towards an individual:

Spirits ever watchful, guardians of your soul,
May your wings bear
The beseeching love of my soul
To the earthly being entrusted to your care
So that, united with your power,
My prayers may radiate help
To the soul whom they lovingly seek!

If you wish to send your thoughts to several—or many—out on the battlefields, you could say:

Spirits ever watchful, guardians of your souls,
May your wings bear
The beseeching love of my soul
To those earthly beings entrusted to your care
So that, united with your power,
My prayers may radiate help
To the souls whom they lovingly seek!

The great events now in progress will be a teacher of love and selflessness; and also a teacher for spiritual worlds—let us hope that they will be! Then the great sacrifices—those tremendously great sacrifices, made by humans through their blood—will be offered on the altar of spiritual beings; and what can be so painful to initial view will then serve to attain humanity's highest aims. The more we imbue ourselves with this feeling, the more readily available will those thoughts be when, after the war, widespread peace is agreed.

The twentieth century is called upon to transform many things by way of destiny, world order and among human affairs. Whatever is achieved in this respect will save humankind from having to repeat this event in future. The victorious triumph of spiritual life is a concept that has often found its way into our hearts during this time. Try to understand how we have been witnesses to events that are intended to be decisive, not for a short time span, but for long, long ages in the evolution of the human spirit! And let us try, from out of this seriousness, to summon the love and selflessness that will lead us—each according to their strengths and abilities—to put ourselves in the right place. Our karma will certainly guide us. And those who cannot at the moment step in to help, do not be downcast. It may also depend on saving some strength for later, when many will need to recognize the moment when karma calls them. May there then emerge—precisely in those recognizing spiritual science here and now—the reflection that what may happen in the outer world becomes ever more evidently manifest, that the beings, forces and will-impulses of the spiritual world work into all world events, into human spirits, into human souls, into human hearts. May a bond arise out of all the grief and pain we have experienced, a bond that connects human souls with those divine spirits who rule, guide and bring about human destiny. Human souls will discover this crucial point. May human souls uncover what is meant by our phrase: May the Christ-endowed human soul discover through its striving.

Now, my dear friends, it may be that we cannot all be involved in the fighting, maybe we cannot all do everything our ideals would wish, but we *can* all participate in these momentous events in the sense just outlined, in the words just spoken. In many and various places across the country—one here, another there, wherever we may find ourselves, to whichever circles we belong and with whomsoever we are humanly connected—these are the places where love can be active, where love gives us strength: that is the place where pain and sorrow, human misery and need call us to action, to think, to participate, the place where we feel we rightly belong, where we long in our hearts to be deeply connected with the other person, to whom we look because both their and our most holy shared treasure is sacrificially protected by their courage and their life's blood.

Let us therefore turn our thoughts, as at the beginning, towards those who—as just described—are consigned to the events of our time:

Spirits ever watchful, guardians of your souls,
May your wings bear
The beseeching love of our souls
To those earthly beings entrusted to your care
So that, united with your power,
Our prayers may radiate help
To the souls whom they lovingly seek!

May the Spirit whom we seek through our science, seek with our hearts, whom our spiritual movement wishes to serve, lead us. May it also lead all humankind, because those under His leadership will not only follow their own goals but, in following Him, will hold all humanity within their sights.

People who know how to trust Christ will find their way rightly. So, my dear friends, we have striven to direct our thinking towards the Christ over the years. May the times that have just broken in upon us prove to be times of testing—which we will overcome—and may we link our souls so strongly with the teachings of the Spirit, that they become our aids in times of travail, that they become a strength not restricted to us but accessible to all humanity! May the Spirit leading us upwards to Christ help us to imbue ourselves with this living cosmic-earthly Christ so that our thoughts may be rightly sent to those about and abroad, where folk- and human destinies are being decided, so that the right Spirit may help them, that Spirit so wisely leading human evolution, bestowing upon it salvation and blessing! Let us do all that we can so that the sacred, sacrificial blood soaking the Earth may, when called upon, serve its vital role in the onward ascent of Earth evolution; so that, out of what is happening on Earth, spiritual progress may come towards physical, earthly evolution, such that it may perceive: Truly, it has been worth spilling blood for the Earth if such progress is brought about.

All those not immediately able to sacrifice their blood must have the awareness to work in such a way that Spirit can permeate earthly evolution; that they must do everything possible so that Spirit imbues Earth evolution and that those having spilt their blood should have done so in aid of something valuable. Because, if we co-operate towards such evolution, looking with unclouded vision at the wider circumstances, then we will be conducting ourselves commensurate with not needing to feel ashamed in face of those at the Front. Were we to fail in this, our eyelids might not after all allow us that unclouded view: were we, on the one hand, to feel integral to our time yet, on the other, to fail to muster the strength to act creditably on such feeling. Spiritual science will embody this credit if it can contribute to giving people such strength, strength which can both support those who have given their blood while likewise strengthening those serving in other ways. Each in accordance with their situation.

Spiritual science will then be able to reflect: I was a means by which humanity, in its time of great travail, had an opportunity to succeed in its trial; then will spiritual science have achieved its divine goal.

With these simple words, my dear friends, I would like to close this evening, which I am so glad to have been able to experience with you.

# Lecture 2

## 3 December 1914, Munich

A lecture such as that given the day before yesterday[21] might easily have given the impression of being one-sided in extolling the virtues of one Folk Soul over another on the basis of mere sympathy. If a spiritual researcher should speak of these matters on a basis of pure sympathy or passion, one might assume that what they said would have little value in spiritual-scientific terms—that what they had to say, being saturated with such fervour, must be fundamentally and inwardly untrue. Now, however what was said yesterday—despite being connected with the deepest knowledge of what present-day spiritual science is permitted to say—may appear to you, it proceeds from the ways and means in which the modern spiritual researcher has to relate to one or another of the Folk Souls.

We know from the basics of anthroposophy that we do not understand the term Folk Souls in the same way as expressed by abstract concepts current in the exoteric world. Quite specific beings—beings of the rank of Archangel, as can be read about in the lecture cycle 'The Mission of the Folk Souls' [22]—beings with a higher consciousness than human beings direct the affairs of nations. We look aloft to these Folk Souls, speak of them as real and present beings, as real as we ourselves are. How can the soul-spiritual element in human beings relate to these Folk Souls? Let us begin by framing this question.

We know how human consciousness oscillates as it alternates between sleeping and waking. We know that people have to awaken into their physical and etheric bodies and that, between falling asleep and waking up, they dwell in their astral body with their I. Once the person, between falling asleep and waking up, is outside their physical body with their astral and I, they are in a region which—as regards their relationship with the Folk Soul to whom they belong in a particular incarnation—is quite different from that in which the individual is when they are in their physical body. They are born into the area of their Folk Soul, as defined by their language and related factors. How does this Folk Soul work upon a human soul, affecting those elements removed from the physical and ether bodies during sleep, yet which inhabit its physical body when awake? How does the Folk Soul of a people, to which a person belongs, affect the individual soul?

It works, in fact, only during the time when a person has dived back into their physical body on waking: between waking and falling asleep. They are then immersed in the forces of their physical and ether bodies; and submerged within these forces are also what I would call the tentacles of the Folk Soul of the people to which an individual especially belongs in that incarnation. We are not only immersed in our physical bodies; we also sink into a certain element of our Folk Soul, living between waking and sleeping within the processes of our physical bodies and within our Folk Soul. We experience in community with our Folk Soul during waking consciousness only that our Folk Soul does not speak directly into our fully conscious I but that it speaks primarily through our ether body into the subconscious of our astral body, that it gives us a certain direction, tingeing and adding nuance to our feelings and temperament. That is the basis upon which we relate to it. Anyone able through initiation to observe what is entailed in a human being diving down into their physical body will observe a meeting with their Folk Soul upon submerging into their physical state. They will also see something else. Once I speak about it, you will soon realize that, within what the spiritual researcher has to say about one Folk Soul or another, absolute objectivity has to be maintained.

Spiritual researchers live in those moments when, by rightly strengthening their soul-spiritual element, by making it possible to be conscious independently of their body, by observing where the human being exists, they can observe them even when they are outside their physical bodies with their astral and I. There the spiritual researcher can see that each human soul, when unconscious between falling asleep and waking, lives and is submerged within the compass of the Folk Souls under consideration for that time. The human being is with the Folk Soul of their nation once they have dived into their physical bodies. But while they are in a state of sleep they are in company with all the other Folk Souls significant for that time—with the exception of the Folk Soul, with whom they dwell when awake in the physical.

Given the opportunity, the spiritual researcher may become acquainted with the idiosyncrasies of other Folk Souls because, as soon as he or she becomes conscious of their own I in their body-free state, they commune equally in soul and spirit with other Folk Souls as when they are living with their own Folk Soul in physical life. This makes it quite impossible—unlike in cases of habitual emotional fervours—to speak preferentially about this or that Folk Soul. But when the spiritual researcher is consciously with the other Folk Souls, then their consciousness shows them that every person—between falling asleep and waking up—is unconsciously connected with all the other Folk Souls, albeit slightly differently from the connection they have with their own Folk Soul. When diving down into their physical bodies, humans learn to know individual Folk Souls in their fundamental characteristics—largely as regards their active influences on themselves—even if on a subconscious level. During sleep or when initiated, one becomes acquainted with the other Folk Souls, not individually, but in relation to their co-operative work. Only one's own Folk Soul is not present. The others work together as if in a round- or circle dance, and one is alive within this circulating activity in the same way as one lives with one's own Folk Soul during daylight physical life. There one co-exists not with the particular features of that one Folk Soul but amongst their co-operative working. There is only one circumstance through which—during body-free existence, that is, during sleep—one can be as if judged; one can quite certainly be condemned to be torn away from the usual communal circling of the Folk Souls to be with only a single 'foreign' Folk Soul. Please understand me correctly! Being alone with a single 'foreign' Folk Soul is *abnormal.* It can be achieved if one particularly passionately hates that other Folk Soul. In doing this—in being alone with this single alien Folk Soul in the same way as one lives with one's own Folk Soul in waking life—one is condemned to being torn away from the circling activity of the other Folk Souls.

Yes, these are objective truths resulting from spiritual research. They show you that the adage often iterated by spiritual science is *bitterly* serious: that what we encounter as external reality is maya, the great deception, and that, behind this illusory veil, lie truths about which those merely content with the veil of maya can not only understand nothing with their reason, but do not wish to understand anything with their will.

There are many, many people nowadays who are not yet able to picture what lies beyond this veil of maya, who cannot therefore grasp that there is an invisible, supra-sensible world in which relationships more utterly different than can be dreamed of exist between human souls and Folk Souls. If you take spiritual science seriously when it points to spheres connected with your lives, you also have to stomach it when spiritual science describes relationships in spiritual worlds into which it is quite uncomfortable to plunge—be it only in thought—while your will also baulks at it. We don't want to take the plunge; we want the truth about many things to be different, so that not only our reason but our will won't resist those intensely serious matters of which spiritual science has to tell and which we allow to pass through our souls.

On the basis of feelings, which can be stirred by contentions as just outlined, we sense that the principle to which our spiritual movement subscribes—which does not differentiate as to race, colour, nationality or any suchlike—is so fundamentally bound with the deeper foundations of our movement that it is quite idiotic for anyone taking spiritual-scientific verities seriously not to represent this primary principle. It is total idiocy to hate the being of a particular Folk Soul because—in our most profound humanity and at our lowest subconscious level—this would entail condemning ourselves to being close to that Folk Soul during sleep, in the same way as we live with our own Folk Soul during our waking hours. Because the normal mode of existing with Folk Souls during sleep is this: to participate in the entire circling round of Folk Souls active at a given time; also, that human beings are not allowed to become one-sidedly partial, both of which conditions are ensured by the wise order of the world.

We have often emphasized that what human beings have to undergo in the years ahead, what they will experience between death and a new birth, depends to a certain extent on the after-effects of their lives in physical bodies between birth and death. From what we have just discussed, we can infer that being together with one's Folk Soul is integral to this embodied life. I said that this communing with our Folk Soul gives rise to certain nuances or tinges. We take with us through the gate of death into spiritual worlds what our Folk Soul has activated in our soul-spiritual constitution by way of motives and impulses, and we have to gradually slough these off. If we think about this, it will become instantly clear that the manner in which we have lived with our Folk Soul will affect our standing as to the after-effects immediately following death.

Let's observe two nations in light of this: the Russian and French people. It is in the nature of Folk Souls that they are active differently within their consciousness from the way in which human beings are in theirs. How are humans active in their consciousness? They direct their gaze towards the horizon of outer facts and are also able to turn it inwards onto their own soul. We know that people differ from one another in some respects. One group may belong to Goethe, whose gaze rests objectively on things, another group to Schiller, who is more concerned with individual inner vision and from that position carries out all that he achieves. Folk Souls also share slight similarities, but are only approximately similar, because their consciousness is of quite a different order to human consciousness. Folk Souls relate variously to diverse individuals belonging to their folk or people: in directing their gaze outwards it will be more of a will-filled gaze, a look that will send its impetus into individual members of a people. They work objectively and centrifugally when turning towards an individual. Or they might exist more introspectively. Such Folk Souls are less inclined to subscribe—one could express it thus—to 'Folk Soul Realism' in expanding over an individual and instead rather to 'Folk Soul Idealism', which dwells more pensively within: to this latter inclination does especially the French Folk Soul belong. This French Folk Soul, as it at present permeates the French people, experiences a certain suspension or halt in its consciousness caused by looking back to an earlier time.

I have often drawn attention to the way in which we possess our usual, physical waking consciousness because we dive down into our spatial body. After death we owe our consciousness to time we spend looking back at our previous lives. We already have an inkling of what is characteristic of a higher consciousness that evolves not in space but over time. So it will not be very difficult to grasp what kind of consciousness the French Folk Soul has. It ignites its own self by looking back to ancient Greece because it is in a fundamental sense recapitulating, re-awakening, ancient Greekness. Ancient Greece is resurrected in the French Folk Soul, just as the ancient Egypto-Chaldea of the third post-Atlantean epoch is revived in the Italian Folk Soul. Hence the Italian Folk Soul has the potential to revive primarily the sentient soul in individuals belonging to the Italian people. The intrinsic nature of the French Folk Soul stimulates the intellectual soul in individuals, as can be proven in many instances. Even historical facts become wonderfully explicable when informed by these general results of spiritual science.

A few such things may be mentioned here. Just consider: what was a unique aspect of the Egyptian Folk Soul? Astrology existed then, directly affecting souls. The souls of this people looked outwards at the movements of heavenly bodies, not seeing the material processes that today's people see, but perceiving the activity of spiritual beings. They related to the entire cosmos in the same way as a person relates to other human beings, knowing that through every feature of their physiognomy a soul is gazing back at them. All physiognomy was seen in this way by the ancient Egyptians: the soul element in nature was perceived. The sense of onward progress into more recent times lies in the fact that what was previously akin to an elemental capacity is now ignited directly in the human physical body, becoming its inwardness in our more recent fifth post-Atlantean age. Just as what the Egyptian underwent was of a more elemental nature, what an

Italian experiences, in recapitulation, as soul-spiritual in their sentient soul is now more inward, has been internalized. What could be more of an internalization than the Egyptian astrology in Dante's *Divine Comedy*? Correctly re-conceived ancient Egyptian astrology, but now internalized!

One could similarly demonstrate the rekindling of ancient Greek qualities, not in individual French consciousness, but in the effects of their Folk Soul's impetus. Particulars of the latest inventions could be followed up, but insufficient seriousness tends to be brought to such investigations. Greece and even the term 'barbarian', as it once called other nations, has resurfaced. It can be confirmed that, in its deeper impulses—I do not mean consciously—ancient Greece is revived in all French literature and art, as indeed it should be. We have before us a Folk Soul that has processed and assimilated all that existed in ancient Greece, a Folk Soul that affects individuals extraordinarily strongly, asserting itself and taking hold of the individual. Consequently, when the individual French soul plunges down daily into its ether and physical bodies, it is also submerged in the weaving essence and incisively definitive activity of its Folk Soul. It encounters this impetus as sharply contoured. For this reason the French individual, in absorbing such starkly definitive weaving activity from their Folk Soul into their physical body, lives primarily within this, rather than within an elemental sense of self, lives more in the imaginative picture they have created—the epitome of what a French person is—that wells up from their Folk Soul. They live in the image of the French person and with this image is associated all that has great significance for them: *gloire*, glory, and so forth. The French person exists in their own image, which wells up from their ether body. This fantasy image is powerfully imprinted and becomes enmeshed with the soul-spiritual identity of the individual; it accompanies them as an intensely articulated aspect of their ether body, even after death into the spiritual world. This ether-image is very hard to get rid of—the image they have made of themselves adheres tightly and is firmly bound to them.

The attitude of the Russian Folk Soul towards its individuals is quite different. Unlike the French, this Russian Folk Soul does not have anything to recapitulate, in the sense of other post-Atlantean cultures, such as that of the French. It is a youthful Folk Soul, who impinges little on ether bodies. That is why, on submerging into their physical bodies, little of incisive character or sharpness of contour attaches to the single individual belonging to this Russian Folk Soul. However, their etherically-woven fantasy images are brought into spiritual worlds after death.

These are some of the differences in the ways individual souls relate to their Folk Souls after death. On the one hand, we see the hosts of such single souls, who have gone through death, taking with them sharply configured images of themselves and, on the other, we see young souls belonging to a young Folk Soul in the East, ascending and bringing with them few sharply defined—albeit ether-suffused—images.

Now we are standing—as I have often explained—on the threshold of that great event of coming times: the appearance of Christ in a most especial form. I need not expound on this in detail today. Ahead of Him, since the last third of the nineteenth century and as a fighter, fittingly preparing humanity for this Christ event, goes that Spirit whom we call Michaël, conquering harbinger of the Sun Spirit. Now, everything depends on this event, imminently to dawn over humanity, being rightly prepared for in spiritual realms. Yet this can only take place if, in spiritual worlds, work proceeds on the pure elaboration of the future Christ to appear in ethereal form to humankind. For this it is necessary for Michaël, in his capacity as harbinger of the Sun Spirit, to fight a battle in spiritual worlds. For this battle he needs the aid of souls who, as a result of their bodies, bring aloft with them only few sharply contoured fantasy images. Thus we see the Spirit Michaël and, among his followers, a number of Russian souls, fighting for the purity of the spiritual horizon, in gruelling battle with souls emanating from the West and bringing with them harshly defined fantasy images. These need to be diffused and dissolved. We observe how this battle between East and West has been in preparation since the last third of the nineteenth century, an intense fight in service of humanity's future, a fight entailing the spiritual East of Europe countering the spiritual

West of Europe: spiritual Russia waging a robust onslaught against spiritual France.

That, my dear friends, is among the most shattering events of the present: seeing how, to the same extent as down here on tactical fronts, the great deception of the physical bond between West and East is being perpetuated, while over there in spiritual worlds the harsh clash of Eastern Europe—Russia—is directed against the European West—France. Here we have one of those instances that have such a shattering effect on the spiritual researcher: where what is behind the veil of the outer world can be seen to be the exact opposite of what appears to be taking place down here, in the land of delusion. But I wish to exhort you—again and again—not to believe that you can speculate about such things. Anyone inferring from what I said about an isolated instance—that the spiritual can be the opposite of what takes place among maya's illusion—who imagines they should seek the spiritual in the opposite of physical maya, would be very seriously mistaken. For there are cases where events in the spiritual world proceed exactly as in the physical. Between these two opposing circumstances—one of which is the connection between France and Russia on physical and spiritual levels—are any number of gradations.

Nowadays there is little feeling for the impetus out of which genuine spiritual science has to be communicated. Our times have to some extent become—if I may put it like this—frivolous as regards what appears newsworthy to individuals. Precious little is asked about the responsibility behind what is to be communicated for the one who is focusing on the connection between the physical and spiritual worlds. Not for personal reasons, but by way of illustration, may I add something about my lecture of the day before yesterday. You see, in that public lecture, where I could naturally only speak in exoteric terms, I was nevertheless not speaking as exoterically as you might believe. I would be happy if, especially in such lectures, you would consider the cultural task spiritual science has, namely, what is behind the selection and manner of expressing what has to be said. These are not arbitrary ideas, randomly cobbled together. Take just one example: I said that, if one wants to evaluate the relationships between individual European nations in this war, one should proceed historically. For instance, by considering that Austria's Balkan mission was at the behest of English[23] politics—that, basically, everything that ensued for Austria came as a consequence of all it carried out on behalf of English imperatives. I said that one has to take account of this, and that, as a result, Austria—and with it Germany—came particularly to oppose Russia; that England abandoned its own task to fight against Germany, while Central Powers came into conflict with Russia. And also because of Austria, motivated by England, being assigned the latter's Balkan mission; and further, by going to the Turks' aid when the intention was to hold back the influences of the Russian East. Obviously, in an exoteric lecture intended for the wider public, one can only hint at what might affect sensitivities in the positive ways they ought to be affected today. Yet what lies behind this issue? Externally one sees English politics on the side of the Russians which, precisely due to an English deed, has had its consequences. We see that externally. The spiritual researcher, seeing this in the spiritual world, can make a unique discovery, a highly idiosyncratic discovery. Let's imagine that the spiritual researcher takes a certain viewpoint, looking upwards from below. They would take a point of perspective below the physical plane and look upwards towards the astral plane. They might also make this point to be above the astral plane. Then they would see what unfolds on the physical plane while at the same time seeing what transpires on the astral plane. They would blend these perspectives. You see, if one looks up from below or from above downwards through the astral plane, one can see through the astral to the physical and vice versa. Now looking at the physical, one sees England fighting Turkey, since Turkey has declared war on Russia. But that is merely maya-illusion, for in truth the astral being of England is fighting with Turkey against Russia. So that one has the theatrical dimension that, in the north-west, England is for Russia and, in the south-east, England is for Turkey, that is, fighting against Russia. It is just that one fact is pivotal for the physical, the other for the astral plane.

If one faces the world with this kind of knowledge, one feels: naturally, one can't share knowledge of this kind externally, with the public, and yet one is prompted to pick out this one point about England's fickle capriciousness in the East. That this fact was chosen is a result of knowing its spiritual context. It is with this example that I wished to illustrate the responsibility with which one has to assemble individual truths while also being responsible for the manner in which they are conveyed.

If one's occult responsibility is properly sensed, one will not randomly cobble something together—in the manner of modern wordsmiths and journalists—but what has to be expressed needs to be gathered from the very being and effects of the time. It is certainly not for personal reasons, but simply to alert you, that I tell you that spiritual science—in approaching the world fully responsibly—ought to be taken very seriously and not confused with what journalism and copywriting puts about—nor the way it mixes material—all of which is a very long way from a feeling of responsibility towards the spiritual powers of our time. Especially at this time, my dear friends, I may be permitted to draw a little attention to the seriousness of spiritual science for, in many respects, our time shows us a serious countenance—an extremely earnest visage—and only those will weather this period well who understand how to honour this stern countenance.

In order to underline this more firmly, I would like to bring before your souls a connection interesting to pupils of spiritual science. It has often been said that spiritual science did not in truth enter the present because it sprang up at the will of someone or other or because someone had been personally inclined to make it their ideal and to spread it to other people, but because now is the age when spiritual beings—who had previously barred this gate to truths later to be revealed to humanity—have now opened it so that this wisdom can flow down into human souls. We are heading towards a time when people must ever increasingly receive this wisdom, which cannot just be absorbed by the soul in the form of abstract concepts nor merely as grey, intellectual ideas. We are approaching a time when what we call Imagination wants to flow into human souls and human feelings. If one could but see through to this, one would say: There they hang above the landscape, like heavy clouds before a storm, hanging in the spiritual world, waiting to flow into human feelings, waiting for human souls to mature. Yes, this is how our time is, indeed it is.

Now, there is a peculiar law: the imaginative element that is wanting to enter into human souls, but cannot yet be received as Imagination into a given age, projects a Morgana-le-Fay-like image, a quantum mirage, down as far below the physical plane as it is situated above it. These Imaginations elicit in human beings passions, feelings, urges and instincts, which are enacted in the form of antagonism. If you take today's eruptions of instincts, the passions with which people abuse each other, they are nothing other than the results of Imaginations, which the peoples of Europe should be absorbing but which cannot descend, and which are instead reflected on the physical plane in the human subconscious in the form of instincts and passions that oppose the truth. We can basically say that everything we are currently experiencing by way of instincts and passions being projected is an expression of the fact that renewed Imaginations wish to break into the world, into human cultural evolution. All that the war so often—and so tragically—propels to the surface is distorted Imagination, which humanity cannot grasp.

Then again—and this never strikes me as being entirely unimportant—I would remind you that one should not say: Every war is transformed Imagination. Wars can be something quite different. Today's is as I described. Generalizing, which affects knowledge of the physical plane, has no significance for the spiritual world. Here matters have to be researched separately and individually.

I would like to introduce a phenomenon from a particular angle in order to explain it. Nowadays we see how members of different peoples pursue each other in hate, how they insult each other. Where does this originate? Now, since we have in deepest earnestness accepted the nature of repeated earthly lives, it should not appear particularly inconceivable to us that the soul, over the course of its repeated lives, passes through various nationalities. Someone presently living out their incarnation in a German body may already be inwardly preparing to incarnate in an English body; someone at the moment experiencing their incarnation in an English body may well be preparing in their deepest recesses for a German incarnation. Human beings are already dual entities—they are dualities. Externally, we appear to the world—not only with regard to our physically-perceptible exterior, but in respect of much else, too—quite justifiably in our physical bodies as they are linked with the weaving being of their Folk Soul. Yet that which will make our next incarnation a totally different one begins to assert itself inwardly. Now, human beings—amongst much else towards which they feel enmity—are most frequently an enemy of their own inmost being. They are most often in conflict with themselves, not realizing that it is their own inner nature that they are fighting. Take an English person, who is predestined, through their soul's innermost impetus, to be a German in their next incarnation. Today we see them fighting their own inner nature—fighting against their next, German incarnation. This comes to expression in their shameless insulting of all things German. Glimpsing their future objective in a German body, they rage against what exists as their inmost being, in the spiritual world. Fundamentally, this is a soul's dispute with itself and only externally, among the maya, is it a case of berating those across the Channel in Central Europe. Basically, what is being cursed is their own soul. Therein lies the deep tragedy—which people have to overcome throughout their feelings and inner motivations—when matters become *bitterly* serious and they compare external maya with what exists within.

This is how we can see the Folk Souls as real living beings who interfuse and permeate each single, separate individual. What each person experiences, they experience in conjunction with their Folk Soul. In outer life, on the physical plane, people oppose each other. Each nation blames the other for the war, believing they are saying something noteworthy. What is this mutual accusation of guilt? The karma of each nation and that of the other nation in question both depend, of course, on what their Folk Soul is experiencing within each nation and the impulses being directed into each individual's ether—and thence also astral—body. This is how individual nations live side by side with each other in relationships that are expressions of their Folk Soul with Folk Soul karma. When the former, through the latter, experiences something or other, when this or that happens through this interrelation, it does not take place without being connected with the deepest karma. Inasmuch as a Folk Soul is a self-contained entity, national karma also exists. Whereas in outer life we believe that one nation harms another in some way, it transpires that each nation's experience is one of national karma. If one nation causes the downfall of another, what takes place in the defeated nation is something it has itself caused through its own karma. If one speaks in the crude terms prevalent in external life about the rights of this side or the other, this is really no different from an old man seeing next to them a child, full of youthful vigour, and asking: Why am I getting older? Why is decay increasingly evident? I see that the child is stealing my energy. By growing up, that child is taking my strength. Rather than acknowledging naturally declining strength, the old person succumbs to illusion. They wouldn't do this, yet I have heard the like of it: 'That child is depleting my strength.' You immediately appreciate that this is nonsense because the causal connection lies within each individual being. It is like this with the karma of peoples. They live alongside one another, and if the one triumphs over the other, the victory is for their karma; even though their victory signifies defeat for the other people, their defeat is provoked by their own karma. So we see that spiritual science is peace-bestowing, though on the other hand it understands that opposing forces simply have to work against each other.

It is precisely in instances such as these that one can hope that attention will be directed towards the fact that spiritual science does not toy with sensational concepts, but the science of the spirit—when taken in its *bitter* seriousness—can really course through our souls, shaking and rattling them and making of the individual who takes it seriously a different being. We must well and truly focus on this: just how superficially we sometimes regard spiritual science as a mere game of reasoning and how we should actually regard it as something that can make of human beings a completely different entity. Much by way of understanding correlations will result if you admit to this.

If two people have differing views of an issue playing out within their sight, one of them will generally be wrong. It will be easily verifiable that one of them is incorrect. But a person's individual life differs

as an attack. Attacks and assaults on other nations only begin when the other is berated, sworn at. These are matters that need to be understood particularly deeply: acting for the true identity of a people means nothing other than what one can compare in individual consciousness with the fact that one can only look after one's own body, see that it is in the best possible working order, yet one cannot do the same for another's body.

I beg you to note that here is a thought which sets the direction for discerning—for evaluating—one which can be garnered from spiritual-scientific sources.

If we gaze into the weaving existence of Folk Souls to what lies beyond gazing, to see what transpires externally, I would say that for the spiritual researcher matters are grave—quite exceptionally grave—at the moment. But it also behoves the gravity of these times, when we have seen some of the most extreme acts of war, that we are challenged to found a new culture, one which takes account of what lies beyond the veil of the senses. Those who evaluate external world events in the right sense will be those who see in them something akin to cyphers or mighty cosmic symbols of a totally new dawn in human evolution.

I said: Not only does reason with its prejudices rise up against what spiritual science has to say about the supra-sensible beings behind external events, but feelings and impulsions of will also rebel. They reject it because the soul has to transform itself, has to sense and feel about much else besides. That is what I said. Yes, it really is one of those truths. We sleep not only at night but in part also during the day; just that at night our desire for our physical body is so strong that it suffuses our astral body and our I, hampering our consciousness. If we now—with this same astral body and same I—descend into our physical body to satisfy that voracity, what we develop by way of consciousness is then flooded with the influences of Folk Souls; consciousness is once again suffused so that, though we believe ourselves to be wide awake, an element always remains asleep in us. Basically, part of us is always asleep and into this sleep can the Folk Soul work because it is not the same consciousness with which we reach our everyday decisions. This diurnal somnolence—which is only masked by everyday awareness—also includes the incoming effects of Folk Souls of other nations. They work in a particular way into slumbering human natures, eliciting albeit different events than during actual sleep, but nevertheless prompting events on the physical plane.

While the German people possessed, for instance, an evolutionary model issuing from the innermost depths of German identity thanks to Goethe, it neglected this in favour of embracing Darwinism. Just as the Italians were to develop the sentient soul, the French the intellectual soul, the British the consciousness soul, so the German was to develop their I. Much in the essential being of the German people becomes understandable if one can feel—and focus on—how everything constituting German culture wells forth from out of their I. The way in which their I is bound up with their most sacred spiritual treasure is a characteristic of the Central European human being.

This can be seen particularly graphically in one phenomenon. If we take occult truths themselves and look westwards, external culture has little connection with what manifests as occultism or mysticism. They remain as two parallel streams. You won't find much concerning occultism in the average Paris bookshop; you will have to go to a specialist supplier. Now see how the matter lies in a German, how everything proceeds from the I in such as Jakob Böhme, how the evolution of German culture is unthinkable without occult impacts of this kind. Think of Goethe and Lessing. Here there are not two parallel streams but one stream in which life is suffused and saturated with spirituality to the extent that you could not subscribe to the materialistic notion that Christ could reincarnate in a physical human being in the way promulgated by Star of the East. That is why the necessity arose—similarly to the present antagonism between Germany and England—a necessity that could not be delayed in leading to war: to separate German occultism cleanly from English occultism. Some may wonder why such a sundering had become necessary. I just wanted to hint at this. Some will actually see a kind of archetypal image in the alignment of facts—or the justification of facts—when reading the letters between Grey[24] and Annie Besant:[25] their manner of proof and the way it is composed show a great similarity in both. With this I merely wished to indicate that what proceeds from the German people is connected with its inmost soul.

If a German is alert—I say this as a fact, without sympathy or antipathy—they will hold with the profound theory of evolution put forward by Goethe, who lays out the sequence of organisms but who obtains the impetus for their array from the deepest recesses of his I. Half a century later, from out of the consciousness soul, Darwin reproduced this, but with a materialistic complexion. The world understood this more easily and even the German world preferred to take up a theory of evolution in Darwinian guise than in Goethean colouring. From the depths of essential German entity, Goethe also founded a colour theory, which physicists to this day regard as nonsensical because the external world has adopted Newton's theory of colour. When were Darwin's and Newton's theories of evolution and colour taken up instead of those conceived by Goethe? When among the German people folk were asleep and another Folk Soul could exert its influence instead. Here we have sleep in the midst of waking. And when people are jarred into wakefulness, they still misunderstand the issue but notice that something is amiss. Then they head for their trinket box to take out the insignia they have been awarded by English fraternities, returning them but forgetting to also return that English-tinted theory of evolution and that Newtonian colour hypothesis. One could cite a strand of Haeckelianism as a good example. Certain things can be experienced here. For example, even today you can experience and hear that in a particular scientific society a lecture has been doing the rounds in various German towns on the subject of how international people's organizations have been damaged by this war and attention being drawn to what—were you to measure it on a larger scale—would be quite correct, but not on the scale that this speaker, with his habitual professorial frame of reference could proffer. Taking scale as a starting point, it sounds very odd when this fellow says: Internationalism must be resurrected as soon as this war is over because otherwise Germany will fail to benefit from a great deal and certain metaphysical elements previously unfolded by the German people might arise again; he said he was happy that this German spirit, with its leanings towards the supersensible, has been swamped by nations with little inclination towards the spiritual. This could be heard during a primarily politico-economic lecture recently: the fear that the German spirit might awaken.

Much could be said, but I just wanted to give expression to one or two aspects of what can be gained if we take what is albeit bitter to a superficial view of life with sacred seriousness, with a seriousness that streams into us like a magical zephyr when we receive spiritual science in its full profundity. It is incumbent upon us to ponder this, to feel this, to sense it in these times and, with such feelings, we may be vouchsafed an overview of our time and may feel united with those who are outside, abroad and having to stand up—with their blood and souls—for all that karma is demanding.

So let us embrace what our knowledge and our task ought to be and what is intended to awaken our caring, with the words:

From the courage of fighters,
From the blood on fields of battle,
From the grief of the bereft
From the sacrifice of people
There will grow fruit of spirit
If, spirit-conscious, souls will turn
Their thoughts to realms of spirit.

# Lecture 3

## 23 MARCH 1915, MUNICH

THE first part of today's lecture will be dedicated to knowledge relating to actual experience, around which our Society's karma has of late skirted, and the second part is intended to shine a spotlight on issues which contemporary events make particularly noteworthy.

In the last two public lectures[26] I was obliged to lay particular emphasis on the way in which, in order to imagine spiritual worlds, it is essential gradually to become accustomed to a new language, a language differing from that which we use when describing what we know—through our brain-bound sense perceptions and our reason—of worlds in which we live. To some extent in support of our friends, I would like to link recent concrete experiences that have played out in our wider circles with events of which I could certainly have chosen other examples; but I choose these because, I would say, they relate most directly to recent experiences and can provide us with concepts about the relationship between the human soul and spiritual worlds.

Ever and again I have stressed that when the soul crosses the threshold on its journey of realization into the spiritual world, among its first experiences is becoming one with what it perceives, learns and undergoes. Here on the physical plane we remain to some extent enclosed within our skin and separate from what we are observing. As soon as we enter—and have anything to do with—the spiritual world, we no longer feel enclosed in the way our skin confines us to our physical body. We feel our entire being to be dispersed, as if identifying with every being and event with which we have dealings. To illustrate this, I will turn to some positive incidents.

An elderly member[27] recently went through the gate of death. This person had for years lived, with all their feelings, with their entire soul, in the Imaginations one acquires when one absorbs—and absorbs with great soulfulness—what spiritual science can offer. It is because it is so important that it is so often reiterated: theoretically gathering what is conveyed as spiritual-scientific Imaginations cannot be the be-all and end-all. It can be a point of departure but is not everything. Such Imaginations must take hold of our feelings and sentience. Even in a public lecture, I was able to explain how the sentient soul is presently more connected with the eternal core of the human being, while what manifests from the consciousness soul touches more predominantly upon what human beings experience of the physical world. That is why it is so important to feel what can be felt when taking in spiritual-scientific knowledge, because such feeling has far greater power to take hold of our souls and to really put them in contact with spiritual worlds than mere thinking, than reasoned deduction. It was with their feelings that the person of whom I was speaking had lived so extensively within spiritual-scientific Imaginations. So I can relate that it appeared to me very soon after their death—before I had even been informed of their death on the physical plane—how this personality, while still within their ether body, was inwardly processing all the feeling- and sentient forces they had garnered, what they had themselves become through living for so long within the stream of spiritual science. What I describe appeared to me unbidden while their ether body was still connected with their astral and I. The person who had gone through the portal of death came and told me that they were now feeling what they had become through spiritual science, what they were feeling now that they were no longer confined within their physical body. And there resounded from the person beyond the portal of death the lines I will presently read out.

You will notice, in the first three lines, that the deceased uses a word which one can hardly justifiably find in one who has laid aside their physical body; but that is not the point. The word that refers to a physical heart is meant symbolically. Here heart stands for the etheric organ of feeling. Here is a case of someone who has traversed the gate of death and whose strongest experience before dying as if summarizes the result of their life, as if to say to themselves: I am now in a situation where I can experience the nature of my self, how the nature of my self appears when I grasp it with an understanding of how—in my feeling cognisance—I have attained it through spiritual science. This is how that individuality, less than two hours departed, let resound the words, which I must say are positioned such that I have done nothing to them other than record what this soul said from out of their self. Their own words served as a eulogy at the beginning and end of their cremation. I read them now:

Into worldwide spaces will I bear
My feeling heart, that it become warm
In the fire of sacred powers' workings;

Into worldwide thoughts will I weave
My own thinking, that it become clear
In light of eternal life, evolving;

Into grounds of acquiescent sensing will I plunge
My soul, that it become strong
For true goals of human striving;

Towards God's peace do I quest
With life's struggles and cares
Preparing myself for higher selfhood;

Towards work-glad peace do I aspire,
Presaging cosmic existence in my own existence,
Do I long to fulfil my human dues,

Anticipating, may I then live
Towards my star of destiny,
Which in spirit realm appoints my place.

Let us hear resounding what this self can sense of itself as a result of it having evolved feelings instilled by spiritual science. It is important to bear in mind that we are dealing here with a personality who, in this physical life, reached a ripe age and that the potential exists in one reaching an advanced age to wish to characterize themselves so that—only after death—this self can fully express itself in its own identity. Thus to observe it one needs do nothing other than give oneself up to—lose oneself in identifying with—that being to enable it to express itself, of itself.

It was different in another instance, when it was a case of a relatively early death. Present events prepare us for encountering cases such as this, when so often people of a tender age are dispatched through the gate of death. Here, in the case to which I refer, it was not the cause it so often is nowadays, but it was still an early death. When a death occurs early, one can say: Had the person lived longer, their ether body would not have been set aside but could have supplied their physical body with forces for decades longer. Someone who passes through the gateway of death ahead of the decades they could have lived bestows their unspent ether body on the spiritual-elemental world. Today countless such unspent ether bodies ascend into spiritual worlds. If in spiritual science we speak of having great hope for the age evolving out of the lap of present events, what comes into consideration is that those who now cross into the spiritual world will become witnesses to spiritual work and through their individualities will send forces into earthly life. Their ether bodies persist as something secondary yet special in that they remain unspent. Large numbers of such ether bodies represent a force which will work on into human beings who will again live in peace once it is attained and will become collaborators in dissolving materialistic world outlooks through their spiritual view of the world.

We can be fortified when we experience how people die at a young age if we can to some extent perceive what is happening.

In the second case,[28] to which the karma of our spiritual stream contributed and at whose cremation I was again to speak after they had gone through the gate of death, the time between dying and cremation was between Wednesday and the following Monday. By then, this ether body had departed and to my occult observation, in the night before speaking, I had to some extent lost sight of that ether body—it was no longer visible. This individual was already at large with their astral body and I. Here was an observing soul faced with an astral and an I. Again the wish arose to speak a few eulogistic words, at the beginning and end of the funeral, that had something to do with the individual. The resulting words were expressed by that person. In that they were released from their physical and ether bodies, it was possible—in what I think were precise words—to accurately encapsulate the nature of their earthly existence. Once again, these words are not mine but are as they should be when characterizing a person who has traversed the gate of death: received through force of Inspiration. Words arose as Inspiration in the observing soul when surrendered to the impression of the deceased:

You walked among us.
The limber gentleness of your being
Spoke from the quiet strength of your eyes—
Peace, soulful enlivener,
Flowed in the waves
Through which your gaze
Rested on objects and people,
Conveying your inner interweaving;
And this essence
Ensouled your voice, which bore
Through your words' hue,
More than the words themselves
Revealed: the veiled being
Evolving in your beautiful soul;
Yet the devoted love
Of compassionate lives
Were wordlessly, wholly brought to light,
This being, who out of noble, serene beauty
Proclaimed with responsive inkling
Cosmic soul creation.

These words were spoken at the cremation and the extraordinary transpired: it was at the very moment—which can only improperly be called a *moment* during awakening—when the heat of the incinerator actually took hold of the physical body of this person. So, for a moment, the opportunity arose for this person, who had gone through the gate of death, to advance their consciousness, not during the funeral service but just as the flames were consuming their body. Then oblivion resumed. Such moments of consciousness that suspend unconsciousness can take place until full consciousness is established some time after death. This instance showed particularly clearly the workings of consciousness beyond the gate of death. Such consciousness experiences time in a form quite different from the way in which human beings experience it when living in their physical bodies; this is significantly demonstrated here. The perception of time by those no longer in possession of a physical body can only be compared with our perception of space. Here in physical existence we can always look back: what we have seen persists. If within time something has taken place, we have to look back on its image in memory; it has to arise in our consciousness. Such is not the case in one no longer bearing a physical body. The disembodied soul looks backwards as we look back in space.

This is how the deceased gazed back at what was being spoken: much as we look back spatially. What was spoken now appeared to their soul. In just such concrete cases is the singularity of the spiritual world made manifest. Now, I just said that, at the time the eulogy was to be spoken, I had to some extent lost sight of their ether body, but a second glance showed that it was precisely this ether body that was able to supply the inspiration imprinted in the words. Once I could again locate their ether body—I mean for my observation—I became aware of where this ether body was while I was speaking those words. It was during the night between Sunday and Monday. I said that I had lost it, but it was only later that I realized where it actually was: I was myself within it. It was a dissolving cloud. The I and astral body had already separated off. Because I was within the ether body I could not perceive it, much like a cloud in which one finds oneself. Yet what was alive in it provided the inspirational potential to etherically imprint the words I was to read.

Here you see the mysteries and intimate proximity of the human soul with spiritual worlds. I would not make so bold as to mention this were it an isolated case, but it was reconfirmed in a third instance. Once again, I was asked to say some words characterizing this third deceased individual,[29] who had lived in our circles. The death of this person was something particularly painful for our feelings on a physical level because this individual had embodied our best hopes for spiritual-scientific work. They had, during their time on Earth, absorbed much of what is currently defined as erudition, knew their way around—was at home in it—and had the firm intention to do what is needed in our movement, which is: to settle into what is now defined as science and so to transform it in their soul that spiritual-scientific insight could be reborn at a higher level. Not everyone is capable of doing this, but it is among the essential requisites of spiritual science. Concordances between science and spiritual science can often lead—in those unfamiliar with spiritual science—to the belief that it is necessary to press ahead with present science and, once fully saturated with it, use it for a lively ascent into spiritual science. One arrives at a certain point where the correspondences afforded by current science with spiritual science appear so convincing—are known to be solid by inner experience—that one cannot be further misled by the material culture of these times.

Once this person had gone through the portal of death, the need to shape the beginning and end of the cremation eulogy in a particular way arose again: a distinct impetus to direct this individual towards the bridge that exists in our spiritual-scientific movement between the physical plane and the spiritual world. It is particularly painful for our feelings here on the physical plane that this person was snatched away from us in their youth. However, it could not have awoken as much hope as it ought to have in the spiritual-scientific stream in which we live were we not certain that forces streaming into spiritual science come not only from those living in the physical plane but that forces also issue from those who have gone through the portal of death and who have been equipped with spiritual science. So the need was obvious to accentuate to that soul: something great has been vouchsafed you, now that you have gone through the gate of death, even now to remain a true participant and co-creator.

Whoever takes spiritual science seriously needs to reckon with the fact that those who are no longer on the physical plane are still to be considered real co-workers.

So words had to be moulded for someone, for whose imprint I was in a certain sense not responsible, words that arose from their essential impetus, as I will now read. You will see what effect such imprinted words have, words that sound as follows:

As a providential hope to us
You bestrode the field,
Where on Earth the spirit blooms
Through the power of soul being
Seeking to reveal itself in researching.

Beings whose love of truth
Knew of your longing since time immemorial;
Creating out of spirit light
Was your earnest life's aim,
One you ceaselessly pursued.

You tended your abounding talents
For the sake of spirit-knowledge's bright path.
Not misled by world-contradictions
A true servant of truth
Transmuting ahead in sure steps.

You schooled your spiritual gifts,
Making them brave and tenacious
When, from both sides of the pathway,
Error thronged you,
Creating space in you for truth.

To your own self revealing manifestations
Of pure light, to fashion
Sun soul forces
That shone mightily within you,
Was your life's care and its joy.

Other cares and joys
Barely touched your soul
For knowledge seemed to you as light,

Bestowing on life its meaning,
On life its true value seeming.

As a providential hope to us:
You bestrode the field,
Where on Earth the spirit blooms
Through the power of soul being
Seeking to reveal itself in researching.

As a loss that pains us deeply
Do you now depart the field
Where the spirit's earthly seed
In the lap of soul existence flourished
And your sense of the spheres ripened.

Feel how we gaze lovingly
Aloft to heights that call you
To another creating.
Send to your forsaken friends
Your strength from spirit lands.

Hear the pleas of our souls
Sent after you in faith:
We need for our earthly work
Strong forces from spirit lands
For which we thank our departed friends.

As a providential hope to us,
As a loss that pains us deeply,
Let us hope that you, far yet near,
Unlost to us, will light our lives
As a soul-star in spirit realms.

It was some time after the following night that the personality in question seemed to resound towards me—not from out of his consciousness but from his very essence, as if in answer—such that it could be felt as an answer to the words above; yet not as though speaking from a personality, his essential core spoke:

My own self to me revealing
Of pure light to fashion

That Sun soul forces
Shine mightily within me
Was my life's care and its joy.

Other cares, other joys
Barely touched my soul
For knowledge seemed as light to me,
Bestowing on life its meaning
On life its true value seeming.

Only then did I notice that it was a transformation of two verses, transposing the second person into the first person form. You can see from this example how something of a correlation set in between the soul who had tarried in physical life and the soul now having gone through the gate of death. I wish to draw particular attention to the fact that these things are transmitted in such a way that one cannot change anything in the wording. You also see that I was not then conscious as to why the two verses had changed character, something I only adduced from the answer from the departed soul beyond the gate of death on the following night.

We need to become accustomed—as in this situation—not to harbour such feelings in relation to spiritual worlds as are felt in the immediacy of the physical world. Please be aware that upon such qualities does a rightly understood relationship with spiritual worlds depend. As a small example of this, I could mention the following, coming as it does from quite the opposite direction. When these difficult days began, the verses we use were given as if direct from spiritual worlds, like the words I use today when I try to lead souls towards those who are amid events out in the fields or who have already crossed through the gate of death:

Spirits ever watchful, guardians of your souls,
May your wings bear
The beseeching love of my soul
To those earthly beings entrusted to your care
So that, united with your power,
My prayers may radiate help
To the souls whom they lovingly seek!

There it says: 'Spirits of your souls'. In Berlin I had to face someone objecting that this was grammatically incorrect and that one couldn't know in the second line to what those soaring wings referred, because if one says 'Spirits *of your* souls', one is addressing those who are living as humans, yet one is turning to *Spirits* of those alive. A pedant could opine that one should say 'Spirits of *their* souls.' We do indeed need to become familiar with the fact that, in the spiritual world, grammar, as it quite obviously and logically pertains in the sense world, does not necessarily apply, and that yonder one requires greater mobility of soul. One addresses them: 'Spirits of your souls' but in the second line it is obvious that one is not addressing one or a number of human beings but the sheltering, guarding spirits. Grammar is not the decisive factor here. We have to be clear that in higher worlds everything is far more flexible, that one doesn't need to direct attention away from the person when addressing their guardian- or sheltering spirit. These are in far closer contact with 'their' person than ever two people are down here. In the latter case, one has to use physical grammar because between two such people no such close bond needs to exist as between a guardian spirit and 'their' human soul. Thus one could say: Precisely by means of words that are so susceptible to earth-bound grammar in the form given, something of the unique character of spiritual worlds is conveyed. Words emanating from spiritual worlds then become an educational template or device. Sometimes one only understands these things much later on and such learning is not as easy as making flippant grammatical witticisms—which is no great art. We have to find our way into this sort of delicate stance towards the spiritual world. When describing the higher worlds, much depends on not reaching for crass expressions acquired here in the physical world, whereby something of its nature is lost. It is easy to find fault with subtle depictions of spiritual worlds—the realm of spirits then loses the distinctive form of its power. In crossing the threshold we enter the realm of the Spirits of Movement. Style itself has to become more agile. Spirits of Form are for the world spread out around us. Style has to befit the realm of the Spirits of Movement. The time will come when a way will be found into such questions and we will not be able to maintain that what is applicable to the physical world can also adequately depict what in the spiritual world is mobile and immersive.

By using concrete examples—to which our Society's karma has led us—I wanted to illustrate and clarify some aspects of the relationship between human beings and spiritual worlds. Rather than outlining abstractly, much can become clearer by transposing oneself into individual spiritual circumstances and, crucially, a feeling can dawn in us that, through our spiritual-scientific movement, a lively interrelation between physical and higher worlds must gradually arise. After the many experiences we have had to undergo recently, one can say: Our hopes can be bolstered because some aspects of our spiritual movement can only exist if we are certain that those who have gone through the portal of death can become our supportive co-workers. This admittedly requires that we grasp with all possible gravity and intensity the content and intentions of our spiritual science.

In conclusion I would like to reiterate what was examined in detail in the Vienna lecture cycle[30] about life between death and rebirth and which it is important to take into account. We could say—because we have to use words that serve physical life—that human beings are in a kind of unconscious sleep after death. Then they 'awaken', though this is not quite the right word, which sounds as though they arrive at some sort of consciousness. That is not the case. Once the person has laid aside their ether body, they do not lack consciousness nor do they exist in sleep consciousness but they have excessive consciousness. They have a kind of overflowing consciousness rather akin to being overwhelmed by blinding light and being unable to see—such is the inundating excess of consciousness after death. We are engulfed by infinitely potent consciousness which first has to be damped down to the level we have acquired according to our evolution in the physical world. We have to orientate ourselves in this excess of consciousness. What we call 'awakening' yonder initially involves becoming accustomed to the far higher level of consciousness entered after death. It involves dulling, dampening consciousness to a bearable level.

Another thing, I must say, is that with each observation, one is increasingly shown how, for particular states of existence the experience of life in spiritual worlds is the very opposite of experiencing the physical world. The following is a case in point, which I'd like to mention. Between birth and death it is usually the case—without higher knowledge—that nobody remembers back to their birth. This is not a matter for anyone's own recollection. If one were to listen to those who claim only to believe what their five senses tell them, one could object: Then neither should you believe that you were once a small child. You only believe this for two subsidiary reasons: because you see that other people begin their life like this and you assume that you did, too. This is a conclusion only reached by analogy. Alternatively, others have told you so. Through communication—not by observation—do we know that we embarked on life by being born. Nobody notices that this is just an assumption reached by analogy. One would need to reflect: I cannot know anything about my physical origin on the basis of my own observation. When looking back over life, we do not see as far back as our birth. It is different between death and rebirth. This can be shown precisely where an inner wish arises to send aloft words associated with—and characterizing—the individual who has gone through the gate of death. This impulse arises from a longing to serve the one who has gone through the portal of death, to aid them, in as swift a way as possible, to receive what they need, namely an unencumbered view of the moment of their death. For as little, in physical life, as one is able to look back on the moment of one's birth, just as essential is it to view one's death between death and rebirth. Death is always accessible to retrospection, but it appears differently from the spiritual perspective. It may have had terrible aspects, when seen from the physical, but from the other side it is the most glorious event one can behold. Death is shown in all its splendour as it wrests spirit victoriously from physicality. This is among the most wondrously beautiful experiences seen in retrospect between death and birth. Here is a further example of the antithesis between physical and spiritual worlds.

One gradually learns to recognize the idiosyncrasies of the spiritual world. These are perspectives I wanted to develop aphoristically for you today. A further viewpoint immediately becomes relevant to what we are experiencing at the moment: the view that alongside the person who under normal circumstances might have lived much longer, an unspent ether body exists as an individual entity with the deceased individual. Only in older people is the dissolution of the ether body of short duration. We are always surrounded by as yet undissolved ether bodies. We are living towards times when this will be very noticeable because, emanating directly from these ether bodies, will an atmosphere be formed such as has hitherto never existed in Earth evolution. One might imagine this to have been similar in earlier wars, but things change because in past times human beings went through death differently. Previously, there were not as many people living enveloped in materialistic modes of thinking. This causes ether bodies to dispense spiritual impulses. Further, human beings will exist on Earth who know this in their feeling and feel this in their knowing. I hinted at this in lectures[31] dedicated, as I say, to the events of our time. What our time wishes to teach us is that—alongside spiritual levelling—we will also need spiritual deepening in relation to symptoms accompanying what will appear in future. Should we not experience as enormously distressing that our times—declaring themselves as they do to being so logical and enlightened, with scientific culture spreading into every quarter through popular channels—that in those same wide circles something which we must regard as judgements based on passions can grab such wide attention?

Anyone heeding the voices which hold Central Europe to be as if enclosed within a vast fortress will soon realize what this passion wreaks in people's souls. You only need to look north- and north-westwards to see aghast how human passions and discrimination can bring us to such a pass. Better newspapers can be especially instructive. How one quarter or another will yell: We didn't want this war! How could those who stand in opposition to the being of Germany, to the region which had the very least cause to want this war—Central Europe—quite so senselessly apportion blame for this war?

In this respect it is objectively possible—due to the very ways and means in which the being of Germany has evolved—to acquire a certain national self-knowledge in a way that is sadly lacking in other peoples. It will certainly be possible, a long time after these bellicose, martial events, for the majority—that is, outside Central Europe—to achieve sufficient overview of events, in some degree to leave behind the most idiotic opinions of the present. To us—who live within a spiritual movement not wishing merely to pontificate theoretically—to us it should be clear that in face of such difficult events an objective position can indeed be reached, one we can ourselves elucidate precisely because we are living through these destiny-laden days. How easy it is for some short-sighted wit to criticize what belongs to the core impulses of our spiritual science. In the past months, much has had to be painfully suffered in this respect. Here we have a spiritual-scientific movement that says it is working lovingly to commit to humanity without differentiating as to race or any other such thing. One might reflect: How can what has lately been put forward by me not be in agreement with that? Before these fateful days broke over us, I warned against construing the principles of equality, equal rights and equal status by inverting them into complete abstractions. Remember how often I said: When people come along saying that Buddhists, Muslims or Christians are just varied forms of worshipping one being, it is like saying that salt, sugar and pepper are all flavourings, so it doesn't matter which of them they use, while sprinkling sugar onto their soup and beer just because they are all food additives. Using generalities like these in abstraction can be comfortable, but any serious seeker cannot allow themselves to rely on them.

If we immerse ourselves lovingly in the essential natures of individual European nations, we come to recognize that the Folk Soul of the Italians speaks to their sentient soul, members of the French nation are approached through their intellectual soul, the British via the consciousness soul, the German nation through their I. It is not by abstractly pouring out love over every nation that one arrives at concepts. The essential nature of our movement will consist in recognizing that the human soul longs to rise to what is universally human while—and through—acknowledging national singularities. Spiritual science can help someone born this time in Britain to muse: Now I understand that the Folk Soul speaks to me primarily through the consciousness soul, through that which governs the relationship of the soul with the physical plane, through that which predisposes a person to be capable of being material. In acknowledging this, they can come to realize that they need to rid themselves of whatever hinders them—on the basis of their nationality—from rising to universal humanity. Such knowledge is always helpful and the important thing is to acknowledge the idiosyncratic essence of each individual nation. If someone of Russian culture were to reflect: A unique feature of our Folk Soul is that it floats like a cloud above each individual, causing the individual to think chaotically when looking upwards to their Folk Soul and thereby to be dependent on finding their way into the productive element of other peoples; were they to do this, they would find their way. Those who through spiritual science recognize the essential nature of the Russian Folk Soul will reflect: Why am I a Russian? I possess the forces I have gained from it so that I may absorb the strength of other nations.

Through spiritual science a German will recognize—and they need to conceive of this with all due objectivity and humility—that, through the way in which their Folk Soul speaks to their I, they are predisposed, predestined, to seek what is universally human through their nationality; that they grasp that what leads them to transcend nationality is the national element within the being of Germany. Herein lies the concretely national element of German nature: that the national element is driven out above and beyond the nation into universal humanity. That is why the transition from German Idealism to spiritual science is to be found in the confluence of German Idealism with spiritual science. It is vital to struggle onwards to concrete conceptions of spiritual realities. Spiritual science provides the opportunity to conceive of these matters concretely. When you hear that the Frenchman Renan[32] says that what he has garnered from German culture seems to him like higher mathematics when compared with what he absorbed from other peoples—which appears to him like a lower form of maths—this is an expression of what characterizes essential German nature. We are now destiny-bound to have to recognize this fact. We must recognize it—can do no other than acknowledge it—yet we have to do so with the same objectivity, accepting that it is our destiny to forge ahead to truly spiritual life if we are properly German in the same way as it is vital that the British slough off materialism in order to attain to spirituality. Differing tasks await the various nations on the basis of their national identities. It is particularly important for Germans to immerse themselves in the spiritual realm of all that flows through German culture. There is no such national imperative for Russians; for them there is only the potential to accrue sanguinary forces—the forces of blood—that enable them to receive the essential being of other nations. It can be seen that the German core essence has learnt much of importance during the evolution of Folk Souls.

Folk Souls, like human beings, undergo their own process of advancement. Between the years of 1830 and 1850 something particular took place for the Italian Folk Soul. Previously, this culture was not as isolated from European culture as it later became. Before this time their Folk Soul was working within the soul, whereas thereafter it reaches outwards, beyond soul qualities, and shapes the physical world towards national identity. While human beings stride onwards to become independent of the physical world, the opposite is true of the Folk Soul. It works first at a soul level then on the body such that—before the sixteenth century—the Italian Folk Soul worked only on souls, later reaching out beyond souls alone into the corporeal, shaping the nervous system and the ether body so that the human being could determine—and then also identify with—corporeal embodiment. They became more brittle and rigid, increasingly shutting themselves off from other cultures.

A similar juncture occurred for the French Folk Soul in the middle of the seventeenth century. The Folk Soul began to turn its sway away from the soul to encroach on the physical, causing the nation to become more rigid and unyielding. For the British, this only happened from the middle of the seventeenth century onwards. Shakespeare does not yet belong to an age when the Folk Soul had transferred its hold onto the body, which is why Germans understand him better than do the British. During the time between 1750 and 1850 a certain transfer of influence from soul to body took place for the German Folk Soul, but it retreated from it once more. In

Western people the Folk Soul first floats higher, then sinks down into corporeality. Those which sank down into the physical earlier rose into spirituality again. Their descent took place between the middle of the seventeenth and eighteenth centuries. Due to this, the German Folk Soul remained more flexibly mobile. It doesn't constantly remain at the lower level but alternates between high and low, taking hold of human beings and then leaving them free again.

These are things which will only be fully understood in future. It must be said that we are not sufficiently capable of empathizing from the depths of our souls with these dark, difficult times yet also with their great and significant potential. The events of these times ought to be endlessly significant for those interested in what is weaving spiritually throughout the world. Once people start to think about the root causes that have contributed to the present state of war, one thing will be clear: the antithetical tensions between Folk Souls will certainly have been a factor in present wartime events. But you will search in vain for causes in the physical world, never finding what clarifies the issue, because their origins do not lie on the physical plane and because it can be said: Spiritual individualities, spiritual impulses, are working into events. Only when this is understood by humanity will any sensible conversation about contributory forces be possible. It will then be accepted that human beings were mere tools, conduits for good and evil forces. To arrive at such a conclusion, a prejudice-free open-mindedness is essential. Suffusing ourselves with what spiritual science can be is not only for our reason but for the innermost recesses of our souls.

It can be important to recognize how much of what can be ascribed to the British is closely connected with national character. There will have to be acceptance of something that has been harrying me since July, since before the outbreak of war. Sundry opinions could be heard at the time. I am recounting objectively and wish to be assured that any personal element be disregarded by you. It was impressed upon me that the world was threatened with great danger because in London a terrible idiot, one *Grey*, was directing foreign affairs.[33] The world considers *Grey* a clever if perhaps devious person. On the basis of intuitive impressions, I could never consider him anything other than an imbecile and am still obliged to regard him as exceptionally stupid, as one whom—on account of his inability to reflect on situations—ahrimanic forces could seek out for the purpose of effecting particular harm. Based on external criteria, it is hard to prove that such a person is a fool. Yesterday I bought a book in which was a letter written by a ministerial colleague of Grey. I only found out about the letter yesterday but have since July thought Grey a fool sought out by Ahriman to wreak calamity. It's interesting for us how the letter writer qualifies his Cabinet colleague Grey:

> It is highly entertaining for us, who have known Grey since his inauguration, to observe how he impresses his continental colleagues. They seem to surmise something in him that simply isn't there. He is one of the foremost sports anglers in the Kingdom and a passably good tennis player. Yet he really possesses no appreciable political nor diplomatic aptitude. A certain tedious boredom in his manner of speech and a rare quality of inertia should be recognized as such. Earl Rosebery once said of him that he made such a concentrated impression because he never had a single thought of his own that could divert him from the task he had been handed complete with precise instructions. When a temperamental foreign diplomat recently commented on Grey's taciturn manner, something that never revealed what was going on inside him, a cheeky secretary riposted: 'If you shake a china piggy bank that's chock-full of gold, it won't rattle. Neither will it rattle if there isn't a single penny in it. Winston Churchill causes a few pennies'-worth to rattle so loudly that it gets on your nerves but ne'er a clink from Grey. Only the person holding the piggy bank knows whether it's completely full or totally empty!' That was indeed impertinent but well said. I believe Grey is basically decent but seduced through a certain vanity to become involved in arrangements best left to those with spotless hands. His excuse is always that, of himself, he is unable to oversee and think anything through. Though he is in no way a schemer in his own right, once a canny schemer wants to make use of him, he can appear the perfect plotter. It has always represented a temptation for political strategists to choose him as an instrument, and he owes his present position solely to this circumstance.

This is an example of how one can be misled if there is no attempt to see things objectively. In this personality, who is not distinguished by any particular shrewdness apart from his personal abilities in fishing, which have nothing to do with the crucial qualities upon which much depends, ahrimanic powers necessarily had to rely on working from the inside outwards so that events actually came about. It will gradually be understood how essential it is to be clear about just such things and how, in the supra-sensible, good and evil need to be recognized as such. Wanting to understand events on the basis of what can be observed in the physical will not result in insight. It will then be understood how various impulses streamed over from the East, how what gave impetus to these events had long been in preparation in the East, just as what can be observed in Eastern Europe at the moment—how factors evolved which of necessity had to light the torches of war—led to war because Western factors engaged with the arson coming from the East for reasons which can only be fathomed if one plumbs the crucial root causes. It will be important for these events to force people—if they want to understand root causes—to look up to spiritual worlds and not to remain rooted in the physical, in which case they will be arguing for a very long time. We will have to see—more than will some others—that for anthroposophists it is vital to focus on a more secure horizon than that presented by experiencing the affairs of the physical world.

Just how restricted the physical horizon can become has been noticeable for some time. For many, historical reflection only began in July. Even some within our circles subscribed to eccentric opinions. The elements of what I would like to say can be found in the lecture cycle *The Mission of the Folk Souls*,[34] given in Kristiania. There it is also described how, in the East, preparations are under way for what will emerge in the sixth post-Atlantean epoch. We are presently living through the fifth post-Atlantean epoch. If you think in the abstract that humanity is rising ever higher from the fifth, into the sixth and seventh epochs, then you can get overwhelmed. But merely pressing ahead is not the way humanity's cultural evolution advances. Up to the fourth culture, there was a repetition of Earth's evolution. The fifth epoch is the decisive one; it represents something newly added, which must be carried over into the sixth era. The sixth culture will descend into decadence, it will be a degenerative culture. This has to be taken into account. Connected with this is a spirit such as Solovyov[35] who, with his habitual qualities, has in a certain respect outgrown Russian folk characteristics and immersed himself in the Western world, so that his philosophy is Western—albeit encased in the temperament of the East—but still, in terms of sentence flow, recognizably Russian. It would be foolish to say that someone steeped in Western European culture could be endowed with something transcending that West-European culture.

Again, these are just by way of disjointed examples, but through them you will hear an appeal to try—through our spiritual-scientific stream—to use these desperate times to understand and to clothe in concrete form all that really can flow into our feelings and sensitivities when spiritual Imaginations flow into our perceptions. Our spiritual science will prove its worth in future precisely because it finds its way through the disturbingly troubled passions of our time.

I am well aware that since the beginning of these oppressive times of ours, neither here nor anywhere else have I spoken of matters in any other way than could be presented to an objective world view. And yet, what was to be heard? You can hear all sorts about what has been going on over the past few months, the state of various matters being criticized in the world at large. One is often obliged to hear the claim that the majority of members only listen to the opinion of a single person, that everything relies on blind faith... How far blind faith has got us is evident at this moment!

Opinion was rife about what I have been saying: 'To while away his time, he uses his occult faculties to test Wolff's Telegramme.'[36] Exceptional trust from someone within our movement to say that I use the truth of Wolff's Telegraphic Bureau to the detriment of Germany's enemies! This is just one example among countless others. You see how the boundless passions overwhelming the world even play into spiritual science. This should not prevent us from seeking the truth in respect of what it is our obligation to pursue. You will understand this.

Basically, it has always been as it is now. What has now been said has always been said and done. I have previously emphasized that this theosophical movement—which has now become the anthroposophical movement—has never wished to develop in any other way than within the onward progress of Central European culture. It has never been a matter of allowing anyone to tow us along in their wake. Seeing this, mistrust was spawned from the English quarter against these Central Europeans who were not devotees of what was being presented by British Theosophy. A sense of truth had to reject the British conception on the question of Christ because it was such that a belief could have arisen that Christ would reincarnate into a physical body, the grounds being that a spiritual coming would be incomprehensible. This proved the impossibility of uniting the two directions. In English publications you now find correspondence from Mrs Besant which in every way calls upon the theosophical world to act against those in Germany. There you find a belated explanation as to why the German theosophical movement had to separate from its English counterpart back then. Mrs Besant says: 'Now, when I look back in light of German methods, as revealed by the war, I admit that the lengthy efforts to ensnare the theosophical organization and to set a German at its head—the anger against me as I frustrated these efforts, the complaint that I had spoken of the late King Edward VII as the protector of European peace instead of granting the Kaiser that honour—all this was part of a wide-ranging campaign against England, and that the missionaries were tools, sent and used by German agents here...' (in India) 'to carry out their plans. Had they succeeded in turning the Theosophical Society in India, with its large numbers of government officials, into a weapon against the British Government, educating them to look aloft to Germany as to their spiritual leader instead of insisting, as they had always done, on standing for the bond between equal free nations, it would gradually have become a channel for poison into India.'

This personality has hit upon what I *then* wanted. So there you see the root cause as to why war broke out between Germany and England. Yet you can see that our present struggle towards all that is spiritual has also progressed. Much of what had to happen then will perhaps now be understood differently.

Affirming occultism is a double-edged sword. It has to be said over and over again that a sense for truth needs to permeate souls intensively so that, through it, salvation and not calamity is brought about in the world. How what has to penetrate into our souls as a result of the events of the present is connected with the way in which we, as keen students of the spiritual, can bear fruit is expressed in the following thought: When peace returns, there will be unused ether forces in the spiritual world which will want to send down strengthening forces. And, from souls enlivened by spiritual science, forces also need to rise up, uniting with those forces from above. Then will what is a blessing for the progress of humanity and what spiritual science is capable of becoming also become significant. If a really good many souls who experience this—truly and objectively—can be mustered, if very many souls can have thoughts illuminated by a spiritual-scientific view of the world and can raise themselves in longing to spirit realms, then will all that is so hard about our times also be valuable for those souls. I would therefore like to bring the context for our spiritual striving to expression in these words:

From the courage of fighters,
From the blood on fields of battle,
From the grief of the bereft
From the sacrifice of people
There will grow fruit of spirit
If, spirit-conscious, souls will turn
Their thoughts to realms of Spirit.

# Lecture 4

## 29 NOVEMBER 1915, MUNICH

THIS is a time when the experience of death—from the perspective of the physical, both in its wider and closer contexts—confronts our souls; a thousand-fold among humanity as a whole, but also within our closer circles, from which over recent months and years the souls of many dear friends have departed through the gate of death. It may therefore be timely to direct our observant gaze towards something with which we in this Branch may feel especially connected from a particular angle: the riddle of death and its associated mysteries. We will turn our discerning eyes towards the riddle of death, not just because we are plagued by curiosity or a thirst for knowledge but because we have assimilated from such considerations a certain amount of what spiritual science can offer us regarding the mystery of death. Closely related to this is what we need by way of strengthening forces for life and how, basically, by observing death, the chasm between two worlds—the physical world in which we live and the world of spirits—can be eliminated. Haven't we often reminded ourselves, by rightly calling to mind actual, concrete deaths, how those souls, with whom we were involved in physical life, remained connected with us after they had gone through the gate of death? Could I not in this very Branch—and in this regard—express that it is among the most fortifying thoughts by which we can accept being sustained that we have friendly souls in the spiritual world who can and have—because of the ways in which they were once associated with our work and concerns here on Earth—become our faithful helpers and co-workers? One does need to emphasize that we live at a time in which we feel duty-bound to work out, to elaborate, this spiritual science, a time in which spiritual science is still misunderstood, and from such misunderstanding and non-comprehension stems the enmity we encounter. Sometimes doubts can arise as to whether, in face of such enmity—an opposition which will truly manifest in ever fiercer forms—we will have recourse to sufficient strength to withstand it in terms of what we are vouchsafed within the physical environment. This is when the fortifying thought can arise that those faithful souls of friends who have gone before us and who are unimpeded by the obstacles which still mount up against us here on Earth may unite their forces with ours. It is from such convictions that we can believe in the victory—if a slow, gradually ascending victory—of our spiritual-scientific work.

When a person goes through the portal of death it is opportune for our souls, if I may put it like this, to experience how they, having laid aside their physical body in the arena of earthly existence, rise and enter spiritual realms, largely leaving behind these physical worlds. If we have acquired a conviction in spiritual science, we may still feel a person's crossing of the threshold of death in terms of their departing the physical world. If the gaze of the spiritual scientist is now directed towards the experience of death, towards a person as they cross the threshold of death, that spiritual researcher's gaze will frame this event rather differently. What primarily forms the focus of consideration is the experience itself undergone by so-called dead individuals, how they themselves experience and feel this passage through the gate of death inwardly and how their existence is further elaborated between death and a new birth. Here it must be said: What initially transits through the portal of death is, as we know, the ether body together with the astral body and I. What the deceased feels, on entering the spiritual world in this threefold form, is that the stage of the physical world, together with all those people with whom they had been connected—and everything else related to it—as though all this were leaving them, as though it were to some extent slipping away underneath them. Then the person having newly gone through the gateway of death lives their way, with their ether body, into the etheric world, becoming one with it. We also know this: to their gaze appears a kind of overview of their experience on Earth in their recent incarnation. This experience can really be compared with a sort of universal dream experience. In undulating, weaving images of great eloquence and deep significance does their life run on for days on end. One could say that this panorama of life expands, during which the deceased feels: you see thus far; your life unravels, ebbs away. And beyond this flowing life, the arena in which you previously existed, also takes its leave of you.

This is a completely etheric experience. Whilst we experience physical-sense existence, sensing as hard and coarse the objects with which we collide, knowing clearly that what we experience through our senses is external to us and that we feel ourselves to be within the boundaries of our skin, the person beyond the gate of death experiences their existence and interrelatedness with the world in such a way that no such great differentiation is felt; they feel as though the contents of their life's tableau were almost identical with their own self. Yes, this panorama at first constitutes their world. In that great panorama they survey what they underwent and it is for them their immediate world, the place of their existence. To some extent, the earthly world sinks away from them and from this ebbing world there projects what they had experienced since their birth within that earthly life, and this all unravels like a mighty, intensely living pictorial panorama, not in dull dream consciousness, but shot through with vibrantly clear consciousness—not just seeing in images but such that everything undergone in differing modes during life is revivified. Every single conversation we have had with other people is heard again, everything we experienced with others, the impressions we shared with them: all this we experience again. It is because everything is flowing, flooding life that such a wealth of dynamism is possible which, crammed into a few days, forms a complete overview—one always simultaneously in front of us—of all that we underwent over the course of what may sometimes have been long earthly lives. We go through this knowing: previously on Earth, one experience was followed by another. You had an experience, you were at the centre of your life's many networks and associations. This one flowed into it, remained a while in your memory, was then partly forgotten. Anon something new appeared and so your life's streams flowed together over the years. Now this is all simultaneity to your soul's eye; now everything is—if I may put it thus—both within your self, yet spread out as widely as the world.

In these days after death one does not differentiate between world and self but both flow together and the world is simply that which is self-experienced. Initially, there is nothing more than what the self itself experienced, within which everything we have ever undergone with others during Earth existence is contained. Then we feel as though everything that is of external-etheric-material nature—which had at first appeared as the bearer of this world of images—were to leave us and as though this world of images were no longer as if observed, but now as something with which our entire being is bound up and which now totally comprises our inner experience. And because we are simultaneously able to absorb those images into ourselves, we are in turn in a position to sense and experience the rest of the spiritual world and to survey it with our consciousness.

Now, gradually, other human souls appear in the widths of the spiritual world, souls who either went ahead of us through the gate of death and are now there, or souls who are still below in physical bodies, amidst physical life. From the perspective of the spiritual world, one views human souls by seeing them in the form of their soul-spiritual nature. What is physical is only perceptible to physical organs but the soul-spiritual element, which clothes the physical, can rise up before our soul-vision. We feel ourselves far more closely united with all that is being experienced by us than we could feel connected down there—namely on Earth—where physical bodies separate us through their inherent boundaries.

There is just one thing onto which we must always hold: words, which all bear the imprint of conditions on the physical plane, have to be carefully chosen when depicting what is spiritual because experiencing in the spiritual world is far more delicate and inward than it is here in the physical world. If we want to bring to mind how a thought representing an experience lying far in our past re-emerges when remembering that experience, how that thought emerges from ourselves when we actively imagine it and now—I would say—think the reality-content of such a shadowy, remembered experience, then we gradually achieve a concept as to how spiritual reality actually arises before us after we have gone through the gate of death. This reality does not, as a rule, approach us from outside as do experiences in the physical-sense world. Imaginations do indeed arise in this way, but with endlessly greater vitality than memory-images, but in such a way that we do not differentiate between I and Imagination in the way we distinguish I from external world here. They emerge from us, rising like memory-pictures, but in such a way that we know: what is arising there, on the horizon of our consciousness, is reality. Here an Imagination arises and we know it to be as much a part of us as are memory-pictures on the physical level. It rises up in full vivacity. We, however, know that we are bound to it and that our I is within it. In this way does the soul ascend, in this way do we feel ourselves to be at one with souls and with the soul-being of the higher hierarchies, which gradually appear. I'd like to say that the spiritual world comes towards our own souls from out of indistinct, dark gloaming in the same way as do those memory-pictures that surface into our souls. It is just that memory-pictures are more twilit, only depicting an external reality, while the Imaginations that arise become speaking Imaginations in that they announce their intrinsic being through a spirit language then unveiling itself—a language that then becomes for us a revelation of souls and of spirits with whom we will—in the most multifarious ways—come together more warmly and inwardly than ever we could be with another human being in the physical world.

You need to make especially clear to yourselves just what initial experiences human beings have when they stride through the gate of death. The retrospective contemplation of their most recent life is of enormous, vast significance for all their subsequent experiencing between death and a new birth, and we can reinforce our sense of its importance if we think how, in physical life, we achieve our I-consciousness—not our I but consciousness of our I. How we arrive at our I we know from our spiritual-scientific studies[37] that Spirits of Form lend us this I inasmuch as we have progressed from Moon-existence to Earth-existence. But this I is at first unconscious.

It becomes conscious by being reflected in our physical bodies. How is it reflected here on a physical level? Well, as you know, you can see it in normal dream life: even in dream life, the I is only very rarely conscious of itself. An I will intermingle, merging with the arising dream-pictures. By which means do we experience I-consciousness during the day? Be quite clear as to how this I-consciousness is connected with all our sense perceptions and with all external experience. If we move our hand through the air, we feel nothing. The moment we hit something, we notice it. Yet we actually notice our own experiencing, sensing what we feel through our fingers. In bumping into the outer world we become aware of our I. In a further sense do we become conscious of our I through the fact that, on waking, we dive down out of sleep consciousness into our physical body—we collide with our physical body. Consciousness of our I is actually summoned before our soul in this collision with our physical body.

Let us be quite clear: I-consciousness must not be confused with an I. Initially, an I remains in the subconscious and is, one could say, incomplete. The true nature of an I will only be experienced by human beings during the coming Vulcan epoch. But an I acquires Earth consciousness because—with the astral body—it dives down into the ether and physical bodies, colliding with them. In this collision with ether and physical bodies does that I become aware of itself; through it I-consciousness arises from the moment when the physical body has become hardened enough for the collision to be sufficiently strong, in other words, from that point in early childhood, the point back to which we can remember.

Now, the soul also needs to collide with something in life between death and a new birth. Here in physical life, it collides with the physical body, which is bequeathed us by the forces and substances of external nature for the purpose of us attaining I-consciousness. After death, between death and a new birth—in order to attain to its henceforward *spiritual* I-consciousness—the soul collides with its own life, which, in the days after stepping through the portal of death, it has been observing, and back towards which it constantly looks. Firstly, life appears to visual gaze, then it becomes an ever-present retrospective. In that, having gone through the gate of death, we live on in the stream of time, we look back upon what we have directly experienced in and through death and—now as a spirit-being—does the soul stride onwards, always looking back and colliding with the panorama of its lived life, which yet remains spiritual recollection. So, just as an I is ignited to I-consciousness by colliding with its physical body down here, similarly is I-consciousness ignited after death by colliding with its own retrospectively viewed past life. By looking back over this do we experience I-consciousness between death and a new birth. Such I-consciousness is different after death but is certainly not any the weaker for it.

What is this I-consciousness actually, here in the physical world? When we want to become aware of our I in the physical realm, it is the case that we are dependent on being shown it by other means within our physical body. Our physical I appears to us in reflection in the mirror of our physical body. We feel quite passive in the genesis of our I, at least when we are not imitating a philosopher such as Johann Gottlieb Fichte. By contrast, once we have gone through the gate of death, we feel ourselves to be perpetually active. Ever and ever again do we, as it were, reflect in our now far more intensive consciousness by looking back on our own life and uniting our I-consciousness with the awareness that we will ourselves—over and over again do we will ourselves, and we are allowed to will ourselves—for we remain indissolubly and enduringly ourselves because the impressions of all that we have undergone also remain inextinguishable. With these words I would like to reflect very clearly what is experienced between death and a new birth. Experiencing consciousness between death and rebirth is quite unlike experiencing consciousness here on Earth. Here on the physical plane nobody can actually, with their normal consciousness, look back on their own birth. One's own birth cannot normally be experienced when observed with everyday consciousness; memory only begins later on. I have previously said here: If people rely only on their own experience in life—on having experienced something themselves—then nobody can actually claim to remember their own birth unless they look back clairvoyantly. If someone says: I won't believe in the spiritual world until I see it for myself; I won't believe what spiritual science presents and I only believe what I myself have seen—one can simply reply: And what about your own birth? You cannot have had much experience of that. So you see from this that only the consequences of even something as highly significant for human life as birth can be deduced by normal consciousness. Our normal consciousness only ever assumes that we were born by concluding that we look quite like the people of whom we observe that they, too, were born, hence we must also have been born. But this only relies on inference.

It is quite different during the time between death and a new birth. As little as one can look back with normal consciousness on one's own birth, does one all the more intensively look back through the remembered panorama of one's life to the moment of one's death. As truly as the experience of birth is extinguished for earthly consciousness, just as truly does the event of one's death remain within the soul's backward-looking consciousness between death and a new birth, but now seen from the opposite side. This may have some gruesome aspects; yet one cannot conclude from this that it is terrible for the individual living onwards to have to constantly look back to their death because, from that perspective, it is the greatest, most wonderful, most meaningful experience a human soul can ever have and because, in ever-radiant glory, it illustrates how the spirit triumphs over material existence. This enduring retrospective to the moment of death is an all-revitalising, all-heightening and uplifting, universally-consciousness-enhancing experience. The soul reflects primarily through this death experience: I live here in the spiritual world, with the spiritual world. To the extent that a soul has the strength to say this to itself does the experience of death hold mighty significance for each newly-beginning onward life.

I was saying: the human being feels how their body and everything that co-existed on Earth now leaves them. They feel how, through their inner activity, they now have to compensate their consciousness, how they have to produce something for their consciousness which was previously bestowed on them for that purpose while their body was their instrument. 'I can exist consciously within myself without my body': the potential in grasping this thought produces a far more powerful awareness than can be had within earthly life. Death gives us this conviction so that you can sense: your body is receding but a time is now beginning in which you no longer rely on colliding with your body to feel yourself to be an I; a time is now starting when you can—to some extent—yourself pour spiritual forces into the sheaths of your soul so as to continually summon yourself to consciousness. Through recognizing that this activity of summoning-yourself-to-consciousness pertains once your body has been torn from you, do you have a real-life impression of inwardly creating an existence. That begins at death, when one has to begin to experience oneself without one's body. Death is the starting point for living onwards without a body, to feeling oneself to be an ego by looking backwards to the event of death. When the gaze of the spiritual researcher—by allowing the spiritual world to come alive within—reaches the point where souls who have gone through the gate of death emerge as if into their inner life, onto their field of observation, in the form of Imaginations, then one learns to know *how* the deceased are experiencing. One learns to detect differences that arise and one can of course only ever describe particular instances. We will look at one such differentiation.

One learns—as if in an arena, a soul observatory—how human souls present themselves after death. These souls are of two kinds: those human souls who have entered the spiritual world earlier, before our own death, whom we find therein as disembodied souls, and those souls who are still embodied on Earth. We are just as capable of empathizing and co-experiencing with these latter souls who remain on Earth. As the arena of terrestrial existence withdraws from us, the potential remains open to know ourselves still to be connected with what was our soul component. Only our physical surroundings vanish from us while our souls expand, uniting with the widths of the universe and, precisely due to this, are we given the possibility of knowing ourselves to be remaining connected with souls and able thereby to experience them still.

But there is a difference between experiencing one quality of soul from the other kind. If we experience a human soul in the spiritual world, we naturally—I would hardly need to say this were it not for those who have grasped nothing of spiritual vision still believing it so—do not encounter it as if approaching it just as one meets people externally, but that one feels the being in question emerging, arising in one's consciousness. Now, in a soul already disembodied, who has gone through the portal of death and whom we encounter, we have an inner awareness that they are present. The impression begins in this way. We are aware: here is a soul. At the same time we have to live into it, to feel our way into it. We have to receive the Imagination of them in such a way that we feel involved in the creation of that Imagination.

I would really like to describe the matter as follows: you feel yourself to be in the spiritual world. The awareness dawns that you are no longer alone, that a soul is nearing. Now it is as if, in the physical world, you are bearing a thought invisibly within you. Yet you wish to make it visible so you take a chalk and draw that thought, making it into a picture. It really is initially like this in the spiritual world. You know that there is a real spirit present. In order to see a soul, you first need to come into contact with it in such a way that you, as it were, *draw it* as an Imagination *into* spiritual space. You do this, knowing yourself to be active in creating that Imagination. And if it is through the music of the spheres that its being allows it to speak to our being—much in the way that our language announces our souls here in the physical world—when it allows the music of the spheres to resound from itself, you feel as though you cannot remain passive. If you hear the speech of a person and you do not wish to think, you need not understand it. You have to participate if you wish to understand someone. This is also what you have to do in this realm. You create a co-existence with them—actively and dynamically—knowing that every part of the soul's being and appearance, which could appear before you, has to be co-created as an apparition, a phenomenon. You create the appearance, not the being. It may also be the case that you don't feel so strongly active but then know: a human soul is present here. Yet it may of its own accord strive to become an Imagination, without our active participation just described. The Imagination appears to us more of its own accord. Then we are encountering a soul who is still embodied on Earth. Once the human being has gone through the gate of death and is gradually living on in spiritual worlds, they learn in this way how to relate to other souls, to distinguish between souls they meet in the spiritual world and those whom it has to think of as being displaced onto Earth.

With this I have specified one of the differentiations that transpire when directly experiencing the spiritual world. Thus, experience, spiritual experience, is also necessary in differentiating whether one is meeting human souls or whether one is experiencing beings of the higher hierarchies. Consider what I have described as the experience of human souls. I said: You encounter human souls either in such a way that you create—or you recreate—Imaginations or that they appear largely of themselves. The experience can, however, be like this: you are aware that a being is present. That being has to appear before us as an Imagination, also in our experience, if we really wish to sojourn in their company. But it will not immediately be possible for us to create this Imagination with any immediacy in the same way as just described, where in some instances it constructs itself largely by its own activity. We need to develop something quite different within us when we sense that a being is present. We need to educe the following feeling: we make way for that being to create within us. We relinquish some forces so that the forces of the being in question can instead stream into us. Whilst we feel ourselves—in the case of a human soul—to be participating creatively in forming the Imagination, we feel in the presence of a being of the higher hierarchies—or from the ranks of the Angeloi or Archangeloi—how these beings themselves create Imaginations within us. In this way do we gradually find our way into co-experiencing in spiritual worlds.

We also know, quite concretely, that this co-experiencing takes place over the course of many long years—its length in relation to the previous life on Earth has often been studied—and that life will run in reverse order. First we have a couple of days of life's panorama, then we begin to live backwards through our lives, but differently from the way in which we lived here between birth and death. We experience the last first, then what came before it and so backwards in spirit until our birth. We experience it by observing our lives, but now from the opposite perspective. I can tell you that we see it from a perspective of *effects*. To take a crude example, once in my life I said to someone: You are an ignoble person, or I injured them in some other way. I experienced something in my life. What *I* felt is something quite different from what *they* felt. *They* felt insulted and pained, *they* experienced sorrow. Now, reliving this after death in the soul world, you yourself experience *by its effect* what you have done. The sorrow felt by the other through our derogatory insult, this pain and sorrow we now experience in its effects on ourselves. Through this retrospective life do we undergo the effects of our deeds as they were experienced in the other person. We can gain a certain glimpse of this post-mortem experience if we turn our attention to a connection the spiritual researcher can uncover between impressions after death and those here in the physical world.

What I am now talking about is something that can alert us to how the spiritual researcher, little by little, gradually arrives at their conclusions; and how it is prejudiced to opine that anyone who has crossed the threshold into the spiritual world would know that world on the basis of their own visions, and that they could answer any question randomly put to them. Over and over again we see that, when a spiritual researcher speaks of this or that in public and engages in a question-and-answer session, how what might from a certain perspective seem desirable in answering a question about all things in Heaven, Earth and all things eternal, it is then assumed: whoever can see into spiritual worlds already knows everything, every single thing that there is to know. That is about as clever as someone here present saying: You have eyes, you know Munich, so describe California to me! In spiritual worlds it is actually the case that one has to proceed step by step, gradually acquiring what needs to be grasped of spiritual worlds; it is naïve to believe that it somehow doesn't apply that everything first has to be observed step by step. It is quite different in spiritual worlds from here in physical existence. Here, in the physical, let's say that you've never been to Heidelberg and yet you want to describe Heidelberg, so you bestir yourself and travel there. In the spiritual world, things have to approach you and you have to evolve inner patience and experiential forces in your soul. Things come into your view once you have sufficiently readied yourself. The Heidelberg of the spiritual world has to approach us and we have to prepare our souls for it to do so. It always depends partly on the extent to which we are blessed as to whether we can experience one thing or another spiritually. It is in this way that the spiritual researcher can very gradually uncover mysteries of the spiritual world and also be instructed about them while there.

Today I would like to talk about a particular result of spiritual research, one not yet discussed here from that vantage point. Once you have developed and made accessible certain inner powers of spiritual observation and watched how the human being tarries in spiritual worlds between falling asleep and waking up—viewing the sleeping human being as a soul as it exists outside its physical body—you find out various things on the basis of gazing which, in one sense, have to be learned if you wish to take hold of something: you notice that a person is in fact continuously active in soul, much more active than when they are awake. While awake, a person makes use of such activity as their body has cultivated, and into this do they, in soul form, transpose themselves and exist. By contrast, during sleep they live within their own activity. In following this, you notice that people relive—differently—what they have undergone in the physical world between waking up and falling asleep. Let's imagine that I have done something or have read this or that: while asleep, I experience all that reading once again, going through it all. Nowadays we have as yet no awareness in normal life that this also becomes I-conscious, and yet it plays out at a soul level, however dully, extending far enough for the soul to actively elaborate what it has experienced during the day. Thoughts are transformed in soul so that they become fruitful for us. We assimilate as the fruits of living what we have undergone during the day. Ever-actively do we work on those fruits of living, those results of life and this is what we do during sleep.

The spiritual researcher can discover something. If they compare this experience of sleep, which human beings undergo, with those undergone by human beings in the years or decades after they have gone through the gate of death, while wandering through their lives backwards, it is interesting that people travel through their lives such that they relive their nights and not their days. As they had looked back on the day every night, it is this that they traverse in the soul world. It is the same as what they had experienced during the day, but now viewed from the perspective of sleep. How we experience this is quite remarkable. We don't usually think about it, but our memory here in the physical world actually only stretches across events of the day. We remember what we did during waking consciousness. Now, after death, we remember precisely those nocturnally-relived daytime, earthly experiences. That is where the conscious memory of our nocturnal processing arises. I haven't expressed this so clearly before simply because I did not yet know it. Such things transpire and appear to one during sequential spiritual research.

One important thing, as it were, steps into the light of day, something important for the consciousness and work we ought to be creating in our Branches and communities. Previously, and from another viewpoint—you can read about it—I drew attention to the fact that life in the land of soul lasts approximately one third of the time spent between birth and death. The reasons for this are elaborated in those books. But the reasons given there are from an angle different from that which I am sharing today. You relive your experiences of the night. How long does one normally sleep? This equates to sleeping roughly one third of one's life. Striding through these nights after death will take a third of one's lifetime. This is connected with length of nocturnal elaborating, something immensely interesting and important. This fact was previously given on the basis of different reasoning. I documented it, for instance, in *Occult Science—an Outline*:[38] a third of one's lifetime is the length during which one relives the latter after death, during life in Kamaloka. Now, from a completely different perspective, one not previously thought of, the same transpires: Kamaloka lasts around one third of a lifetime on Earth, but now from the angle that one relives one's *nights*. So you see, these things arise over and over again and are immensely supportive and strengthening as proof for the veracity of what spiritual science can offer human beings. You seek a truth from a certain angle and arrive at it from elsewhere, at the fact that Kamaloka endures a third of a lifetime. You confirm the same fact from a diametrically opposite direction. Results of this kind are mutually supporting. This can often come to one, assuring one while giving certainty to those who cannot yet research for themselves. I have often mentioned this congruity. By really following—as individuals together within the life of these Branches—how such topics are researched do we gradually conquer for ourselves an inner certainty and the power of conviction, even though we may have to exert ourselves over long periods along our own paths to knowledge in order to reach our own experiential conclusions.

Now, in conclusion, I would like to share a truth with you, one of particular interest for our time, though always of general interest. In a public lecture[39] I spoke, from one perspective, about deaths that can take place when, say, someone in the bloom of youth is hit by a bullet: that in one sense their physical body is taken from them. I spoke about—and have previously shown from various angles—what becomes of those unspent forces. Today I want to add another slant to that experience of death.

How do those pass on and enter spiritual worlds—those from whom their physical body has vanished—not due to illness or old age but who have lost their physical bodies forcibly by bullet or other injury? What becomes of their unspent forces?: this was what I explored. How they actually enter the spiritual world themselves becomes a mysterious riddle. In times such as ours you see so very many souls entering the spiritual world. Their bodies have been taken from them by external means. They differ sharply from those souls whose bodies have been taken by old age or illness. To explain and understand questions such as these, one has to be able to place what is correct alongside what else is correct in spiritual worlds. You have to be able to ask: With what does one have to combine a phenomenon, which has become a riddle, in order to elucidate it? It transpires that you have to place the phenomenon alongside something you can experience in the physical world. Now, we want to characterize experience in the physical world initially by looking towards those crudely materialistically-minded spirits who are not willing to rate anything other than what can be starkly conceived of with sense perceptions and which, because it makes a crude impression, they designate as existing. But there are other things in this world that make life valuable and these others are ideals. Admittedly, the most crassly confirmed materialists will say: You can't eat ideals; they don't exist in any proper sense, they're just thought up. But people who actually work towards truly cultivating, elevating and vitalizing Earth existence are those who import ideals. Whatever does not exist—in the crudest materialistic sense—has to be brought into the course of Earth existence to the end that this life be made valuable. Idealists are in a sense harbingers from divine worlds. For ideals are like messages from divine realms: they need to be rightly introduced into the world yet they do not originate in the physical world. You cannot observe ideals nor can you experiment with depicting them through experience. Nevertheless, ideals are like messengers from a spiritual world.

The human soul who, through a bullet in the bloom of youth has been bereft of their body, ascends through the portal of death into spiritual worlds, leaves behind not only unspent forces—to be used as I indicated earlier—but also brings into the spiritual world a quite distinct consciousness. Such souls enter the spiritual world differently from those who could complete their lives or those whose body has been taken from them through illness. Such souls enter spirit-land bearing thoughts about what might have been, down there in the physical, namely what their own lives could have been from the point onwards, at which they sacrificed themselves. All that could have taken place over the following years of their natural lives—as far as capacities are concerned—had been assigned to the physical world. It might have been possible, let's say, that two years after they died, their body—as a physical body—might still have been on its feet among others. Now they are no longer present. Something which might have existed in the physical world is there no more. This is what a soul, whose body has been taken from them, now takes aloft into the spiritual world.

Now it also needs to be announced aloft to the spiritual world how—down there in the world—something intended for the harsh conditions of existence is not living out its days amid that harsh material existence. This announcement is for the spiritual world akin to a declaration of ideals in the physical world. These are the 'inverse idealists.' Down here life can proceed such that potential is not realized, that souls return from the physical world, having forcibly encountered death. Among those up there who have not experienced this, an announcement is made, signifying the same as does a declaration of ideals here. Here in physical existence it can be declared: not only that which makes an impression on the senses is of value, but ideals are something precious, stemming as they do from spiritual realms. In the spiritual world, those whose bodies have been taken from them announce that here is something effective which, albeit existing differently in the sense world, enlivens the spiritual world just as ideals vivify the sense world. This is a highly significant result of spiritual research and it makes clear to us that sacrificial deaths are just as meaningful for the spiritual world—not only, as I set out yesterday, for the physical world—but equally for spiritual worlds. Among the souls living in spiritual worlds are those who look back on a course of life lived out, but there are also those who have learnt that situations can be truncated with a jolt, and these are in some respects the inverse idealists of the spiritual world.

This is how life's phenomena, life's riddles, gradually reveal themselves and—in times such as ours, when so very much of a mysterious nature can be presaged from blood and sorrow—one really does gain a sense how for the first time spiritual science can place the human being centrally into the whole totality of life. Humanity marches on. Previously natural science did not exist; it has emerged from the dark gloaming of souls' striving. Spiritual science also has to arise. Humanity of the future will not be able to dispense with it. Nowadays it has many opponents, but human beings will increasingly sense the enigmas of existence and with them an ever greater need to approach such mysteries of life through spiritual science. This must ever and anew be resurrected in our souls as the thought which unites us with our spiritual movement and which in one sense points out how we are seeking something within our spiritual movement which has to become ever more widespread amongst humanity, something we need to hold onto through all the naturally occurring adversity of the present.

Today I would like to emphasize—on the basis of today's considerations—just how seriously our times should now be warning us to do everything within our power to really embed spiritual science in human evolution. To that effect I would like to strengthen this exhortation and make it all the more forceful because the conditions of the time do not allow us to be together as often as usual. Let me therefore direct this appeal to your very souls: that during these times of war we work within our Branch groups all the more faithfully and devotedly, even though the co-operative work among you—with, for instance, me—may only rarely be possible until more normal circumstances are restored. Travelling around the world is presently more difficult than usual, and it may be that we have to learn—really, really strongly—to rely upon ourselves in working within our individual Branches. Doing whatever we possibly can in this respect will be immensely fruitful in the sense of the spiritual striving that must flow into human evolution. For again and ever again do we need to be directed towards this thought: the great sacrifices having to be made by such countless numbers of human beings at present—which are inwardly so enmeshed with all the mysteries and pain death buries within human evolution—that these events can only rightly relate to our soul life if we are able to observe human affairs and historical progress from the wider perspectives of spiritual science.

It is not my intention to focus on all the hindrances and obstructions that may have reached your hearing, though they had to be discussed at a certain place.[40] Yet these issues have shown how essential it is that, quite factually, we become convinced of the need for—and effectiveness of—this spiritual-scientific movement, and that we separate from it all that arises out of our personal wishes and whims, as these will create hindrances and obstructions to the right progress of our spiritual-scientific work. Spiritual science is so replete with content that we can engage with it quite objectively. Let us often—over and over again—powerfully remind our souls just how easy it is to allow personal, vain or conceited ambitions to infiltrate what we should actually be getting hold of: the spiritual life pulsating throughout the world, which we should be allowing to inspire and seize us.

Certain events have recently played out within our movement that are close to our souls and thoughts: alas, blood is flowing out there, where large swathes of humanity are struggling for aims whose significance cannot today be gauged, and yet a spiritual movement exists which could—quite factually—provoke interest in the fact that one need not direct one's attention towards what is merely of a personal nature. Yet so much of a personal quality is still to be found here—just at a time when souls ought to feel obliged to empathize as one with these great events. This is a source of pain: that the potential for working together on what ought to be an impersonal project should still be fraught with so many personal issues.

Well, especially today we need—continually and repeatedly—to look up from our individualized lives at what European humanity—and the whole of humanity beyond it, too—is experiencing and say to ourselves: The right aims, achieved through adversity, will only come to fruition if humanity's future evolution is suffused with what spiritual science can bequeath to it. If the fruits of the blood, the pain, the sorrow and loss, can be united with thoughts distilled from spiritual science and survive into the future then, on the fields today demanding so many sacrifices, there will one day blossom a spiritual life that dignifies such sacrifice. Looking towards such times, we will close with these words:

From the courage of fighters,
From the blood on fields of battle,
From the grief of the bereft
From the sacrifice of people
There will grow fruit of spirit
If, spirit-conscious, souls will turn
Their thoughts to realms of Spirit.

May a good many souls among our number turn their thoughts towards spirit realms so that what may blossom and bear fruit from their efforts becomes a blessing, not just a personal one but a blessing for all humankind. In this sense do we want to cultivate our work most intensively—whatever life may bring—all the while holding firm to our task of working onwards together!

# Lecture 5

## 18 MARCH 1916, MUNICH

We would like to use this evening to turn our attention particularly to an occult-historical consideration, while the day after tomorrow to one of a more purely human-occult nature. Although I wish to take as my starting point a question—one to some extent prompted by necessities, in face of which present events do need to be considered—this won't lead me into warming up old topics nor revisiting bygone contentions, but will serve to express something that needs to be said. For that reason, I wish to start with a question, one I will not immediately answer, but which will be answered later on by way of the various thoughts I wish to broach. I want to start from the question: Why has Mrs Besant been wanting—since the outbreak of war—to denigrate our German movement in such an outrageous way in her English journals? Why did her campaign of vilification begin at the outbreak of hostilities and why does she continue it now in such an unbelievable manner? The following remarks may provide a few clues in answer to these questions.

The public lectures[41] I am holding in connection with our spiritual movement obviously have to be delivered in a way that is accessible to the public. Underlying each sentence spoken, far, far more is implied and each sentence is predicated upon an interconnection between certain facts. Today I will say something about these interconnected facts.

I have often drawn attention to the fact that we are living in an age in which it is absolutely essential that occult-spiritual knowledge should flow throughout all cultures. Now, the occult stream, the spiritual-scientific stream for the evolution of humanity has never actually been completely severed. But you have to break not exactly with prejudice but with a sort of premonition—something quite prevalent even in our circles—if you want to form the correct view on subjects that ought already to be familiar to you. You have to break—it cannot be phrased otherwise—with a certain addiction to dreaming, with that somnolence towards which some of those approaching our movement are easily drawn in their longing for a degree of cosiness for their souls, for something that will convey them warmly through life as they hear about what can affect them so warmly that they come to believe in the higher determination of the human soul—all of which is quite right—but which can entail high levels of lulling in the feelings. This can be seen only too often among those who welcome spiritual science affecting them without concurrently putting the necessary effort into securing clear, reliable conclusions as to what spiritual science can be, about life's everyday occurrences, how realities interweave within every individual life.

It has often been noted, when explaining human evolution, that the fifth post-Atlantean cultural period, in which we live, has the task of developing the consciousness soul based on conditions general among human souls and how, in the following sixth post-Atlantean epoch, Spirit Self will have to be carved out. The fact is that certain human capacities at present found slumbering latently in Eastern Europe among the Russian people will have—quite fundamentally, actively and consistently—to co-operate if they are to become effective during the sixth post-Atlantean age. For this it is vital that Russian humanity—if it is not to be led astray by its 'intelligentsia'—is strongly irradiated by certain qualities deeply embedded in the Russian Folk Soul. Drawing attention to these qualities: this Russian Folk Soul has in its entire nature and bearing something one could almost call feminine, something adaptable, something lending itself to absorbing whatever cultural evolution has offered it.

Connected with this is the fact that the Russian individual has always—throughout the course of the evolution it has undergone—imbibed predominantly Eastern, orientally-tinged forms of Byzantine religion that pervade Russian culture. So far the Russian Folk

Soul has barely been inwardly productive, negligibly creative but, in its most eminent sense, highly assimilative. That is why so little can be said about an onward progression of Russian Orthodox religion over the centuries, over the course of which this Russian-Byzantine-orientated religion has been at work among the Russians. Those who have participated in a ceremony in the Russian Church—however fleetingly—will be able to feel how strong is the oriental aura-like quality suffusing such ceremonies, how to some extent aureate-gilded qualities are brought into the immediate present. That is the one thing.

A second thing is this: inherent in this Russian Folk Soul lies the tendency for individual Russians to have little sense for the forms of thought which, in Western and Central Europe, necessarily constitute, structure and stratify social life and its onward development. An underlying feature of the latter is, for example, the adoption of narrow judicial modes of thinking in European social structuring. The Russian soul has little comprehension for this suffusion of social life with conceptual tropes, which confuses what it would like to consider the free, emotional enacting of its destiny. Russians do not wish to be confused by thought constructs externally plaited onto social forms.

A third characteristic is that to which Herder felt so attracted[42] and which really is inwardly connected with what one can call traits of the Russian Folk Soul. This trait was not originally uncovered in Russia itself—in other words it was not conceptually singled out in Russia—but by Herder himself, borrowing widely from Slavism and Pan-Slavism as he did: further proof of that nestling Russian adaptability. This third aspect shows a certain peaceable quality, a non-aggressive nature with regard to spiritual life, a nature more passively given to devotion. Aggressively acting on behalf of some dogma or other is foreign to the Russian folk character. So here is a third characteristic.

Of course such characteristics—precisely due to differing circumstances and the complications always present in human life—can be perverted into their opposite. Through the sort of national seducers we are presently dealing with, almost every one of these three traits is inverted into its polar opposite. To those within spiritual science this need not be marvelled at.

We see therefore—and we would be able to see this more clearly were we to fill it out with a few more brushstrokes—but you see that in Eastern Europe there is substance that needs to flow together with what emerges far more actively from Western Europe's evolution. Precisely the polar opposite character traits can be observed in the West of Europe. It was alluded to what could be actively brought forth for humanity over the course of this evolution into the fifth post-Atlantean epoch and how it is to be further evolved if such matters as were again spoken of in yesterday's talk were not slept through; such as, for instance, when I characterized the receding tone of German spiritual life.

For those who can observe the course of spiritual life impartially—impartially, that is, despite it being presented in physical reality through the most terrible distortions and caricatures—and who can watch the inner stimuli in this spiritual life, it is nevertheless clear that whatever is to be found in Central European spiritual life has, for a specific reason, to contract a marriage with what flows from the natural disposition of Russia. A kind of co-operation has to take place between what is produced by what I'd like to call the unique nature of this Central European spiritual life and what can be absorbed through certain purely natural qualities of the European East.

Were you to study this Central European spiritual life more closely, namely that trait to which I have now publicly drawn attention, you would see that, certainly, spiritual science as such is not yet encompassed within it, yet it does actually contain the seeds for spiritual science. I have often intimated how Fichte speaks of a 'higher sense'. Goethe speaks of an 'observing power of discernment'.[43] Schelling[44] speaks of the soul's need to elevate itself if it wants to penetrate the mysteries of existence in pursuit of what he calls an 'intellectual outlook'. The better to understand this, one needs to direct one's attention to the works Schelling accomplished in his old age, 'The Philosophy of Mythology' and 'The Philosophy of Revelation'. A deep grasp of Christianity inhabits these works, which is not yet understood. A spiritual conception of the world is alive in a work such as, for instance, 'The Deities of Samothrace', where Schelling attempts to fathom the mysteries of the Samothracian Kabiri. Nowhere else among recent spiritual life can consciousness be seen of the fact that, in Christianity, one is not dealing with a sum of dogmas nurtured in the name of Christianity—which is actually a side-issue—but that the main issue of the Christ event is that the Mystery of Golgotha took place; nowhere does this confront one more powerfully than in Schelling's 'Philosophy of Revelation'. All this is replete with potential for development and ought to lead us to such evolution as we have often sketched out when thoughtfully looking towards all that Central Europe must produce within the fifth post-Atlantean time frame.

Now to Western Europe! Looking at Western Europe, you need to be clear that it is suffused throughout with an historical and traditionally-imparted occultism which nowhere arises in an organic, living way from what lives in exoteric life, such as the true modern occultism that comes from the spiritual stream that flows through Goethe, Schelling, Hegel and so forth. The occultism existing in the West is only loosely connected with external science. It would not, for instance, be possible for England to make any similar connection between an occult science and the actual striving for knowledge as implicitly found in the German Idealist world view. It is unthinkable that what is genuinely and externally English in, say, the philosophies of Bacon of Verulam,[45] of Spencer,[46] or that English-tinted Darwinism—or, then again, more recent pragmatism—could find any bridge between what exists in the various occult Orders of the West with what is true of German Idealism. What runs throughout these multifarious occult Orders has to come to an end and can form no lawful bridge with external worldly science.

However—regarding these Western Orders and particularly certain high-level Orders—there is historically transmitted knowledge, which each takes into its ambit, and I'd say also specific knowledge about the European position in the world, whose prime secret, as outlined above, is: on the one hand Eastern Europe is preconditioned as if by blood to receptivity, but that which lies to the West of

Eastern Europe is predisposed to develop capacities that need to be absorbed by the East. Leading personalities among Western Orders are doubtless privy to this fact. Where such leading personalities elaborate the basic tenets of their occult activity, there is widespread talk of such associations.

Something quite specific is connected with these fundamental ideas in the West. When looking into them, they can best be seen where they have become most rigidly overweening and conceited: within the British Orders. A concept is current among those at higher levels of initiation—historical grades of initiation, in which they are not actually, in real life, initiated—that the Anglo-Saxons, on the basis of their own folk identity, have to bring about a sort of cultural marriage between themselves and the Russian folk identity. For those within Anglo-Saxon occultism, in the sense just outlined, see this as a means of dissipating the deepest occult driving forces of Græco-Latin *being* or constitution. That is their thinking. For the fourth post-Atlantean cultural epoch which, as we know, came to an end around the fifteenth century, what evolved out of Greek and Roman culture—also in terms of the occult—was the decisive factor. However, Anglo-Saxon society has to slough off this Græco-Roman component during the fifth post-Atlantean age. This is something presently required, something that has to be put into effect and realized. All those adhering to this doctrine, subscribing to what is a dogma of will or intent, know that the fifth post-Atlantean cultural era must wear Anglo-Saxon features, must bear the imprint of Anglo-Saxonism. They also have a definite image as to how Europe is to be moulded in future. Their view of a future Europe is one in which the spiritual life of Central Europe must at all costs be suppressed as something that must be prevented from flowing out into humanity as a whole. This is to be ignored as if it is an insignificant detail.

All things Anglo-Saxon contain this as a more or less unconscious doctrine, spreading out into all other Orders having some connection with, for instance, the *Grand Orient de France* and into all West-European secret societies. An underlying tenet at work with varying degrees of unconsciousness is this: Central European thought and knowledge is not to be taken into account in the fifth post-Atlantean epoch and will not be allowed to do so. Everything is to be orchestrated such that the fifth post-Atlantean age bears the imprint of Anglo-Saxonism. This is the reason why something akin to a marriage between Western- and Eastern Europe has to be induced—to the neglect of Central European life. The war we are now experiencing has been constantly spoken about for many, many years within these occult Orders and has not been depicted in any less terrible detail than is being proven. It is naïve to believe that this war just broke out without being foreseen by many people and as though war had not been widely discussed. A great deal has been said about it! On every hand you will find extrapolations about the impending war being introduced and elaborated, especially within Anglo-Saxon Orders or fraternities. Over and over again you find it being expressed that a great European conflict has to take place. The parameters of a future Europe are being drawn up. It is known that, in the sixth post-Atlantean epoch—for which some Anglo-Saxon quarters use the materialistically-tinged term 'the sixth sub-race'—the capacities mentioned, which have to do with what I'd call certain blood-qualities of the Russian people and, through all this, a sort of confluence of Western European qualities with those of a Russian nature, must be brought about. You always have to think clearly about these matters and keep them firmly in view, otherwise you will sleep through what the occult movements of the present actually represent.

In this connection I would like to draw your attention to a fact, one I have never forgotten because it cannot be forgotten. When Mrs Besant was making her first foray[47] to us in Central Europe, a gathering was arranged in Hamburg, where she gave a lecture. I put a question to Mrs Besant: If we want to start a Central European spiritual movement, how would it relate to the fact that, at the beginning of the nineteenth century—at the turn of the eighteenth to the nineteenth century—a unique spiritual life was to be observed germinating precisely in Central Europe? Mrs Besant answered: 'There would of course be little understanding for the contexts underpinning the matter.' At that time—albeit in abstract, conceptual form—a sort of spiritual knowledge was emerging within German life. But because humanity could not make use of it, it could only unfold in purer, more elevated and truthful form within English spiritual life, and then only later. It may be uncomfortable for some that symptomatic responses such as this are not forgotten by me. And they will not be forgotten.

Now, in the last third of the nineteenth century an unusually significant phenomenon relating to the spiritual development of Europe was heralded, one extending across to America. This phenomenon—which appeared only to manifest externally in the form of a personality—was of greater significance than one is inclined to accept. That phenomenon approached us in the form of Helena Petrovna Blavatsky.[48] The outer fact is a given, but is only an expression of deep inner spiritual connections: that Helena Petrovna Blavatsky emerged from the Russian people, with all the characteristics of the Russian people and, amid these great, centrally formed spiritual qualities, with a high degree of psychic ability.

One needs to have a concept as to what the appearance of such a phenomenon in the course of humanity's occult evolution means in order to honour it and follow the example I am about to give with understanding. Among Western Anglo-Saxon Orders, secret societies and so on, who concern themselves with occult ideas in the way I described, it became known—and a lively stir ensued—that a unique personality, originating from a Russian folk background, was displaying traits of a future human evolution that were concentrated in outstanding psychic capabilities manifesting in a singular mediumship. All quarters were astir. Animated questioning broke out among these Anglo-Saxon Orders. Just how lively this querying was can be expressed as follows, even if it has to be compressed a little. The people who are actually the doorkeepers or sentinels of such Western Anglo-Saxon movements said among themselves: It is significant that such an individual should waken precisely among Eastern humanity—something to be pondered—and a position has to be taken on the matter. The real question arose: How do we deal with a strong psychic attribute that might betray certain deep universal secrets? How can this be made into a conduit that can channel the future Russian element so as to combine it with Anglo-Saxonism? The aim was to channel Blavatsky's capacities, to attract them into the Anglo-Saxon sphere of influence and, at the very least, to harness Blavatsky's psychic abilities to present such occult doctrines to the world as it was those Western Orders' aim to present: to demonstrate how a certain science of the future, permeated by occultism, must appear—this was their goal. Human thinking was to be led—thinking which can so easily be manipulated—towards what could lead over from the fifth to the sixth cultural epoch, but in such a way that it be suffused with the motives and goals rooted in Anglo-Saxon occultism and its dogmas. In this way was the psychic personality of Blavatsky to be used, in order to implant in her what needed to be historically conveyed: articles of faith existing within Western occultism.

At first, things proceeded, I should say, much as they were intended to proceed. Blavatsky bestirred herself in trying to settle into the spiritual life of Central Europe. What this entailed will become quite clear if we observe more closely the occultism contained within this Central European spiritual life. This spiritual life had always brought occult-spiritual elements to the surface and an occult-spiritual element can still be discerned in certain, albeit exoteric, literature. It persisted throughout the fifteenth, sixteenth, seventeenth and even into the eighteenth centuries, right until Jesuitism arrived and externally—but only externally—ruined everything. But it was alive throughout those times. And if we today speak about the way in which—in a certain purely ideal form during the times of Goethe, Schelling and Fichte—a deeper striving came to prominence, we must nevertheless be clear that this deeper striving was rooted in Central European occultism, in Central European evolution itself. It was into this stream of Central European spiritual development that Helena Petrovna Blavatsky came—at first through what really was a good process—so that all that later emerged through what I might call the subterranean channels of the human personality into the psychic life of Blavatsky was at first saturated with all the occultism still living on from later medieval times within Central Europe.

However, something different had taken place earlier within this Central European occultism. Western occultism was not merely fatuous nor stupid; it could even be thought to be quite clever, in the sense that appearances may often appear extremely bright. I would not, however, include Grey and Asquith[49] among the latter as I don't wish to gain a reputation for considering present English statesmen among the cleverest. And yet, outstandingly significant people have lived within occult Orders, people who were equipped with exceptional shrewdness and who were able to bring it about that almost everything that could be externally transferred was brought from Central European occultism to England in order to be revivified in England through albeit extensive exoteric and worldly literature.

To anyone who knows how matters really stand, it is clear that, if they pick up something by Wynn-Westcott or another English occultist who knows a thing or two, or if they follow more closely the writings of Laurence Oliphant,[50] all of whom concern themselves with occult English literature: that in producing it you are prepared to clothe what was a product of Central Europe—one which had to retreat in Central Europe because a more materialistic development had grabbed centre stage—in English or West European garb. For this reason, I'd say, it is so hopelessly depressing, ever and ever again, to witness how certain Germans could not do enough to indicate just how 'English' all spiritual striving must be and that as much as possible should be transferred there. People don't know that all that proceeded from medieval German culture was transferred across to England and is once more being reintroduced—in English guise. You could even do some nice little pieces of research which would, for example, reveal that, if you were to set an English translation of an occult work next to a more thorough and scholarly work of medieval German, the two things would reveal grotesque discrepancies! It would become clear that highly spiritual writings within medieval evolution would be covered with a layer of dross and subsequently re-imported into Europe, now smothered in British materialism—all without making it known that it was originally brought over from Central Europe itself.

At first Helena Petrovna Blavatsky was suffused with what was alive in medieval spiritual life. What had been perpetrated through her was not fully in her consciousness; her nature was simply a high-grade subconscious psychic. Now, however, the ambition persisted that everything of a mighty future-orientated nature should be subordinated to Western Anglo-Saxon interests. This urge lived powerfully. Connected with this compulsion—I could certainly describe all the relevant processes, but I will have to just sketch them out as we have limited time—lies the fact that, on a certain occasion, Blavatsky was induced to appear at a certain Order in Paris.

So, Blavatsky appeared in a Paris secret society, on the one hand possessing those deepened Russian occult qualities, on the other steeped in a whole measure of genuine knowledge—call it Rosicrucian or whatever you will—stemming from Central Europe. There she was, right in its midst. By virtue of what lived in her soul, she was an immensely strong soul, a soul which could strongly assert what inhabited it, one also that would not just go along with being merely regarded as some elevated psychic medium, as people in those occult Orders in Paris would have liked. For what especially exercised people was her ability—when she considered it beneficial—to share with the world all her occult experiences, because she had absorbed them into a sort of higher psyche. Otherwise one could have said to the world: You see, what we have to tell you is not just based on theory but appears via a supra-mediumistic route; it bursts forth, seed-like, out of a Russian nature, out of a psychic personality who is indeed highly psychic. Had one wanted to explain it in such a way, then Blavatsky would have needed to be a far less obstinate, self-willed personality. She would not have put up with any such thing. This is why we see that she demanded certain conditions be set in that Paris secret society, conditions I will not enumerate—the time will come when this will be possible—but they again issued from out of that Blavatsky thrust. She felt: those in the West want their Western dominion promoted, inasmuch as this can be boosted through occult means, but I'm not allowing myself to co-operate with that! Because precisely then, among all the remarkable goings-on in Parisian secret societies, she felt herself to be a

Russian and she set limitations—which, as I said, I won't enumerate—for her stay in that Order, conditions which could not, even in the remotest of instances, be respected if such Orders wished to continue being reckoned with by the world at large. She set conditions which could effectively have shot through the entire history of France! That is why they shut her out. There was a feeling that she had been excluded just in time for her not to have discovered too many of that secret society's secrets.

Various other events followed, among which was the fact that, I would say, she acquired a taste for participating in the great events of the world. So she had herself received into a different Order, an American Order. Here she did not set conditions as she had done in Paris but behaved in such a way that what she had wanted to achieve by openly setting conditions in Paris she could achieve in an American manner. And together with a man who was extremely dissatisfied with conditions in America at that time, together with Olcott,[51] she had great plans for life in America—plans which put Western occultists, insofar as they were Anglo-Saxons, in a state which one could describe as seething! Seething in a way that neither Dr Faust nor Richard III ever seethed, as Goethe once said when in a particular frame of mind. Apart from that, what then happened—which had not yet happened in Paris because, after all, Blavatsky knew too much, had seen through their intentions too clearly!—was that something arose which certainly—when measured against age-old sacred occult laws—cannot be fully justified, yet which had to happen in order to prevent a great misfortune, which would otherwise have befallen. A meeting of American and European occultists considered what was to be done and decided, after much discussion, on measures which amounted to what in occultism is called placing someone in occult imprisonment. This occult imprisonment consisted, through various processes, in causing the striving—that is, the spiritual striving—of a person to be as if sealed within a sphere, so that the person concerned could only ever see their striving thrown back at themselves and was unable to see beyond that sphere. Into just such an occult sphere was Blavatsky now placed.

Outwardly, the matter was handled such that during this imprisonment she was in Asia.

But now humanity's evolution brought with it certain corollaries. As I said, what can be recounted is not always exact in every detail—in other words, the details are precise but one has to leapfrog over some of them due to insufficient time, though they may be shared on another occasion if so wished. Anyway, it then came about that leading Indian occultists tried something politically advantageous to their people: to effect by occult means that Blavatsky be released from her occult internment. And everything to which she had initially lent a Central European colouring, which had in turn been overlaid with all that those in Western Europe had wanted to induct into her now became coloured with Indian bias and a complex occult occurrence began to be played out, as it were, around the poor Blavatsky. One day she was free of her occult captivity, but all that was deposited in her soul by way of occultism had now taken on an Indian colouring. Added to this came the more unconscious influence of Olcott, who promptly fled Anglo-Saxon occultism for these brands of Indian-coloured occultism, in order once more to restore them to serviceable use. So it came about that into the place of Blavatsky's previous guide another such leader stepped, one whom—in like fashion with the last one—she continued to designate with the name Koot-Hoomi. But the second, subsequent guide of Blavatsky was basically—as those initiated into such matters know—none other than someone in Russian service, a scoundrel pursuing quite different aims from everything Blavatsky and her devotees were conveying, instead of honestly disseminating occult knowledge among humanity; a personality who above all had grandiose political goals, who carried out a sort of Russian espionage and who wanted to steer and lead matters so that—albeit from the other side—the spiritual marriage between Russianness and Anglo-Saxonness would be accomplished.

All this, which made of some extraordinarily great truths something altogether suffused with pernicious material—of which some is contained in the book *The Secret Doctrine*—can be traced back to the grounds just indicated. It can also be noted that the decidedly

Russian colouring that entered the entire later direction taken by Blavatsky through Koot-Hoomi did not, after all, suit some eminent high-level English occultists, and certain occult circles closely proximate to the Anglican Church set great store in opposing the bias-colouring just described. An elaborate and large-scale story was being played out in all of this.

Above all, we need to be clear that Helena Petrovna Blavatsky was an extraordinarily significant psychic personality, one in whom—due to her psychic constitution—the most diverse striving and streams worked. There were in those days, namely at the start of Blavatsky's appearance in public, multi-directional tendencies to prepare particular political issues of the future in such a way that people were to some extent overwhelmed by occultism. A certain type of occultist knows only too well—if you will forgive the harsh expression—that nothing hoodwinks the world better than giving out some occult teaching or other for a start. And if, behind such occult teaching, there is no inclination to totally honest truthfulness, people dumbed down by occultism can be led anywhere at their behest. This is the tendency of occultists belonging to the grey or black varieties, and these very often pursue distant political goals by carefully preparing for them far in advance. Not for nothing are—or at least, were—some secret societies in Britain, but also in France, repeatedly taught about Poland's future destiny and how one is to act towards the various intentions and currents among the Polish people. Not for nothing were they so often coached as regards the way connections were to result between Romania, Bulgaria, Serbia and associated territories in the Balkan peninsular, and how particular political undercurrents were to be primed so that the intended outcome could be fostered. Vast tracts of politics are carried on in Western European secret societies. I'd like to reiterate: substantial politics are fomented there.

Whereas Blavatsky, as a psychic personality, had never allowed herself to be persuaded into promoting purely Anglo-Saxon occult aims, she was nevertheless viewed as dangerous by such as, say, higher-level occultists closely involved in Anglican circles, whose sole aim was that indicated earlier. It was initially thought that they could implement their aims through people of little talent, clueless about politics, who were already within such movements. There were great hopes of success in guiding the ways of one Mr Sinnett.[52] Under conditions described, it is quite easy to manoeuvre and steer someone not grounded in recognizing as the highest possible axiom a genuine occultist must cherish: that of unconditionally safeguarding human freedom, virtue and dignity. Ever and again does one need to exhort that any occultist—or indeed anyone looking into occultism—keeps vigilant watch over their soul in respect of this essential requirement. Similarly, Mrs Besant was fairly clueless in finding her way into issues but she also contained a strong Anglo-Saxon bent, so that whatever worked through her did so successfully. When you consider the complicated nature of the stream into which she was placed, you will understand something about Mrs Besant. But you really need to go into these issues to understand them even slightly.

My dear friends, it is extremely important that our genuine, clear discernment allows us to survey outer circumstances without being drawn into sundry occultisms; that we retain healthy human common sense in judging external situations and do not allow ourselves to be baffled by all manner of mysticism. We need to discriminate unambiguously among life's processes so that we are equipped against falling into the sorts of shady, occult quackery issuing from some centres, whose aims are anything but pure truth and from which extend methods of fishing in sinister depths to further their aims and purposes. It is urgently *crucial* for our movement that it erect the clearest barrier between its honest striving for truth—proceeding as it does purely from knowing what our times require to be embodied in a universal spiritual movement—and every other occult strand seeking improper justification, and against which one is not allowed to raise the objection that it ill behoves anyone to be interested in matters of their kind. We need to distinguish between the mere superstition that overcomes those who 'know'—in the worst sense of 'know'—and put up clear barriers between them and our spiritual movement, within which our stream must remain bright. And we must never be in any doubt as to the side to which we *do not* belong!

That is absolutely essential. Otherwise one can lapse into bewildered states, from which the worst possible devastation can result. Because such things are openly discussed in more materialistic circles—and will undoubtedly be used by evil-intentioned sources to ill effect in future—I would like to draw attention to them today—and may have to again tomorrow in public—to open people's eyes to what is often regarded as occultism, but with which we wish to have nothing to do, so that we are forearmed and braced, when the time comes, to defend our honest spiritual-scientific striving against being lumped together with those sinister elements.

Let's take just one example: as I said, I mention these matters because they are now becoming known and because we need to express how we think about them. In Paris a personality lives—one quite clearly aligned with the aims of a particular secret Order—who has mediumistic faculties that affect people and who is admired as a medium yet who operates within the occult circles just characterized and who—in part subconsciously, partly consciously—allows such occult streams to flow through them. This person publishes an almanac;[53] in that of 1913—which appeared in advance in 1912—we read, in relation to Austria: 'The person who believes they will reign in future will not reign. Another, younger individual—whom nobody yet believes will reign—will indeed reign.' And in the almanac of 1914, which appeared in 1913, this assertion is repeated in more emphatic tones.

Those who are happy to be duped may well be astounded, if they so wish, by the prophesies of this Paris medium. But those with a brighter spiritual life might also like to draw such conclusions as are made visible there. If you take the Paris newspaper—one comparable with the tabloid *B.Z. am Mittag*, a paper called *Paris Midi*—around the time of the above almanac's assertions, you will find the distinct wish expressed that the Austrian Archduke Ferdinand be assassinated. In that same paper it is opined—just when the three-year period of military service was being negotiated in France—that, should it come to mobilization, in those first days, Jaurès[54] would be murdered! Put this alongside all the shenanigans being carried out today—designed to draw a veil over the secrets associated with the murder of Jaurès—with the fact that the person who published that almanac travelled to Rome during the first days of mobilization in August 1914 in order to influence specific circles in an anti-Central-European direction. Keep all these facts together in mind and try to form a view as to whether you have before you a prophecy or something fundamentally different, something I need not further elaborate for you. But do learn from this and investigate in whose service a person may be who allows themselves to be duped; also the occasions when something appearing here or there in a magazine or almanac is later enacted yet said to be prophecy! Clear, enlightened judgement is essential if you think just how much corrupt deceit may be hanging from the skirts of occultism.

We can look further back. These Western European Orders or Lodges have, since the beginning of the nineteenth century, had their ambassadors yonder in Russia. People may say that Masonic or similar Orders were not tolerated in Russia. All the more did they blossom in secret and their fruits were all the more powerful. Anyone who studies the history of Slavophile philosophy and Pan-Slavism will need to look for their roots in Russian secret societies. Whenever one of their number was caught, they were sent hither or thither or shot by firing squad; but they did exist and the Western European occultism described to you was indeed allied with Russian spiritual life.

You need to have some insight into the deeper connections that exist if you wish to make judgements about world processes. And just because so little can be said about these issues and because we are for the time being somewhat blockaded in, but also because some pieces of information would be missing: the time will come when it will become apparent just what roles were played in Western Europe's entire unleashing of war precisely by these Western European Orders, whose strings—and more than strings!—lead back to English ministries, to Parisian ministries and so on; also how Masonic Orders played a huge role in Western Europe when it was a matter of bringing about Italy's annexation into the so-called Entente. They made themselves very, very busy and were in turn connected with Eastern Europe, with whom they were on good terms. Of the German Masons, both of lower and higher grades—who, as part of an international world league were obviously widely connected, who exchanged 'fraternal greetings' with one another and who set great store by brotherly co-operation—it can be said in mitigation that they were too stupid to suspect much about the whole story in which they were embroiled. This needs to be strongly underlined in their exoneration. It is the most significant aspect of Central European Freemasonry—like many others not actually within its ranks—that it was duped, right to the last moment, and that among them were some for whom there had been the potential not to be deceived.

How often has it had to be emphasized that one has to maintain clear judgement and be prepared to reflect upon such interconnectedness precisely when one engages with occultism! At present we need to be awake to such matters in our circles. Much of what has been said and what has flowed into our movement over the years has not been sufficiently taken into account and has been far too little heeded. For this reason there are some aspects of our movement, especially during these times, that are cause for distress. Our Central European movement really is based on quite different foundations from other similar movements. Just think of one thing: that we can compare our Central European movement with a living being. It has the quality of a living being. When founding an association, one which people may join and then leave again, that association cannot be likened to a living being. There is much wrong with the way in which Weismann[55]describes living entities, but one thing is correct: that a living entity leaves behind a corpse once its soul has departed. This applies accurately to our Society, as opposed to other associations. Our Society contains the substance of life, in that it gives out lecture cycles to its members and they then retain them. When other unions dissolve, members drift apart and no body or corpse is left behind. One can have the most beautiful ideals and then separate again. But think how it is when we part: the sum total of the lecture cycles remains. That is the corpse! That attests to the fact that we do not operate on straw-like principles nor programmes but base ourselves upon what is alive. This different quality will be found by anyone observing us. Quite apart from that, our entire movement has had to take the form it has. How hard it has been, I must say, how endlessly difficult, to steer our small ship through all the hazardous rocks you will by now to some extent recognize if you look at everything that had to be done so that what had to come into its own in Central Europe—despite all Western Europe's ensnaring machinations, which were in place from the outset—could tear itself free. Faced with all that, one can become disheartened when seeing in present destiny-critical times that so much personal strife—which, far from decreasing has since the beginning of the war been on the increase—has been running rampant riot within our movement. This propensity for souls to be diverted into personal concerns in face of all that is great within our movement has come intensely to the fore. There is something quite depressing, my dear friends, in noting—in these times—that there is such precious little consciousness demonstrating that one truly *stands within* this movement and does not, as with other associations, just leave the moment this or that doesn't suit one! We cannot protest that so-and-so many are innocent in what is happening, because, especially when based on occult footings, the facts have to be taken into account.

In face of this it must be said: If such goings-on are possible and have been happening then—in the form the Society is constituted—onward work is not possible within the Society! Work cannot continue if consciousness does not make space for the fact that this Society is something living, something real and true, and is not some association out of which one can just step when things don't suit one. Obviously, nobody can be prevented from so doing. That is not the point of what I am saying. If awareness of this doesn't exist, one can only say that the things that have to be achieved by our spiritual culture will have to be carried out by means other than through the Society, which would in that case be merely a hindrance. What has to suffuse our movement—and which will make everything right—is the purest, the most honest striving for truth. Just that: the purest striving for truth. Because, firstly, we have the task—by means of this pure striving for truth—of bringing a new element into the spiritual evolution of humanity. For this reason, it is essential that certain things be understood.

It is of no minor importance that I draw your attention to the following. Over and over again it happens—though also considered a minor factor—that one person or another comes to me and doesn't ask me anything about soul life or suchlike, but something one would ask a doctor. I constantly have to remind people that they should confidently be consulting a medical practitioner working within our movement. That's essential. Obviously, it is only right that the purest arts of healing and correct medicines are used in conjunction with our movement. However, if I am myself to remain within the field in which I am intended to work, then all that's entailed in medical advice needs to be kept at some distance from me personally. For just such reasons does it have to be made clear that it is in fact a sort of allaying of fears if one says: Official medicine in the wide world doesn't amount to much, so I'll turn to something else. All the more does it behove us—at least, it ought to behove us—that what we want to attempt is not carried out in an underhand manner but takes place with complete honesty and openness and that there is no tendency amongst us to circumvent laws nor external practices. For a start, it is primarily a matter of guiding such conventions round and enabling sensible, forbearing give-and-take to seize its place in human evolution. Everyone needs to know that, if they do not wish to be treated by external medicine, they have to contribute something of themselves so that the tyranny of medicine ceases. They should not be seeking all sorts of pre-emptive remediations by covert shortcuts. This doesn't just apply to the odd person who happens to be active within this Branch; it applies to everyone inasmuch as it is correct. But what I emphasize over and over again has to be taken seriously: turn to our medical doctors concerning medicine. Of course, everyone will find me ready with friendly advice, when needed; but the principle and direction needed are clear and must be understood today.

I have tried to at least sketch out some useful steers to sharpen your view of events that necessarily had to happen. It might be good to give a little thought to the timely cutting of ties by our Central European spiritual movement from all the rubbish lately heaped in Besant's direction, which now so strangely threatens to be the worst kind of betrayal. For it has to be said—though I absolutely don't wish to reheat old disputes—that among the articles being reprinted in Mrs Besant's English journal there is, for instance, the laughable assertion that all my efforts were in pursuance of being voted President of the whole Theosophical Society, so as to go to India to force her, Mrs Besant, from her sphere of activity, the purported reason for pursuing this aim being that I and those affiliated with me were in fact agents of the German government who wanted nothing short of a sort of Pan-Germanism to replace—through sundry occult machinations—Anglo-Saxonism and, from a base in India, to unseat the English government! These accusations are now to be found in far more strident form in articles by Mrs Besant. She knows how to talk drivel of this kind in other areas, too, things worthy of sitting alongside all the Alcyone nonsense.[56] Admittedly, one now hears that Alcyone has been stripped of the honour of becoming the bearer of Christ. Well, in appointing Alcyone, others had to be deposed, didn't they! There was always one person or another being deployed according to need. Even the heir to the Russian throne, the young Alexei, was considered in certain esoteric circles to be endowed with the distinction of becoming a medium for Christ! The previous one had, of course, to be toppled. Earlier, there had been others in contention, even several simultaneously! Well, yes, when each of them was forbidden from telling the others about it—always only mysteriously hinted at, you know—one can have several simultaneously!

But you see, if you take all this flippantly, you will be overlooking what I am about to mention: it was in 1909, when the worst of the Leadbeater-Besant-Rummel issue was getting going—in other words, the first of those worsts—in a Society that was intended to be international. A longstanding friend of Mrs Besant, who had always corrected the scientific mistakes in her books, Mr Keightley,[57] was at the time connected with the movement that was to be founded with

Mrs Besant and based in India. At the time I was asked whether I'd like to take on the Presidency of that international society. It was offered to me from India. 1909 was the year of the congress in Budapest. In the presence of witnesses, I told Mrs Besant that this Presidency had been offered to me. Admittedly, I only told a few people on board a ship in advance of telling Mrs Besant this: As regards this occult society, I wish only to be one thing and that is to represent whatever needs representing within the German folk region; outside this I do not wish to take up any occult position. Yet now she dares to claim in a newspaper that I aimed to be President, based in India! I have often spoken about objective untruths in relation to many issues expressed by Mrs Besant. But when one experiences how I specifically told her that I did not ever want to be anything within the Theosophical Society other than, at most, General Secretary of the German Section or some related role, then one is no longer talking about objective untruth but one may as well say: No such objective untruth is being offered by Mrs Besant but rather—as with the Jesuits and their allegations—we are talking about conscious lies. Anyone wishing to defend Mrs Besant today has to take on board being told that they are defending a conscious liar. If you include the Jesuit accusation, the matter in hand and the whole campaign being undertaken by English chauvinism against what we are intending here, then we can talk about a systematic campaign of lies being under way.

Whoever finds this too strongly worded needs to reflect that nothing said by me ever intends attack, but is only spoken of by way of defending itself. This ought to be taken into account by all those who constantly insist that both sides have a right to a fair hearing. In our case fairness reigned supreme in that eyes were simply shut—at least immediately afterwards—to what was true, even on our own turf, as it were! These present fateful times should at least teach us to view things in harmony with truth and in full seriousness—and then act accordingly. For it is after all true that all these hundreds upon hundreds of casualties dying will have done so for the salvation of humanity if here on Earth souls can be found who—over time and with the right attitude—understand how to think and feel! What is being prepared in spiritual worlds—if viewed rightly by those who understand—will be transformed into forces for the future; forces that can be transformed by souls who comprehend and possess occult sensitivity into progressive forces for humankind. If this is not understood then the events of the present will pass by and all the forces of sacrifice made by vast hundreds of deaths will, in spiritual realms, be directed into the hands of Ahriman. In this situation I have always said:

From the courage of fighters,
From the blood on fields of battle,
From the grief of the bereft
From the sacrifice of people
There will grow fruit of spirit
If, spirit-conscious, souls will turn
Their thoughts to realms of Spirit.

# LECTURE 6

## 20 MARCH 1916, MUNICH

IT is essential—while gradually assimilating what we are calling spiritual science—to bring goodwill towards what is initially something of a blueprint of imparted concepts and conceptual interconnections, I'd say, and to fill these out with genuine Imaginations of what can at first only be communicated in the form of general outlines.

You see, this is what we say: The human being consists of physical body, ether body, astral body, I and so on. That is quite correct, for a start and, if we can put it like this, we then have to orientate ourselves within a comprehensive framework of schematic concepts. But over the further course of acquiring an understanding of spiritual science, you will need to engage more closely with what has been schematically presented.

Closer to home, as it were, within our Society and among what is being offered to audiences, we have a large number of lecture cycles. But these lecture cycles contain comparatively little of what we might wish humanity—or at least small enclaves within humanity—to know as a matter of urgency.

If we term physical body whatever can be seen externally with physical senses, can be viewed by science and is related to reason, experiment and observation, nevertheless underlying this physical body is, as we know, an ether body.

Today let us firstly cast our spiritual eye over these two elements of human nature. Spiritual science per se, it would seem, needs to say least of all about the physical body because it is the only element available to physical science, the only element it has any intention of observing with its methods. The physical body—even if initially viewed in terms of what somatic science deems it to be—can only be understood in its due significance and standing in the world if the higher members of human nature are also acknowledged and focused upon.

Now, you will remember that the physical body—in the form, we could say, that it clothes or envelops the human being when on Earth—could only arise during that terrestrial stage of evolution.[58] It had already received its spiritual rudiments during ancient Saturn evolution and was in process of continual transformation over the course of Sun-, Moon- and Earth evolutions. It had metamorphosed under the influence of what was taking place throughout ancient Sun-, Moon- and Earth epochs. It was in transformation due to the fact that an ether body was being embodied on the Sun. This physical body had to change from the state in which it had come over from Saturn and become different once it became suffused with an ether body. It had to transform again on the Moon, when it was further saturated with an astral body. Not only did the astral body amplify the entire human entelechy but the physical body was altered in that during the Sun era the ether body had to some extent precipitated inwards, during Moon the astral body had been added, whereas on Earth the I was gradually being shaped from all sides—albeit initially within the ether body—but also within the physical body itself.

If we now turn from the human to the cosmic, we need only recall what we have so often spoken about and what is contained in our lecture cycles. We therefore know that, when the first rudiments of the physical body were made possible through what we might call an *inpouring* from Spirits of Will—from the Thrones—its onward metamorphosis during ancient Sun was enabled through Spirits of Wisdom, the subsequent transformation during ancient Moon through Spirits of Movement and the changes wrought on Earth—that is, all that had to be refashioned on the physical body due to the I indwelling it—was effected by Spirits of Form.

This is a very important aspect upon which we need to focus. When a physical body approaches us on Earth, we have to think of it as I-endowed. Being I-endowed, we must further think of it as having received a form particular to itself and appropriate for its time on Earth. During Moon, on the other hand, only inner movement suited to ourselves was received. The shape befitting the earthly person had to be received through a gift from the Spirits of Form, in due concordance with the fact that an I was to be implanted within it. We can therefore say that this physically-formed earthly body is shaped as it is because it had to become the bearer of an I. In bestowing on the human being their I did the Spirits of Form bequeath to physical bodies the contours befitting them as bearers of an I.

The beings of the other realms of nature also received their forms. If you read the sensitive descriptions of ancient Moon, you will see that all beings are described such that one cannot speak of them having the form they now possess; they are described as being mobile or labile. Think back to the descriptions in *Occult Science—an Outline* or in other lecture cycles: they are described as possessing a certain mobility. Other realms of nature also only received their shapes from the Spirits of Form once on Earth, that is, as I'd like to put it, received their shapes in their abiding, permanent form.

Let's look at the kingdom next to humans on Earth, that of the animals. The realm of animals also inhabits form. It has been displaying the forms it presently does only since Earth evolution. But just think about the differences between animal forms and human forms! Our gaze sweeps across the surface of the Earth and we find certain differentiations between individual people—differences belonging among other areas of narrative—but we do find certain external differences in terms of form. All the interesting peoples being deployed by the West Europeans [British and French] at the Front against Central Europe of course look very different from the population of Central Europe. So our gaze observes differentiations present across the globe as regards individual people's configuration and shadings. Yet when comparing differentiations between the peoples of the world and those between different species of animals, you will have to concede that the latter contain endlessly more species and types than are contained within humanity. We can speak of a single species of human being as opposed to widely varying species of animal forms. A difference as stark as that between a nightingale and a lion is not to be found in the human realm. Were such great variance found among humans as is the case between nightingale and lion, nobody could claim that there were no differentiations among humans. Whereupon your contemplation would confirm that the animal kingdom contains a vastly wider range of species than can be found among us, the universal species of human being.

Though what I have just described is perfectly correct, it is nevertheless, from the standpoint of spiritual science, only to a limited extent accurate. Because the following is also correct: in your observations and thoughts about the human physical body, now add the ether body and imagine that a certain experiment were possible—one that cannot of course possibly be carried out: piece by piece to dissect the physical body and, before starting, to call Spirits of the higher hierarchies—Angeloi, Archangeloi and Archai—to effect a withdrawal from the human in question such that they would cease being active in their ether body. Two things would need to happen: let's assume one would not want to maltreat the human being, but one would need to withdraw everything belonging to their physical body. One would then have to bid them withdraw every influence emanating from the three hierarchies of Angeloi, Archangeloi and Archai so that the ether body was totally reliant only on itself, uninfluenced by anything else at all. It is un-swayed, is set in the physical body, and this latter has its firm shape, as bestowed by the Spirits of Form. It therefore has to defer to—to comply with—this firm shape. If you put a very soft lump of rubber into a glass, it will adapt to the shape of the glass and be unable to retain its own shape. On taking it out of the glass it will spring back to its original shape. Similarly, the human ether body adapts to the form which the physical body imposes on it, not possessing its own form. If we remove the physical body, this force, to which the ether body has to adapt, falls away. Yet even then it would not acquire its own shape because, into this ether body, Angeloi, Archangeloi and Archai are working, something we will look at more closely later. We now bid them to leave, so that the ether body can follow its inherent forces alone. The etheric body would now bounce outwards, adopting its own elasticity. Were this to take place visibly, you would see how the ether body expands and takes on its own shape.

What would happen? You would have before you the entire animal kingdom! The ether body would divide itself into portions, would apportion itself into the shapes—at least into those of the main species—of the whole animal kingdom. What this means is: human beings bear within themselves—etherically—the entire animal kingdom! It is only bound together, on the one hand, through the shape of the physical body and, on the other, by the activity of beings in the three named hierarchies. It is absolutely true that the human being bears—in potential form—this whole animal realm within their ether body! Viewed from this angle, the entire animal kingdom is only differentiated from that of the human in that each animal species has taken to itself and evolved to physical manifestation its own form, which also co-exists in the human etheric. So that, when we look at the animal kingdom as manifested on Earth, it is in fact the widely dispersed human ether body.

Here is something remarkable. Around the turn of the eighteenth to nineteenth centuries, within the evolving world outlook of Europe, there appeared in more detailed form what can be found in personalities such as, for instance, Oken.[59] The natural scientist Oken could not yet, in the context of his times, speak of an ether body, something alien to him. Yet among his writings the remarkable phrase can be found: 'The animal kingdom is the dispersed human being.' In other words, he had an imagined conception of the truth. This concept entered his spiritual horizon at a time when those great Central European ideas were in process of developing. That is very interesting! This concept also appeared on Schelling's[60] horizon and you will find a similar statement among his writings. But those who could not commit to such ingenious but obviously by no means conclusive thoughts—because more detailed facts were not yet available—were scandalized. You must imagine that what Oken could not yet know existed in the form of an inventive idea in his soul. I'd like to say that he had the feeling that the individual members of the human being are actually a composite of animal forms. He had the courage to express this, but the fact that he did so scandalized academic philistines appallingly. He had also asked himself: What is a tongue? He couldn't know that an ether body was required so he opined: A tongue is a cuttlefish.[61] Underlying this assertion, however, is what I have just been discussing. Just imagine what academic philistinism made of that: the human tongue is a cuttlefish!

If you want to gain insight into the course of human spiritual life, you need to be broad-minded and open-hearted. You have to be prepared for the fact that the seemingly nonsensical can in fact harbour great truths. Thus Oken categorized the human being as follows: the tongue is a squid or cuttlefish, other organs are other creatures and so on. This was fundamentally a more detailed reiteration of the ancient human view that singled out only the primary species and classified the human being into four main animal archetypes: Lion, Eagle, Angel and Calf [sic].

Thus one can say: the matter is not actually quite as simple as that, but human beings do in fact contain the whole animal kingdom within their ether bodies. As a philosopher might say, they contain the *potentiality* for this. Now, you must bear something in mind to avoid any one-sidedness. If what we have just cited were not to take place, if—apart from the physical body holding together this entire animality—the Angeloi, Archangeloi and Archai were still to exert their forces, then, on passing through the gate of death and shedding their physical body, what I have just described would come into effect. In that case, when the ether body is left behind a few days after death by the astral body and the ego, that element really would disperse, falling elastically into the world and the entire etheric animal world would arise from out of the human etheric world. Experientially, this is not the case. It does not arise. It doesn't proceed in this way from the human being, but the ether body detaches itself quite differently, by dissolving and becoming woven into cosmic ether.

What have we here? Beings from the hierarchy of Angeloi, Archangeloi and Archai work on our ether bodies, preventing its etheric unity from being splintered into the animal kingdom. What is actually taking place? You see, I'd like to describe what is happening by drawing, in the first instance, on a comparison. As people on Earth, we work, making implements or machines out of wood or iron.

Wood or iron are our material basics and from them we fabricate our appliances. Our task is the disposition or arrangement of matter. But the iron or wood has to be extracted from the Earth. We need these raw materials and we extract them from a realm that lies below our human realm.

If you now imagine that above us dwell the Angeloi, Archangeloi and Archai; they are not in the cosmos for the purpose of enjoying a perpetual 'Sunday rest' but they, too, have their work and tasks. What is the actual work of the Angeloi, Archangeloi and Archai? When at work they also need material—just as we take iron or wood from the Earth—and this they process. The materials processed by Angeloi, Archangeloi and Archai are our ether bodies! Much as we process the wood and iron of Earth into implements do the Angeloi, Archangeloi and Archai elaborate in our ether bodies—they are the raw materials on which they work. We humans go around on Earth thinking—if indeed we think any such thought—what we bear in our ether bodies, carrying them around as though they were our property in the way that our lungs are—when all around us an entire hierarchy of Angeloi, Archangeloi and Archai are elaborating structures for the spiritual world, which are used there for our lives. They extract from our ether bodies what is to be used in spiritual worlds.

Whose help do these higher beings call upon? Lifelong, we are thinking, from the moment we begin to think until our very death. The essential aspect of thinking—as you will have gathered from yesterday's public lecture—consists precisely in the fact that thinking lives and weaves in our ether body. It continues living and weaving into our physical body. We believe that, in physically embodied life, the thoughts we form are our sole property. But what our thoughts contain, what we cultivate in our thoughts, and back to which we can remember, is to some extent just the inner surface of our thought life. Particularly in respect of our ether bodies do the Angeloi, Archangeloi and Archai work throughout our thinking life. It is not superfluous that we, as human beings, think. Neither is it superfluous for the physical Earth, nor indeed for the cosmos. Because what we transform in our ether bodies through our thinking between birth and death is used as material and elaborated in accordance with higher principles. During our lives, while we are going about the world as thinking beings and only seeing our thoughts from the inside, those thoughts are worked upon by Angeloi, Archangeloi and Archai so that, after our death, what results may be embodied in the cosmic ether. When our astral body and our ego lay aside our ether body, then—if I may phrase it coarsely—they sew the web of our ether body into the cosmos, that web whose essence has resulted from the manner of our lifelong thinking. Henceforth this belongs to the cosmos. As human beings, we live not only for ourselves; being human entails living for the entire cosmos.

We know that, after our sojourn on Earth, Jupiter, Venus and Vulcan epochs are to arise. As preparation for this, everything has to be woven into the cosmos in the form of forces. Work is needed for this to happen. Included in work required for this is, for example, what I have just described: that Angeloi, Archangeloi and Archai are active in accord with our thoughts. A slightly different material ensues from the foolish or stupid thoughts we entertain during our lives, which in turn differ from our more sensible or sage thoughts. Depending on which sort of material we supply to them are those—crudely put—'etheric machines' elaborated, which then enable the onward evolution of the universe to proceed. Thus, when after our death our ether body is assigned to the cosmos, the work of the three hierarchies named is likewise conferred thither.

Let us look at the human astral body from a similar perspective. Whenever we make observations from differing standpoints, different relations with neighbouring realms will always result. Someone who can't read—and included in reading is the potential ability to synthesize—they may encounter many contradictions in the phenomena described. But this only stems from not focusing on the points of view from which issues can be illuminated.

Our astral body exists in similar relation with its earthly environs as does our ether body. Our ether body is—or encompasses—the entire animal kingdom, from the perspective I outlined to you. Our astral body is the entire plant kingdom. I would have to describe our astral body as being related to the plant kingdom exactly as I spoke of the ether body in relation to the animal kingdom. All the plant species on our Earth exist within it. And once again it is a fact that, were all the higher hierarchies not to work on our astral body after we underwent the reverse experience of our life from death back to birth, while the astral body was gradually being sloughed off, nothing else would arise other than that the astral body would be discarded and exist as the entire plant world at large in the world. Yes, indeed, this entirety would assemble itself into a globe shape, in accordance with its own elasticity. And yet the astral body cannot coalesce into a sphere because, during our lives between birth and death, Spirits of Form themselves, Spirits of Movement and Spirits of Wisdom—and even to some extent Spirits of Will—have been working on our astral body.

When we have spent years or decades freeing the astral body—back in reverse order over the course of our life, as so often described—from its cohesion with earthly life, then this work on the astral body provides Spirits of Form, those of Movement, Wisdom and Will with what they need for their work *embodying* into the cosmos that which they need to incorporate into it. What is embodied in the cosmos in this way certainly benefits us and has to exist in the universe; it is also woven into the cosmic fabric, but differently from what was described earlier. When our ether body is cast off, it is straightway sewn—or I could say woven—into the universal world-ether. However, what is woven from our astral body in what appears as the work of Spirits of Form, of Movement, of Wisdom, of the Thrones, this works in concordance with our I as it undergoes its time between death and rebirth, containing such forces as have to be active in order that we are able to return to a new incarnation. For vastly much is involved in our being able to embark on a new incarnation! Actually, what superficial physical science today knows about the construction of the skull and the brain is considerable; in fact, so much is known that there are a huge numbers of people for whom there is simply too much to know. But when you consider the extent of what external science knows about the skull and the brain—how that wondrous construct is created, down to its most minute constituents—how little progress would be made by external science in actually generating them! We are faced with a momentous mystery. Those of limited outlook whom one might think of as dullards or 'stuntlings' make short shrift of this mystery by claiming that what is handed down through the generations is spontaneously self-perpetuating, that the human head simply self-generates within the mother's body.

You can understand that people might say this, but how clever it is may become clearer from the example I'd like to bring. Hypothetically, we could imagine that there were beings in Munich who could see a great deal but *with the exception of* human beings and their activities. It is conceivable that such beings might exist in Munich who could not perceive human beings and their activities. Such beings blind to humans and their affairs might, for instance, see clocks. They would be aware that clocks exist and how they were assembled, yet not see the human watchmaker assembling the timepieces. They would just see the components coalescing without the hands carrying out the assembly, though might possibly see the various tweezers, callipers, collets and so on with which the parts are gripped; in short, they'd see all the components self-assembling out of thin air. What concept would such beings have of a watch? They certainly wouldn't think there were watchmakers in Munich—they would deny that completely. They might think: Oh, how frightfully superstitious to think there are clockmakers, knowing as we do that clocks spontaneously self-assemble.

This is exactly the sort of assumption people make about whatever gradually takes shape over time on a physical level: that it spontaneously self-generates. In truth, every single thing that arises does so through the actions of the beings of the higher hierarchies and not just due to the mutual interactions of fathers and mothers, nor is the human being evolving within the mother's body created 'of its own accord'. No, the entire universe, together with the beings of the higher hierarchies, is involved in the process.

Evidently, the whole cosmos, high into its loftiest regions, is involved in the creation of everything connected with the head, but especially so in the human head itself. Physical science will itself realize—and the levelling up of physical science with spiritual science must ultimately be brought into equilibrium—and learn to think differently about embryology, as indeed to consider differently all the organs. Those other organs, as will be discovered in the not-too-distant future, are strongly dependent on inherited factors. Far less is the human head thus dependent. It is only constrained by its bond with the other organs. Spiritually speaking, the whole cosmos really is involved in the creation of the human head, participating spiritually and being actively focused into the maternal body.

The fact that people don't see forces at work—as, for instance, a farmer doesn't see the forces active in a magnet—is no proof that these forces don't exist. What is present in the human head is in one sense prepared, elaborated in relation to what each human being brings, within their I, from their time between death and a new birth and which is then further transmuted by Spirits of Form, by Spirits of Movement, by Spirits of Wisdom, the Thrones, all working on a mighty hollow sphere. What is being worked on here is vast in extent, a sphere into which everything is incorporated. Imagine an immeasurably great sphere into whose global surface is embedded everything to be processed in accordance with the degree to which the human being has given over to the great cosmos the contents of their ether body. This forms something we, as it were, endorse or sign, if I may express it thus; that is to say that which has been brought with us from the assimilation of the astral body. The time comes—beginning with what I have called in one Mystery [62] context the midnight hour of existence—when this sphere begins to shrink, gradually becoming smaller and smaller; and this sphere, which is being transformed by higher Spirits in accordance with the earlier incarnations of the human being concerned, ultimately becomes so contracted—ever smaller and smaller—that it unites with the germinal human received into the maternal body. From this evolves primarily the form of the head. This emergence of the shape of the head is a wondrous mystery and is a result of *centuries* of work by the higher hierarchies.

Just think how humans' perception of their relationship with the world can be deepened by knowing how they are placed within the entire cosmic context! Human beings, in bearing their heads, need to consider—in all humility and obviously without pride or arrogance—just how little they contain of the wisdom required to form the head bequeathed them. Human beings bear the contents of the entire cosmos within them.

Viewed in this way, spiritual science gains enormously by being the point of origin for perceptions or feelings which—in an arrogant soul—can become treacherous. I alluded to this in the second Mystery Play[63] where Capesius, in conversation with Benedictus, senses the approach of verities of this kind: that the divine services of the Gods are necessary in creating, in bringing forth, human beings. Many—especially those susceptible to however unconscious a self-regard—deem themselves all the more elevated on account of this. Human beings can appear monstrously important to themselves. It is more prudent to nurture a sense of how little consciousness one possesses of all the wisdom necessary to bring about a self!

You might of course share the opinion of those who object: Fine, but why do people need to know all this? They can live perfectly well without knowing all these facets. Therein lies a huge error. In truth, they cannot. We are living in just such times as make us prone to the aberration that we can live on Earth perfectly well, eating breakfast, lunch and dinner and so on—and can carry on much else besides and notwithstanding. But this belief is not founded in truth. Eventually, human beings have to be brought round to the fact that their belief is not grounded in truth.

On the basis of the above, I now bring in the example of Karl Christian Planck[64] into public lectures: that extraordinary person who lived a solitary existence in Ulm for years on end and whom the University of Tübingen failed to appoint to a then-vacant Chair because nobody recognized the significance of the man. Of course, stunted intellects will say that, towards the end of his life, he became so nerve-wracked that he said all sorts of self-important things that can be construed as megalomania. Stunted people would say that. But anyone, like Planck, who had not fully endorsed spiritual science, would still suffer from their nerves under such treatment by their fellow humans; and yet Planck could say what he did in the opening speech of his *Testament of a German*, in the wake of those words of the ancient Romans: 'Ungrateful fatherland, not even my bones shall you have!'

I brought in this saying of Karl Christian Planck's—uttered before he died in 1880—as it reflects so well what now confronts us in our European World War. That man of idealistic outlook was well qualified to see reality because the inner strength he had developed—as one able to plumb the founts of existence through thinking—is also the most practical thinking in the world. The sort of practical which people who reckon they have eaten Practical by the spoonful is not actually practical. Only someone who has gleaned what springs from genuine founts of life experience—in spite of humanity's brutality and after all warranted striving has been crushed to death—can claim to be practical.

I am bringing this example to demonstrate how the human power also vital for outer practical life—that clear, incisive thinking—can only arise when the human soul is enriched by spiritual-scientific truths. How can people of our time believe that human life on Earth is viable without having any idea of spiritual-scientific knowledge? Because they are so infinitely short-sighted! If they weren't so myopic, one could prove, purely externally, how wrong those are who say that people need not worry about some spiritual world: they would be born of themselves, would bring themselves up. Some sort of education would need to be on offer, but today's education comes up with the sort of massively clever educational principles that reach the dizzying heights of Foerster's Pedagogy.[65] You would then become one of those stolid citizens who put their mind to what they have to do to feed and water humanity—themselves included.

Humanity has not always been like this. Thinking it is possible to live on Earth at all without some spiritual knowledge is a recent phenomenon. External proof of this is plentiful, and I'd like to posit to you an example I've outlined in various Branches. We could probably find a Munich example if we had time, but here in Munich we don't have such time. This was found recently in a Hamburg Art Gallery and arose as follows: let's think of that great symbol at the start of the Old Testament, the temptation of Adam and Eve, which we know to be the luciferic temptation. Isn't it the case that when this is painted today—no matter whether realistically, idealistically,

Expressionistically or Impressionistically, in Futurist mode or whatever—people will generally believe it to be in accordance with reality, even if they paint Adam and Eve in varying degrees of horribleness. They will include the tree, the snake, as large as the tree, with its reptilian head, but certainly with a snake's head. Can this be called realistic, in the true sense of the word? I don't think so, my dear friends! Leaving aside all mention of modern women, not even the original, archetypal Eve can have been of such limited acuity as to be seduced by a real snake! That can hardly be considered realism! Just think of a real snake, slithering through green grass: is the archetypal ur-mother Eve supposed to have fallen for its wiles? Even a present-day snake, gliding around as an actual creature, can only be thought of as a symbol of something else.

But now let's remember which concepts we need to associate with this luciferic seduction. It is after all luciferic! The serpent can at most be a symbol of Lucifer. Associated with this image is the fact that the being Lucifer remained behind during Moon evolution. Nor can this being be seen with physical, earthly eyes. With Lucifer still remaining at the stage of Moon evolution, he can of course not be seen with normal, physical eyes, only with one's inner eye. He can therefore not resemble any terrestrial snake, which *can* be seen with physical eyes.

You have to imagine Lucifer in the way that spiritual science can. Just think, human beings bear their head as the element that is the furthest developed of their limbs. On this hangs by the most fragile of means—just look at a skeleton—as if hanging; the rest of the organism, albeit the spinal column and cord also hangs from the skull. Yet what develops later, physically speaking, was formed earlier. Were we to go back in evolution and see Lucifer with our inner eye, we would naturally have to see him at his Moon stage, preparing the earthly human head. You would see a human head, not yet quite solidified, internally mobile, still polymorphic, variously-shaped, and from it hanging something resembling spinal column and cord, which could be imagined as something akin to a snake's body. You would have to paint Lucifer like this, with as ambiguous a face as possible and from this head a serpentine body dangling, which is approaching the primal beginnings of a human backbone. This would be a spiritual-scientific image of Lucifer.

Now, there was in that Hamburg Art Gallery a thirteenth or fourteenth-century painting by Master Bertram[66] depicting the biblical story of creation, where this paradisiac symbol is painted in such a way that Lucifer—in the form I have just described—thoroughly accords with spiritual science's image. So, in the thirteenth or fourteenth century, Master Bertram was able to depict Lucifer correctly, as spiritual science can confirm. You can go and see it—it is a historically factual image.

We have often spoken of ancient, atavistic clairvoyance, which only gradually faded away. Yet what Master Bertram painted is an indication that, right into the thirteenth or fourteenth centuries, there was still the potential for Lucifer to be correctly depicted in the sense of old atavistic spiritual science. It is therefore possible to prove by external means that it was only a few centuries ago that people became so devoid of spirit as to be as godforsaken as they now are. You'll find plenty of similar examples.

What this means is that what those stunted minds take to be the primal, everlasting nature of the human soul—looking out through one's eyes, combining impressions with reasoning—has only been a quality of human souls for the past few centuries. Previously, all human beings were aware of a connection with spiritual worlds. This died away naturally over time. And yet we find that as late as the thirteenth or fourteenth century, people existed who could paint in accord with ancient vision. It is important to take note of facts such as this. From examples such as this it can be seen how atavistic vision—which, as we know, had to make way for the elaboration of free will in humanity—still persisted, living on in souls of that time. Because the consciousness soul had to be evolved, that ancient spiritual science had to die out.

Today spiritual science needs to be retrieved. As far as a spirit of creativity and inventiveness is concerned, humanity is still living on legacies passed down from the spirituality of old—in every area of life. Today, if someone has an idea about something that did not previously exist, it is due to old spirituality still working on. But it will only be fifty or a hundred years before all inventions and ideas impelled by true creativity in human evolution will have vanished, including in branches of mechanical engineering, if spiritual science does not work fruitfully for humanity. Spiritual science simply has to embed itself actively into the entire evolution of humankind from now on, otherwise the soul life of the human race on Earth will become sterile and unproductive.

We face this sterility in varying degrees, but especially strongly among the arts. Here the impression is particularly compelling that people are largely spirit- or god-forsaken, unable to find and to insert mysterious elements into works other than what has been prefigured in nature; in other words, when the inner fructification of the spirit is totally absent.

These aspects are on the one hand. They show us how essential it is that we human beings become aware that—as truly human totalities—we are interwoven with beings of higher worlds. You can think of people—there are still some today—who are not aware that air exists; for them it is just empty space. At least, it doesn't rise to their consciousness that air exists. Yet the physical body is basically unthinkable without its surrounding air—what are we physically without our surrounding air? We tend to think of people as contained within their skin, but that is a stupid thought. Here is the air, one moment it is within us, then once again outside us. Does air not belong to the human being as much as the muscle in their physical body? Do you not contain what was once external to you? And then again, vice versa?

Just as our physical body is at one with air, so are we—as regards our soul, as regards our ether body—at one with the beings living and weaving throughout the universe in the form of Angeloi, Archangeloi and Archai. With our astral body we are at one with those beings who likewise live and weave throughout the world, the Thrones, the Spirits of Wisdom, of Movement and of Form. They are continually at work in us, just as air is always working in our physical body. Knowing this gives us the right consciousness of *being human.*

That is one aspect of the matter. There is another side to it. I would like to call up an image of these two aspects by way of your imagination and for the purposes of some necessary considerations. Just read *The Brothers Karamazov* by Dostoyevsky[67]—it is a graphic example. Four personalities, among others, appear in this work, the four sons of the old Karamazov: Dmitri Karamazov, Ivan Karamazov, Alyosha Karamazov and Pavel Fyodorovich Smerdyakov, putatively a Karamazov. The effect this novel exerted particularly on Central Europe was quite remarkable. It would take me too long to talk about all the ways and means by which this work, *The Brothers Karamazov,* takes shape out of human life and courses through a soul such as that of Dostoyevsky. But I will just say this: One can greatly admire the artistry and incisiveness of his psychology—as people nowadays call it, knowing as they do so little about what really constitutes *the art* of psychology—and for his finely observed lives. Nevertheless, anyone who may not have absorbed spiritual-scientific concepts and percepts, learning that the human being consists of physical body, ether body, astral body and I—whether written on a chalkboard or in colours, as was often done for the sake of memorizing—anyone who has not absorbed this intellectually but who has gradually, over a lifetime, come to experience these elements in human nature, in the way we aim to do over the years, may have an uncomfortable feeling about the largely chaotic depictions in *The Brothers Karamazov.* However, it does contain many fine observations on life—if you only focus on externals. For instance, the eldest of the Karamazov brothers has a different mother and has quite different character traits from the two middle brothers, Ivan and Alyosha, and the fourth, who is rather childlike, has yet another mother. Old Karamazov is a frightful, phenomenal bounder who carries on all sorts of monkey business, so that this Smerdyakov has an idiosyncratic relationship with the mother[68] and it is not made clear that he is a son of Karamazov senior—but I won't tell the story now. Yet when you look at it from the angle as to who the mothers of the four Karamazov brothers were, you may have the feeling: there's more to all this than meets the eye! It is noticeable that a European would not go about describing things in this way. Central Europeans tend to describe in far more conscious ways and, in descriptions, wouldn't bring in so many subconscious factors as does Dostoyevsky. They would *assemble* more, and in assembling facts they know about, would have less of the richness of a Dostoyevsky, who doesn't take the route of what he *knows* but transcribes from life itself. Life is indeed richer than the human soul can know, due to the spirit existing behind it.

In face of all this, you may feel: much has passed through an endlessly chaotic spirit—through a spirit made chaotic by his epilepsy and through a seriously unhealthy soul—because in our time, just as in nature, human life inclines one to reveal the one thing or the other. Then you may come to a point—if a real sense, a real concept, of what is understood by physical body, ether body, astral body and ego has been acquired—of realizing that in the four Karamazov brothers human presences are represented whom one understands rightly if one reflects: one brother presents as a person in whom one element of human nature predominates, where the physical body primarily is active. In another brother we face a being more predominantly given to activity in the ether body—this being where its activity is centred; in the third brother the astral body comes to the fore, whereas in the fourth brother the quality of an I is more pronounced.

It really appears like this when you read *The Brothers Karamazov* by Dostoyevsky and inwardly observe those four characters, such that you might reflect: because of that whole human vortex affecting the writer and causing him to write chiefly out of the unconscious, these four elements of human nature have the effect that in one the ego, in the next the astral has the upper hand, and so on, so that, overall, these four Karamazov brothers are like a dismembered human being, somewhat akin to the way in which the animal kingdom is a dismembered ether body. So you will find, if you care to look into it more closely, in Smerdyakov Karamazov a predominating physical body, in Ivan Karamazov an ether body at the forefront, in Alyosha an astral body and in Dmitri primarily an I or ego. If this at first seems strange, it is nevertheless viewed from a point of reality and not as one would construct it. In fact, one would probably construct it quite differently, yet there it is when viewed in its inherent reality.

Herein lies an oddity: that a writer who created chiefly out of his subconscious and whose soul was chaotic due to his epilepsy should be nudged towards reality, and who also becomes related, via his astral body—again in his unconscious—with all that lives and weaves throughout the world. For, my dear friends, we can well believe that not for nothing are we—like Dostoyevsky—already standing under the gallows waiting to be hanged, as others had been before him; waiting and about to be hanged when, at the very last moment, a reprieve comes! This is something that releases quite different feelings in a human soul from those in a soul which has not undergone any such event: to be hanged at any minute. That needs to be taken into account.

All this demonstrates, I'd say, how reality can affect a contemporary soul in such a way that, throughout an entire novel, it can depict four brothers, archetypically endowed as I described, who can only be understood if one knows about—and is able to feel—this structure. Then you will also understand why, for example, the one overwhelmingly possessing etheric qualities and the one who is predominantly physical in body should be descended from a person who has suffered frequent hysterical episodes. Many other details fall into place wonderfully once you take this into account.

From the above it becomes apparent towards what our time is forging in a folk-region which, as I have so often described, is suited to some extent to giving up the qualities of its blood, qualities that ought to form a connection with Central European qualities, as I outlined the day before yesterday. Understanding what is happening—including by those who are unconsciously woven into this phenomenon—can at present only be achieved with a background in spiritual science. It may seem inane to say that, but let us for once give it expression: The world is profound, and an ability to know or judge something is not the easy matter those people nowadays imagine it to be who lead lives in the way that some do. People of this ilk dream their way through life in a daze, not knowing the first thing about what is taking place around them.

Enormous events lie ahead and it is not easy to draw people's attention to them. Do you not after all belong—not least through your karma—to those who, bit by bit, commit to such things, who listen to them and eventually get to grips over the years with concepts as to what underlies the surface of life? Those outside this movement can sometimes be given hints, but this may not go very far. Then there are those markedly clever individuals who believe, above all, that those who can *talk* spiritual scientifically, who resort to this assertion or another, know no more than their words; and those who have no idea that everything has to be retrieved from an all-encompassing source of knowledge, but from knowledge that can be corroborated down into its every detail and which becomes especially interesting when such details are substantiated.

That certain things in human evolution need to change will be apparent to you from the two facts I juxtaposed: on the one hand, I showed you what is contained in the human being and, on the other, how to view events that are actually taking place. If someone who has no training in microscopic work looks through a microscope, they will generally not see much. Similarly, the person looking into life in the nineteenth-century East will not generally have seen very much if they remark that Dostoyevsky also lived there and wrote a book called *The Brothers Karamazov*. And because in the content of that book a subterranean element is alive—because it is actually present in himself—and is combined with what in turn exists in the East, the concept has arisen in Eastern consciousness relating to a particular approach to life which they call 'Karamazovshchina'. Whatever is experienced in imitation of the life of the Karamazov brothers is called Karamazovshchina. Yes, it is hard to say and is a more qualitative concept than the Munich idea of 'Strizzi-ness'[69] which is far more abstract. Over there it is more concrete and, obviously, not the same in meaning. But the concept occupies a central place in life there and is also applied to art. People know that to understand contemporary life it is essential to have—in terms of soul background—what can only originate in spiritual science.

Similarly, from the external processes so often confronting people nowadays—and from a thoughtful observation of the facts—the same necessity of which I have been speaking is evident, and this I sought to illuminate from two perspectives.

The following is an especially depressing aspect of present times. You see, long before the war began, generalized opinions had been expressed: certain people were held to have delivered outstanding results in their various areas of expertise. There were no particular reasons to oppose them, as they had achieved a great deal, in the sense of present culture, which is materialistic. Then war was declared. These people spoke out, letters were written. It is quite unbelievable what people—regarded the world over as outstanding—could write once war had broken out! Just read the letters they wrote after the outbreak of war, or read—on another tack now—the letter written by the man—I do not need to share his views with you—who was considered a remarkably committed free spirit: Kropotkin![70] What kind of senseless, arch-idiotic letters he has written since the outbreak of war! These are things which, after all, carry a great deal of weight.

I would like to say: At the moment it is particularly evident—at a time when humanity is facing fast-moving, enormously portentous events—just how little such people, even though they may be exceptional individuals, are of sufficient stature as regards their thinking to face what has broken into their otherwise comfortable, humdrum daily lives. The best of these—in their own regard—are the ordinary philistines; not, of course, from our standpoint, but in terms of modern opinion. Well, they continue to carry on living and holding forth, each opining from their own standpoint. These personal outlooks: how do they usually come about? It's well known that nowadays people don't respect authority and have their own self-generated views. The views they hold are by and large just based on having forgotten in which paper, magazine or programme they heard a given opinion. These are their own views! They differentiate between other, foreign views and their own; the salient feature of these latter is that they have forgotten the source from which they were absorbed.

All this indicates that much—very, very much—has to become quite different, particularly in respect of spiritual life, and that people will have to get used to not going through life in the way materialists do, who are in fact forever dreaming about the world. They of course imagine that others are the dreamers, but the truth is that materialists are the dreamers who never wake up properly. The way spiritual life is regarded really has to change and the fact that it has to become quite different needs to penetrate into the consciousness precisely of those who want to bind the essential live nerve of a spiritual-scientific world view with their own hearts.

We have had to have a more serious exchange of words on the occasion of my present visit for the simple reason that today matters stand such that we have to take every opportunity—opportunities that may not always present themselves so easily. At the moment, travelling around is difficult. All this is connected with what I have repeatedly mentioned here, which can in turn be seen in the context of all I've said again today.

Today I again said that our ether body cannot be seen merely as the bearer of our thoughts, something we drag around and regard as if it were our property, after which it just evaporates. No, it does not simply evaporate! It is the element that becomes woven into the universal cosmic ether after entire hierarchies have worked upon it.

When hundreds and thousands of human beings—as is the case at present—are prevented by death from wearing their ether bodies for decades—as would be normal for the span of a human life—and when so many young people are given up to spiritual worlds, to ether worlds, then what I have so often described comes about: these ether bodies remain present, with the portion that would have been allotted for their use now available for the world itself; because no forces are ever lost. These will be up yonder. But as to what effect they will have up yonder will depend on the state of souls down here. Those souls who will in future be able to find strength for spiritual progress will know: many have undergone a sacrificial death; their ether bodies are still present. If we can become conscious of them—if we are conscious of their forces, which can radiate inwards towards what has been left behind—then a great spiritual revival will be enabled. But there must be souls on Earth who are receptive to what is spiritual, to a spiritual perception of the world. Then what abounds in spiritual worlds as a result of all those sacrificial deaths will be made fruitful for the Earth. Otherwise this will become Ahriman's spoils! Because it must not simply be made fruitful for the Earth—these things don't come about of themselves—but it has to be made fruitful through the mediation of human souls.

For it depends on as many fitting human souls joining—in their thinking and their feelings—with the forces remaining in the unused ether bodies of those who have undergone sacrificial deaths: upon this will it depend whether a future cultural epoch on Earth will be able to use them in furtherance of that future spiritual age, or whether this abundance becomes the spoils of Ahriman.

Think this thought meditatively, my dear friends, and it will become significant for your souls; then will what I have often spoken here—and with which I also wish to close today—indeed turn out for the good:

From the courage of fighters,
From the blood on fields of battle,
From the grief of the bereft
From the sacrifice of people
There will grow fruit of spirit
If, spirit-conscious, souls will turn
Their thoughts to realms of Spirit.

# Lecture 7

## 19 MAY 1917, MUNICH

TODAY I will take as a starting point something that might guide us in understanding what surrounds us and the questions we face. Our times need to be grasped in such a way that human beings can place themselves into their midst, in possession of a deeper and more spiritual understanding. Yet on every hand, there is a deep aversion to spiritual conceptions of all things human. This aversion is actually such that any attempt at a spiritual understanding—a comprehension of such impulses as seek to underpin our difficult times—is rejected from the outset as impossibly fantastical and childish. Nonetheless, the reflections we are able to pursue together here—and which cannot, understandably, address immediate conditions; as you know, they simply cannot—are dedicated to what can lead in some measure to our own understanding and can, with some effort, arrive at truly more profound points of departure.

In order to understand times in which the deepest human forces are to some extent churned into disarray—times in which those deepest human forces are also at work, if for the majority quite unconsciously—it is essential that we don't just talk around all sorts of ideals and topics but that we seek our understanding from a higher vantage point, one spanning the entire evolution of humankind in a general sense. We have always sought—within our spiritual-scientific studies—to arrive at a broader overview across human evolution, and the most diverse aspects of this have been covered. Today I would like to bring something from yet another, slightly different perspective.

We know that a contributory factor within human evolution was undergoing what we call the great Atlantean catastrophe or Flood.

We know that those now living as humankind can be traced back to certain evolutionary conditions that pertained before that Atlantean flood, and that we usually designate those early post-Atlantean epochs as Ancient India, the second as Ancient Persia, the third as Assyrian-Babylonian-Egyptian, the fourth as Græco-Roman. We inhabit the fifth and have to see how this fifth era is to be sloughed off as we move into the sixth.

Now it is a matter of seeing how inwardly, how spiritually—I would almost say: how humanly—evolution among humanity could proceed, how it could take place at all after the Atlantean catastrophe. People who are generally averse to seeing things in context today tend to think: a human being is a human being and the way souls are configured today is the same as it has always been since humankind has existed. Retracing in reverse order the way in which humanity is viewed nowadays, one does albeit arrive at primitive conditions, which thereafter descend into animality. This materialistic interpretation of evolution cannot stand its ground in face of a spiritual-scientific method of observing. For the further—and ever further—we go back in human evolution, the more do we find that the fundamental impetus, the forces underlying evolution become increasingly spiritual; though, if we are seeking accurate insight, we first need to grapple towards the right concept of what is spiritual.

The fourth post-Atlantean epoch is of prime importance for today's age, the most significant in the context of the Earth's entire evolution. It is the age into which the Mystery of Golgotha radiates. It challenges us to view the preceding times as a kind of preparation for the Mystery of Golgotha and the times following it as a fulfilment of the impetus brought about by the Mystery of Golgotha. However, if we go back over Atlantean evolution, we find that the fifth epoch within Atlantean evolution[71] is the most crucial in the span between Lemurian times and our own. For it is that fifth age in Atlantean evolution of human life that is the most incisive, and where we find the point of origin for what we may call the predominantly *soul-level* development of post-Alantean times. Going back into Atlantean times we do not find the animal-humanity of which materialistically-determined Darwinism is so fond of speaking.

We find a humanity possessing a life far more dampened or dulled than post-Atlantean humans. When speaking of dullness of soul life, one would like to say—though the comparison remains a superficial one: the dimmed, dreamlike soul life of Atlantean times resembles the dimly dreamlike soul life of present higher mammals. However, this would be an entirely lame and limping comparison because present-day animals do not experience in their dimly dreamlike consciousness anything like what the humans experienced in their own dreaming consciousness during—and almost until the end of—the fifth Atlantean epoch.

What, then, is the essential hallmark of ancient, dreamlike Atlantean consciousness? Forgive me if what I say sounds materialistic; but one only recognizes what is material once one has command over it, when one is aware of spiritual stimuli. So, the main trait of humanity in those times was that they lived such that their soul life and their life of eating and nourishment were very closely allied. You might object that a close enough relationship exists between the soul life of some modern people and what they consume! That's quite correct and we know that large swathes of present humanity in no way underestimate eating. That in itself need not be designated a reproach. But the difference between the inner experience of tasting food, that feeling of wellbeing experienced by modern humans when combining food with corporeality, and what Atlantean humanity experienced—it is about them that I am now speaking—is actually a great difference. Atlantean humans would eat, they ate this nutrient or another, taking each substance into themselves and, while combining each with their physical existence, conscious knowledge would arise within them as to which elemental spirit had suffused that material. They would not—in the manner of modern humans—gulp material down in colossal unconsciousness but were conscious with which elemental spirits they were amalgamating during the process of combining material with their corporeal existence. Their metabolism was simultaneously a spiritual exchange: their mutual interaction with elemental spirits.

It was the case that we could designate materials as bearers of one or another elemental spirit's impulsion—or even as a being—such that humans felt, with their food, that spiritual forces were entering them. In digesting this, it was felt that a spiritual stimulus was at work within, that the human was not simply sitting and digesting—as they would today—but that they were physically saturated by one or another spiritual-elemental being. Thus materialism, such as it holds sway today, could not possibly exist. You could not claim only to believe in existential mortality because spiritual stimuli pervaded both human and their digestion. In one sense, one only had to eat to be an anti-materialist. Descending into the dim dullness of subconsciousness is an essential achievement of this fifth Atlantean epoch. Eating and digesting became to some extent less spiritual; yet there remained something in the sixth Atlantean epoch, which was more spiritual and that was *breathing*.

Today, when human beings breathe in or out, it comes into their awareness that they are breathing air in or out—that, at least, is what a chemist will tell us. In remote times this was not only conscious but—and this persisted throughout the sixth Atlantean epoch—humans were aware that, in breathing in, they were inhaling spiritual-elemental forces into themselves; and in breathing out they were exhaling elemental-spiritual forces. From its outset, breathing has been an inherently soul-spiritual process and cannot be seen as a purely corporeal-physical activity. During the last Atlantean epoch, what had until then pertained diminished somewhat and later remained only as a memory: when hearing tones or sounds and seeing colours, an awareness remained that—in the tone that could be heard, in the colour that could be seen—spiritual forces were radiating into eyes in vision, into interior life in the hearing of sounds. All this was present in the dim consciousness of those times. Humans achieved more lucid consciousness but at the cost of their more spiritual consciousness, and they had to give up the spiritually-transfused mutuality of their interrelationship with the outer world. Each age has its particular idiosyncrasies. Just as individual humans traverse the ages of life and their effects on the disposition of body and soul are varied, so does humanity's entire evolution go through various states, and later conditions differ from earlier ones. It would be foolish for someone of fifty or sixty to believe that what constitutes their physical-spiritual identity could conjure back their state between ten and twenty; it is just as laughable not to be able to distinguish between the various stages of life and their specific qualities. Likewise, it is eccentric to think that what pertains in later ages of life's evolution was necessarily species-appropriate at earlier ages. Things never return and they differ in successive stages of life more than you might think.

I have taken it upon myself to find out something about the stages of human life in post-Atlantean times. Anyone just proceeding from analogies can also look at human evolution and say to themselves: Just as an individual goes through childhood, youth, adulthood and old age, so also does humanity as a whole. However, if you observe properly and delve into the actual interrelation between facts, that is not the case. You can't simply rely on analogies; only when you take spiritual science seriously can you find what underlies matters. And it appeared to me that this was something different from what one might perhaps summarize by saying that, similarly to an individual human being, humanity goes through stages of youth, adulthood and old age. But this is not so. I found out that humanity in the first post-Atlantean cultural epoch—that of Ancient India—was indeed at a certain stage of life, though not at one which can be equated with youth, but can instead be compared with an individual aged between fifty-six and back to forty-nine. So that if one wants to compare the age of humanity as a whole with a period in an individual's life, it should not be compared with youth but with this riper span. Following this comes the cultural epoch of Ancient Persia. In developing further, humanity undergoes an age span comparable with an individual life that is not youthful but ranges backwards from forty-nine to forty-two. Individuals grow older but humanity grows younger! The Egyptian cultural period therefore has to be compared—in individual terms—with the stage of life between forty-two and thirty-five. The Græco-Roman cultural period is comparable with an individual stage between thirty-five and twenty-eight, and the present, fifth post-Atlantean cultural period can be compared with an individual's age between twenty-eight and twenty-one. If we ask: How old is present-day humanity? We would need to answer: It is currently aged around twenty-seven. You only realize all that has contributed to humankind once this remarkable mystery of evolution is presented to your soul. For that is how this comparative matter actually stands.

All this has definite consequences with regard to human life on Earth. What is entailed in that during the first post-Atlantean cultural epoch the whole of humanity experienced an age between fifty-six and forty-nine? It means: an individual human being would of course experience that they were firstly one, two or three years old. But the fundamental feature of humanity—into which each individual settled—presented a quality which an individual person only experienced between the ages of forty-nine and fifty-six. That is why so much original, archetypically-elemental human knowledge comes to the fore in that epoch, wisdom at which we can wonder in a humanity so old, a humanity which had, as it were, settled into such maturity and age. A whippersnapper of twenty-five would absorb from the aura of humanity whatever was filled with wisdom, much as one would from an older person. Wisdom was dispensed over all humankind, morality was absorbed and, through growing into oneness with the aura of humanity, wisdom was valued, much as one would value a grey-haired head for the reason that it had matured into greyness. Thus did a feeling of devotion and piety flow out over human cultural life which was both natural and taken for granted. This had the further effect that people—in respect of their individual development—could grow beyond what were gifts common to all only when they reached the age of fifty-six. Only then could you speak of really individual development, only then could individuals raise themselves above the groundswell of what approached everyone externally. Actually, many people did not achieve such inner development as corresponds with the maturity between the ages of forty-nine and fifty-six. They were regarded as children; they felt like children who can sense all around them the spiritual contents of humanity's age.

The following age—that of Ancient Persia—brought forth fewer lofty revelations and cultural impulses than the wise elders of the first post-Atlantean epoch had shared with humanity through their association with spiritual beings. All humankind evinced only a maturity comparable with the individual human stage of life between ages forty-nine and forty-two. Those who wished to outgrow the general aura of humanity could only undertake this after age forty-nine. Yet these grew—through their individual progress—into a maturity that could only blossom after the age of forty-nine.

Similarly, during the Egypto-Chaldean epoch, the aura, into which human beings grew, may be compared with the individual's stage in life between the ages of forty-two and thirty-five. In Græco-Roman times this was between thirty-five and twenty-eight. It is a remarkable feature of this Græco-Roman age that the individual's central point in life coincides with the central point in the life of humanity as a whole. It is just that while humanity in general flows downwards, the individual ascends. This underlies the unique harmony of Greek culture, a harmony of which present humanity lacks any concept. When a Greek reached thirty-five, they remained in one sense an average person, remained forever thirty-five had they not evolved an individual element in themselves that transcended the aura of humanity as a whole. Care was therefore taken in ancient times that an individual was enabled to evolve ahead and aloft.

Then followed the fifth post-Atlantean age, the era in which we now live. During this fifth post-Atlantean period humanity will live through a stage in life which can be compared with an individual's age between twenty-eight and twenty-one. This means that someone merely abandoning themselves to the universal flow of existence, someone who is only concerned with soul life to the extent that they are simply human, does not progress past the age of twenty-eight. If such a person makes no effort to advance their soul individually, to make some spiritual progress, they will remain twenty-eight or, rather, will not mature past twenty-seven. Universal humanity can endow us with no more than it does by aiding us to reach the age of twenty-seven. If we do not, in our present age, seek to *fire* and to *bestir* ourselves with regard to our individual soul forces—the forces which can elevate us beyond the general, universal stream of human existence—then, though we live to a hundred, we will never go beyond the age of twenty-seven. Whether we are manual workers, professors or whatever: if we fail to seek spiritual development, which will endow our souls with concepts such as external humanity cannot give it, we remain twenty-seven in age. We will of course grow outwardly older because time cannot be held up; but our souls only achieve a maturity of twenty-seven in absence of our own evolutionary efforts. You really cannot understand our times if you do not bear in mind the unique trait just described. Over the years, I really have asked many questions pertinent to our time, questions about life, about the evolution of culture, about human misery, about what delights present humankind, what torments it; the key to understanding our present is the fact to which I have just alluded. What is lacking in our times cannot be grasped without focusing on this fact.

We encounter philosophies at whose exposition we can only stand amazed because they remain at the stage of declaiming generalities and have not the slightest ability to pitch into actual reality. Why is this so? I put this question to a single personality. I found that the originator of Eucken's philosophy[72] is a man who has all the fire of a person who cannot transcend the age of twenty-seven. Certainly, he can talk—he has, after all, reached a considerable age—in a slightly rough voice, moves with different gestures and has learnt some additional things. But this betokens nothing; his whole manner is no more mature than age twenty-seven. You can bear such twenty-seven-year-old mannerisms throughout your life. This becomes particularly noticeable when people try to bring their ideas to bear on life, when they harbour ideas about ways in which life is to be managed.

Now we come to a slightly perilous area; so let's approach it by looking for the widest possible examples. I have asked various present-day people—those who have the task of intervening in modern life, making interventions concerning the way in which contemporary phenomena are to be governed by their ideas—how things are going for them. There is a typical person of this sort. I have made great efforts to be direct on the subject and not to beat about the bush, but there is no point in pursuing the matter unless the subject is based in its concrete manifestation. If you go looking for someone who is inherently of the type that can never transcend the age of twenty-seven—who will never have more mature thoughts than someone of that age—you find those of this particular type, strangely enough, in the most extraordinary places, for example, in the form of a President of the United States of America. If you study the various programmes that person has promoted, they bear the imprint of the type of person who cannot move beyond the age of twenty-seven because their soul has never absorbed the slightest element of anything other than what external life has brought their way. Admittedly, people of this ilk can be gifted to a greater or lesser extent—talent may well be granted them—but the ideas they develop are, in terms of maturity of outlook, of clout, practicality and common sense, still only twenty-seven and will mature no further—though they live to be a hundred—if they don't start to deepen themselves spiritually and to supply their soul with the power of fire from within.

We live in an age when we have to direct into our souls whatever is to transcend the age of twenty-seven. By twenty-seven people are not practical nor life-savvy; they may insist as they will, but they are not yet practical in real-life terms. That is the reason why the ideas of Wilson[73] are so impractical and erratic and why they please so wide an audience. They appeal to people with the same force of delight which youthful ideas can deliver, youthful ideas that take the form of sundry declarations about people's freedom and suchlike. That's all very nice! That's the way a world is ruled which demands effectiveness of ideas: you just keep making sweeping declarations about peace and then—war is all the more violently unleashed!

One would so much like to engender a feeling for the potential of ideas that really penetrate reality, ideas that have clout, ideas that can grow together with reality. Ideas that are merely declarations, nice ideas, particularly youthful ideas that are thought so pleasant, are spread around. But we need ideas that connect human beings with reality. What kind of lovely new idea is it when someone jumps to their feet saying: The world needs to be orientated anew! The best that can come from suchlike are the words themselves! That is the one and only nice thing: the words themselves, because one can then talk about them and that is certainly pleasant. It's also nice to say: The hardest worker should be deployed in the right job. Great ideas! But what happens when the hardest worker happens to be the nephew or the son-in-law? Nothing actually gets done with nice ideas; only genuine knowledge of reality carries things out, only a capacity for knowing what is real and genuine.

Here is one of the views to be taken into account if you wish to understand today's culture more deeply. The peculiar nature of the times exhorts us to realize how vital it is for human beings to deepen their souls, and that they seek to achieve—through their own progress and to benefit their later years—that which humanity is no longer being universally given. It is obviously easier to talk—in the manner of Eucken—of renewing life, of gaining inner mastery over life, of all sorts of things whereby one can elevate oneself in youthful fashion; all of which are no use for anything but declamations. And if political programmes are produced with ideas such as those of Wilson, then the upshots are incalculable! This is much easier than seriously researching, seriously deepening your search for reality and penetrating the hidden impulses of life.

If our spiritual-scientific movement is truly to have deeper significance it will, above all, have to salvage the will to delve into humanity's actual evolutionary impetus and be prepared to take hold of the great connections in life, otherwise everything in our spiritual science will remain mere theory. And mere theory is worth nothing, however much you may wish to associate with theory feelings that make you seem to be elevated. Only and solely what can delve into life—what is able to grasp life—is of any real value. All sorts of mysticism—in which people seek to find this or that within themselves—can come up with some very nice results, but we need to be able to look away from ourselves towards humanity's great tasks so as to understand, above all, what we have need to understand, what we ought to understand. Otherwise the most important aspects of spiritual science will simply be ignored. Over the years since we have experienced our anthroposophically-orientated spiritual science, a great deal of important things have in fact simply been swept aside unheeded.

If only those dear friends would remember the answer I would always give—over many years—whenever I was asked how matters stand regarding reincarnation because humanity is constantly increasing. If those dear friends might recall the stock answer always given: It could be that humanity will very soon experience the decimation of humankind taking place, especially in Europe—then you will gauge what was meant if you look back and remember the tone in which this was said. Whenever an increase in population was mentioned, the answer was: A time might soon come when, in the most painful ways, populations may decrease. Spiritual science is not about responding with theories to the superficial and casually felt needs of some people, but of answering questions posed by others that arise from the impulses of the times. In accepting spiritual science, it is preferable to grasp the gravity of what needs to be said and enfold it in one's heart than satisfy curiosity—however upstanding it may appear.

This is what I wanted to convey, my dear friends, in the first part of today's considerations and which—taking due account of the situation—is intended to lead to a deeper understanding of our time, something we will tend to further over these days.

As the time designated for general considerations is running out, I would like—without causing anyone to claim I am cutting back on actual anthroposophical content—to move on to something requiring a few words of introduction. But I cannot move on to that before recalling some souls who have left the physical plane for spiritual life, of whom some were close to those sitting here today. It is not possible to go into all their individual names. Our dear friends present will accordingly orientate themselves towards the appropriate uprightness of feeling in face of all those who have left the physical plane for the spiritual. That said, I cannot avoid commemorating the name of one man who, after quite some hindrances, found himself so beautifully to be in heartfelt inner harmony with anthroposophically-orientated spiritual science and who, just in recent times, had taken on responsibility for representing this in a public-facing capacity, accomplishing much of significance. I am referring to our dear friend Ludwig Deinhard,[74] at whose relinquishing of his body to the physical elements—and departure into spiritual realms—our dear friend Sellin[75] spoke such beautiful words. He must be all the more esteemed in that, despite quite some resistance, he found accord with our stream, not on the basis of blind faith nor with a follower's adherence but lately, in ever worsening times, he unstintingly—with all his soul—stepped up to a wide public on behalf of this spiritual stream. I will not shy away from stating explicitly that I count the way in which Ludwig Deinhard stepped into the public arena on behalf of our movement among the most exceptionally valuable deeds.

May I then call to mind Professor Sachs,[76] who died recently and who pursued a great concept throughout his life, a great musical-technical idea, and who always knew how to connect the modest work in which an individual can be immersed with comprehensive ideas, and with whom it was truly uplifting to speak because what he wanted as a human being always fed into a great artistic will. We can count ourselves fortunate to have such people in our movement.

In the wake of such inspiring thoughts, I am obliged—once again, obliged—to raise a less uplifting issue, inasmuch as what in some respects contributed to occurrences—and to the incisive measures I was obliged to take—involve my participation in the spiritual-scientific movement to be served by the Anthroposophical Society. Over the course of time, what was, to a high degree, intended to be a blessing in cultural evolution—the anthroposophical movement—has, due to many of its manifestations, largely evolved into something of an obstruction rather than the spiritual movement I intended. There is no point in glossing over these issues; that would be particularly pointless where there is a danger of several aspects connected with the Anthroposophical Society becoming obstacles for anthroposophically-orientated spiritual science. Please allow me, therefore—after all, we have worked together for many years and ought to be able to discuss such things without reserve—to deal with this quite openly and in the way it weighs on my heart. In general, one might say: Something has become habitual within the Anthroposophical Society that has no right to continue existing in that form because the judgement of the present world as to what anthroposophy intends is all too easily clouded by what has hitherto been taking place.

Taking one detail as our starting point: in the world at large it is often said—and this has become general usage—that I myself come under attack less on account of spiritual-scientific matters and more frequently due to some aspects of the Society. One of the allegations levelled is particularly prominent: that a blind belief in authority reigns, that there is blind following and that much is done out of sheer devotion, and so forth. Were I to raise my own objection to this, I would have to say: For the most part, what ultimately takes place is what I consider to be the right thing, what I might consider desirable. I do not believe that in any other Society so little credence is given to what are actually the specific wishes of someone working within it. Even if that appears otherwise, it is nevertheless the case. Only nobody need take this amiss. Shutting one's eyes and burying one's head in the sand, that is indeed taking it amiss.

My dear friends, I have been hearing quite a bit about moods in the local Anthroposophical Society in recent days. When I came into the foyer this evening, I was enveloped in the most devout waft of frankincense. Do not imagine that someone who directs their attention towards practical and inner life would harbour a particular wish for their evening of speaking to be encumbered by reaching for an *externality* such as this devout frankincense, or that they might take a headache home with them due to such devout waftings, not to mention how frankincense might look, wafting out—forgive me—into a profane world. It may seem unpleasant to mention things like this, but they are, after all, symptomatic. Just ask whether any such course of action has ever been initiated by me. But that is just by the way.

However, the most important thing to me is the way in which the membership feels their connection to be with all that flows through anthroposophically-orientated spiritual science in terms of *spiritual life*. You see, and as you know, a multitude of attacks—partly in print, partly about to be printed—have come into the public domain. If from today's external world there are attacks on spiritual science, it is hardly to be wondered at nor need one experience them as especially painful; it is only natural and quite obvious. That can be countered. Spiritual science really need not fear factual discussion. Maybe one need also not be embarrassed by what is spiralling aloft from the membership. But the following does indeed gravely harm the strength that our movement should possess. One can say that one thing is certain in this movement and above all in this Society: that the most benevolent intentions and measures, the most compassionate admonishments regarding members' behaviour are here drenched in the most toxic gall and enveloped in a cloak of betrayal, of denigration, of the most highly personal of confrontations, all of which points in a direction very well known to us. Things being done, possibly for mystical reasons—I don't know—in terms of pure invention, total untruth, are actually nowhere more blatantly evident than here. The will to behave rightly in this regard is not nurtured with sufficient energy. In fact, neither is the will to see these matters in their true reality pursued sufficiently energetically.

The seriousness underlying a spiritual-scientific movement, the scrupulous way in which it has to be represented, should at least be studied. What each individual can contribute naturally depends on their life-situations and the most varied circumstances; but you can at least study what exists and not give yourselves up to all manner of mad notions. Objective factualness and an absence of personality-based bias is especially needful within a movement dedicated to purely spiritual perspectives, and nothing is more destructive than when those most personal interests, vanity or ambition jut into the ranks of our movement. Certainly, such things crop up in masked or embellished guise, but we need to look for their true countenance, observing them such that we arrive at the truth of a matter. If anyone writes about a series of offences or disputes, knowing perfectly well what motivates them, knowing perfectly well how what is being attacked ought to be due to the unique character of spiritual science, then they are not doing enough if they just refute everything sentence by sentence. Stating and refuting can achieve much, sometimes everything, but very often it is not a case of what is being said; the reasons may lie somewhere quite different. If somebody tenders a piece of writing to the Philosophic-Anthroposophic Press and it has to be rejected, and the person concerned becomes an antagonist, then the original causes are not to be sought in the articles proffered by that individual, but elsewhere. One doesn't discover the truth if the most important aspect—the actual reasons—retreat into the background.

If a person concocts some attack or other based on specious esoteric effects, their foolishness is unmistakable to anyone who is not blind, and you would be going astray if you failed to trace utter fabrications back to their factual context. It could be that someone is behind them, say, someone who once lived in a small central German town, who suddenly hatches the idea of becoming a prominent figure. First they might seek to become imposing on a small scale, then by writing to Frau Dr Steiner and asking how they should transcend their narrow, small-town circumstances. Should they marry into a business or effect upward mobility by other means? When it is then indicated that we cannot concern ourselves with decisions about marriage and so forth, they are still not put off. Things move on; they come and take part in some events, perhaps introducing themselves in a large meeting and in full voice declaiming a Schiller poem without having the slightest idea about speech. Laughter might follow. Their ambition is insulted. Later they wish to be a great painter and they pursue this idea to some extent. Everything is done to support them in their learning and they are welcomed. The person concerned wants only to become an artist but finds learning uncomfortable. They don't actually want to *become* an artist, they want to *be* one, and if others can do no more—out of their own inner conviction—than offer learning advice, that's construed as insulting. They are, after all, a genius and it is a cheek to suggest that they need to train! Others do what they can to support this person's learning, but that in itself is insulting.

Further scenarios along these lines could be cited. Such are the true reasons why someone would feel they have to become an enemy of such an awful Society. All sorts of material is then written. What is written is almost beside the point. Much else could of course be written, because the real causes lie elsewhere. And so it may continue—and it probably will—and may take on quite different dimensions. All such things have, in fact, not the slightest to do with spiritual science itself. But they can develop with great intensity from out of a Society attempting to establish itself, not upon the objective basis which spiritual science itself can provide, but within which all manner of cliquish personal social relationships are sought. As you see, I am merely alluding to a tendency; it may be possible to say more in the coming days. Yet all this does not originate in spiritual science itself but can be traced back to prevailing notions about what should happen in the Society. It is precisely those who have been most cared for who most often do the rounds in spreading denigration and sheer fabrication.

It is for reasons such as these, my dear friends, that I need to reach for incisive measures. I beg you at least really to name both two parts of this present reprimand, so that no further aspersions nor betrayals arise, as might happen were only one part to be passed on. If a reproach such as this is hard for some to take, then please remember that it is as hard for me as for those concerned and that I am just as pained that it is necessary. So please don't turn to me but to those who have caused this reprimand. Look in that direction for causes, but also look for what has to happen in future by recognizing, when looking in that direction, the source of such disloyalty. It is most frequent where personal issues come into play. Certainly, I have stood by everyone requesting personal advice. As regards esoteric matters, personal information tended on the whole to be somewhat superfluous. As for esoteric issues, I will always take care that a good alternative is available. But because personal issues have led to this point, it is essential that from now on everything takes place in full public light. I will take care that each can come into their own esoterically, but I will no longer be receiving—on behalf of the Society—those seeking so-called private esoteric consultations. I will—without exception—have to end these private meetings so that they do not become a source of denigratory material. If that is difficult for anyone, this measure has become necessary for two reasons: firstly, because consultations are not essential for the pursuit of esoteric life. I will bring proof of this very soon. You will shortly have a full replacement for the discontinued meetings—which so often resulted in members bringing issues that had nothing to do with esoteric life. Secondly, because in so doing, I am recording that the claim that people's inner lives are not being cared for is one drawn out of thin air. Just read *Knowledge of Higher Worlds—How is it Achieved?* It is not required for anyone to achieve a personal goal within a certain period of time. The second aspect inherent in this measure—one which I beg you not to forget—is that I absolve everyone who has hitherto had private consultations of any undertaking or promise—something anyway never given—of any obligation not to speak about their private consultations. As far as I'm concerned, anyone can say as much as they like about what I discussed with them, as I have nothing to hide. Whoever so wishes can share everything. Everything from the past can also be placed in the full glare of the public domain. This is the way in which we will best achieve a distinction between lies and truth. It will be the best means of creating a benchmark against which the level of duplicity within our movement can be assessed. But these two measures belong together. I will say it yet again: Those only sharing the first part of this reprimand are not presenting it in its true light—they belong together.

I would still like to mention one more thing, my dear friends; if this is difficult for some, then please turn to those local places you will most easily find, turn to those who have made these measures necessary. It is not acceptable that what the spiritual-scientific movement ought to be for the world should be made impossible by cliquishness within the Anthroposophical Society, because precisely in this way is the living element at the very core of spiritual science exposed to the misunderstandings of the world at large. Do you really think that all the tasks that need to be undertaken in the context of the Society are accomplished for my personal satisfaction? I have been accused of deriving from the Society some benefit for this or that project because, for instance, building work in Dornach had to be undertaken. Do you believe that I could personally have had more concern invested in the Dornach building than any other member who takes our work seriously, or that I could have been personally ambitious in seeing it built? Had the building not become possible, I would have been the very last person not to subscribe to its necessity. What the Dornach building was required—for vital reasons—to represent could not be embodied in any other way than that dictated by its inherent lawfulness.

The drastic measures just mentioned must ultimately be adhered to because, though I have been talking about this for decades, the seriousness of my words has never been taken to heart. Perhaps, now that these measures are in place, they will be. Other societies exist in which behaviour of the sort occurring in this Society has not occurred.

This, my dear friends, had to be said for the sake of our friendship and could not be allowed to remain unsaid. Whoever is serious about the anthroposophical movement will find their way even if, in face of the seriousness of the situation, measures such as these become necessary. For the movement as such is too sacred to be allowed to be extinguished just on account of assorted personal aspirations, in which direction more than enough has been going on. Those of our dear members—and there are very many such—who work out of devotion and sacrifice in the movement and in the Society will be the last to complain about the measures imposed and will consider them all-important. I don't think I'll be misunderstood, particularly by those who are genuinely and seriously concerned for our movement; they will concede that I am justified. There will also be those who will say I am wrong; I will be content to accept that judgment.

Time has moved on. I will continue tomorrow with the reflections I have instigated and perhaps add to what I have had to say about aspects of the Society. It has often been very hard to watch some of this.

# Lecture 8

## 20 MAY 1917, MUNICH

FROM yesterday's talk you could see how, in our times, human beings find themselves in the midst of humanity's overall evolution. It was shown—to some extent by human evolution itself and by what comes towards individual personalities—how this evolution has increasingly awakened a drive to fire the inner soul, to awaken it, because humans have become ever less able to make progress in external terms without drawing on their inner resources. That is the gist of what spiritual science intends: to lead human individuals towards the possibility of striding ahead, whereas in ancient times—simply because each human was born into humanity—they had a given number of experiences that endowed them with a certain level of maturity. You will feel that knowledge of such a fact—as outlined yesterday—is of immense importance and fundamentally illuminates what is needed by human beings of our time.

One can only enter into this properly—in the sense of a spiritual scientist—by looking with wide open eyes at the ways in which present humans relate to human evolution as a whole. Infinitely significant discoveries can be made here; but these discoveries have to be made in such a way that one is in a position to evaluate the facts. There are people today who feel it necessary to extend their soul beyond its boundaries—in other words, beyond the age of twenty-seven. But the courage and energy, which today creates such wonders in the external world, that courage and energy to really unfold inner soul forces are not found so frequently today. That is how it comes about that we meet people who, in their own ways, strive to find something other than what exists in the surrounding culture and tasks of the times. Yet they lack the courage to approach the working methods, attitudes and ethos that long for something genuinely new, that is, for spiritual science. We find that such people do not clearly say to themselves but instead they feel: In times gone by the surrounding world bequeathed more to humans, so we ought to look for what the world once gave humanity; we need to regain access to those ancient gifts once more.

That is the reason why those more inclined to long for the spirit take refuge—I'd say, due to a lack of strength—in all sorts of long-superseded, long-surpassed stages of human evolution. Examples of this abound. One such is very typical: the writer Maurice Barrès[77] who, with youthful impetuosity, wanted—one could say—to storm the spiritual heavens, then sought to join some new spiritual movement or other but, lacking the requisite courage, found his affiliation with Catholicism, as do so many today. Yet it is an odd attitude that seeks their path in a backward instead of a forward direction. The words in which Barrès describes his striving towards Catholicism are the predictable testimony of someone lacking all courageous drive or energy of soul who, because they can muster no will to seek anything new, clutch at what is old. How he clutches is what is typical. Just take the words of a spirit such as Barrès, a product of today's education, who stands fully within it, and from it has evolved his inclination towards Catholicism: 'Seeking what is yonder is a waste of effort. Maybe it doesn't even exist!' Just think: after aligning himself with Catholicism, he speaks of yonder worlds in terms such as these: 'Seeking what is yonder is a waste of effort. Maybe it doesn't even exist! However much we grab hold of it, we cannot experience anything of it. Let's leave occultism to the Enlightened and the street entertainers. Whichever form mysticism may assume, it contradicts reason. So let us just give ourselves to the Church'—Just think about that!—'firstly, because it is indissolubly bound up with France's tradition. Further, because it has been formulated with the authority of centuries and has great practical experience of the ethical rules it must teach people and children. And, lastly, because, far from supplying us with mysticism, it directly defends us against it, commanding the voices of the mysterious groves to silence, setting out the Gospels and sacrificing the magnanimous anarchism of the Redeemer to the needs of modern society.' Here you see the motivation of someone typical of the present, driven to search for the spirit in their own particular way: grasping for what humanity—without human effort—once possessed. He just takes it without making any demands on the real sense of what he is taking. One might call this cynical or frivolous were there not considerable seriousness and striving behind it. And that is just what is so ominous and disastrous: the serious nature of the striving itself becomes frivolous because of its relation to *time*. Don't take such words lightly! The most damaging disservices to our time are rooted in the fact that human beings are always inclined to take things flippantly. Countless other examples similar to that of Barrès could be cited. They would all demonstrate, in their multifarious ways, the attribute of our times just mentioned.

We ask ourselves: What is the underlying reason for this? We ask this because it is important to recognize how we need to do things differently. We can only find our way properly forward if we have some insight into the present calamity, into what underlies an attitude such as this. We have to look back a little over human evolution if we want to understand the present—and we do need to understand it—if we want to make headway. If we go back over the evolution of European humanity and associated Asiatic populations—we only need to go back as far as the first third of post-Atlantean times—we find what even external research confirms: that people could clearly differentiate between the three basic elements of the human constitution; that archaic, dimly dreamlike awareness arose enabling them to distinguish between these three attributes. This is why I gave particular emphasis in my book *Theosophy* to the fact that these three fundamental constituents have to underlie the overall structure of the human being. Going back, we see that human beings viewed humankind as comprising body, soul and spirit. Just think what confusion reigns today—even among those seeking clarity—in terms of an overview of the human constituents of body, soul and spirit! You can scroll through philosophy after philosophy, you can study Wundt,[78] who is not only well known in Germany but studied worldwide 'with passionate resolution'[79] and you will see that the man cannot differentiate between soul and spirit, despite that ability being amongst today's most basic requirements. When did it widely come to light that people were muddling up soul and spirit? As I said, you will find this everywhere: the human being is divided into body and soul and—mixed into the soul without any distinguishing features—also some spirit. This came to sharp expression in the year 869 at the Council of Constantinople, when the spirit was abolished, banished—forgive the harsh expression—because the teachings then formulated culminated largely in creating the doctrine that human beings contained a thinking soul and a spirit-like soul. The spirit was therefore dispatched and a still-sensed fragment of it smuggled into the soul, whereby it was claimed that the soul has thinking capacity and some spiritual attributes. Then followed the Middle Ages with its—in many respects—admirable scholastic research. Yet this still existed under the vigorous constraints of that doctrine [of 869] and any so-called trichotomy or threefold stratification was severely frowned upon. The spirit had to be omitted everywhere. This defines the way in which soul and spirit are considered—or rather not considered—by modern academicians who, according to their own statements, carry out premise-free science. They simply don't acknowledge those premises, as set out in the resolutions of the Council of Constantinople in 869. The fact that the academics have no inkling upon what they actually depend is the reason they deem themselves to be unconditionally premise-free. Those are the facts of the matter. They need to be heard and energetically focused upon—there is no point shutting one's eyes to them. If anthroposophically-orientated spiritual science is to become for human beings what it is intended to become in accordance with the laws of human evolution, such things have to be kept in view, while an understanding of the threefold structure of the human being—as body, soul and spirit—has to be restored to humanity. Just as, on the one hand, the body exists between birth or conception and death and is the physical facilitator of consciousness, so must the spirit be recognized as the spiritual facilitator of higher consciousness, which human beings have to develop between death and a new birth. This is deeply allied with the momentous inner circumstances of life in modern humanity.

Let's take something typical of our times. Thinking—about which we must say it has become an abstraction, though the occasional person may transcend this abstraction—is largely based in public life on three abstract ideas. Nowadays in the world at large we see these three abstract ideas being brought to bear against Central Europe. This central area of Europe will only take up its spiritual task if it accustoms itself to making the three abstract ideas into concrete ideas, ideas that are drenched in reality. These three concepts were driven into consciousness with great fervour at the end of the eighteenth century in the words: fraternity, freedom and equality. They almost remind us of three quite concrete concepts, which are only now understood in abstract terms but which were embodied in human consciousness in terms conceived as appropriate to the reality of those times. They remind us of faith, hope and love. But let's stay for a moment with fraternity, freedom and equality. It is spectral, shadowy thinking that seeks to actualize these three concepts across the modern world. Everything of this ilk, in pursuit of which human souls make such efforts, rests upon the fact that people have no inclination to penetrate reality. They can do no more with these three great cardinal concepts than they do with the new policy of realignment: that each human being should be deployed in the position best befitting them. They announce nice ideas, create abstract concepts out of those ideas, but have no inclination to commit to reality. This reality consists of an understanding of spiritual science.

In the same way as spirit and soul are intermingled in confusion, so are freedom, equality and fraternity jumbled together. The idea of fraternity, of brotherliness, will only be capable of being rightly grasped by humanity once you are clear that human beings only fully exist on this physical plane with one of their constituent elements: in corporeal incarnation. We exist on a physical level, in physical embodiment, which connects us with all humankind through blood and other commonalities. Just think back to olden times about the way in which physical humans related to other physical humans. They did not just contain what they inherited from their parents, but also encompassed the immortal element which accompanied them through births and deaths, configuring itself into corporeality over the course of incarnations. In ancient times, as I outlined yesterday, human beings were capable of co-experiencing what was spiritual in the environment while eating, breathing and digesting—it was one of their capacities. Due to this, they incorporated something largely instinctive, which we might call an agglomeration of feelings, sensations, concepts and imagination, which governed their attitudes and behaviour towards their fellow human beings. This was instinctive in them and we see it decreasing over time. The terrible eruptions of hate which we now encounter can only be understood in terms of their real underlying cause, if we understand how the old instincts are on the wane. These hateful instincts are far more serious than is acknowledged today. Terrible things will be experienced as a result of this condition. And if what needed to be overcome in evolutionary terms was not conquered, the instinct to hate would become ever greater and greater. Even if individual people largely tend—in an age of freedom from authority and premise-free science—towards being led by the nose, sensations streaming up from their subconscious hinder this. Such people tend to look for all sorts of leaders; the more aberrantly and unconditionally they seek to follow such leaders, the more are they exposed to the danger of their apparent love degenerating into hatred. This is not something that can be overcome by criticizing, because it is deeply rooted in human evolution and the more human love is just preached as an abstract idea—and abstract fraternity likewise—the more does mutual antagonism unfold. This is another truth upon which we need to focus most seriously and deeply if we are to understand the present. What has to happen is that an outlook that accepts repeated earthly lives—that accepts reincarnation—has to be transformed into feelings, into perceptions. Just being a theoretical adherent of reincarnation doesn't amount to anything!

Taking as a whole what we have attempted to draw together in order to extract from the laws of human evolution, as they pertain over time, what enables us to focus on concrete facts and not just abstract ideas: there exists in every human being an element that traverses births and deaths, and this transforms abstraction into experienced perceptions—not into instincts, as they previously existed subconsciously, but into conscious instincts with which people can somehow be challenged. Nowadays there is an all-too-strong desire to take up the idea of reincarnation in selfish terms. How often have we seen people desperate to know all about their own previous incarnations! This cannot be the practical outcome of the concept of repeated earth lives. A genuine outcome would entail learning increasingly to see every individual you meet as though they contained far more than could be lived within their single earthly life. What is often called a feeling of distance may arise, which—in due proportion—is a feeling for finding the right relationship towards the other person: not deifying them yet seeking ever more deeply to find within them the element enduring through eternity.

It is false mysticism to brood endlessly within oneself. The kind of mysticism we need is of the sort that guides us towards practical but empathically human knowledge, so that we avoid judging any individual from the outset as being either sympathetic or antagonistic, but are instead conscious that every human soul is actually an infinite riddle. If this idea is seriously taken to heart, what streams from out of repeated earthly lives, what pours into our souls is something which—if rightly understood in the context of modern humanity—ought to be experienced as brotherliness. This brotherly love will not—in typical manner—seek ever and again to help others in a form pleasing to ourselves, but it will want to commit to helping others in ways appropriate to them, so that they are helped in accordance with their own deepest self. A thought such as this will also prevent us from the cavalier criticism that so often erects barriers between us and others and which hinders us from seeing impartially what lives in the other person. Only when the concept of repeated earthly incarnations is alive in our souls—practically and vigorously—will the idea of brotherliness assume the right form and represent what human beings have in common, what they mean for each other through being embodied.

A second aspect of human evolution is that we not only acknowledge the physical nature of the human being—the only aspect to which materialism wishes to admit—but that we recognize the human soul, that we ascribe to each person a conscious soul.

We are not ascribing a soul to someone whom we endeavour to subjugate to our own ethos; that is, if we are of the opinion that we really are respecting their soul while expecting them to share our way of thinking. We have to grant a soul freedom; it cannot merely be ascribed to its body. Freedom is the only salient feature between souls, the only quality that matters. And the root of freedom is freedom of thought. Once you properly understand this second element of humankind—a soul in addition to a body—you will no longer confuse freedom and fraternity but will instead say: Brotherliness is necessary because humans have to establish for themselves a social order defined by fraternity. A social structure defined by fraternity has to come about but, unless people are enthused by really practical ideas about brotherliness, they will find no state structures within which human beings can sensibly live together. If people fail to recognize—within these state structures—that human beings live not only as physical bodies but also as soul entities, they will never be able to conceive of freedom in the right way. This is because freedom lies in soul-to-soul conduct and not between bodies. The freedom required by bodies arises automatically as a necessary consequence of inter-soul freedom having become widespread. This, however, requires that we finally learn not to foist our own thoughts onto other people but allow each soul its own valid direction of thought. Above all, we need to acquire a sense for reality, because in no other areas can one sin more than in those of science and religion.

I can only ever refer—by way of example—to something that happened in a south German town. I was giving a lecture about wisdom and Christianity. Being southern Germany, there were two Catholic priests in the audience. Afterwards, they said to me: According to what you said today, one cannot object—in terms of content—to what you claim, yet one cannot agree with it. I asked: Why? The main issue, they said, is that you say all these things about Christianity, such as can be understood by those with a certain level of erudition and certain requirements and so on. However, we are looking for a manner of speaking that is accessible to all people; we shape our thoughts such that everyone can agree with them. I replied: Your Grace, you know that the way you and I think about what humbles us all, what makes us all devout, comes to both of us. Both you and I can imagine this and each one of us will of course be totally convinced that our image is the right one—unless we have developed a sense for reality. We would be peculiar old fogeys were we to create ideas, whose suitability for all humanity we were to doubt. But what you or I think suitable for all humankind—each according to our individual development—is not the point. That is ultimately irrelevant and we need to transcend that through proper, active, practical self-knowledge. The decisive factor is to study reality and to ask: What dictates reality? What does time and its contents teach us as to what people need? What do people's longings teach us? From this another question arises from the one you posed, namely: Does everyone go to your Church nowadays? If you are to speak to all people, wouldn't they all flock to you? They couldn't avoid answering: Admittedly, not everyone still goes to church. I then said: So you see, among those in today's audience were mainly those who no longer go to church but who also have a right to find their way to Christ and it was to them that I was speaking.

One should not—just on the basis of one's own opinion—conceive ideas as to what people need, but rather in accordance with what reality is telling us. It is less comfortable to study reality. You have to keep adjusting how you deploy your observational senses and have sufficient willpower to ask repeatedly: What are the real needs of the times? How do things stand? What are they asking of us? Unless this practical sense—which has to underlie freedom of thought—has infiltrated people's souls, we will not achieve corresponding soul-to-soul relationships. Just as the social fabric, towards which humanity must aim, is dependent on us arriving at truthful insights—in the sense of spiritual science—into corporeality and the idea of fraternity, in the same way do we have to grasp and make real concepts of soul and freedom of thought in the areas of science, education and religious ethos.

A third element is the spirit. If it is now possible to reinstate the spirit in its rightful place and to reverse what the Council of Constantinople decreed in 869, then what may pertain practically for human life in future will also be valid for the spirit. Today we have two tendencies: one follows the same direction as the Council of Constantinople, which translates into banishing the spirit. A monistic world view strives to banish the soul likewise. Those of the opinion that natural-scientific monism contains so much tolerance—in today's sense of the word—that it could never bring itself to overturn a Council and expel the soul as well are mistaken in their thinking. The propensity mentioned is prepared not only to proscribe the spirit but also the soul. Those who today are mini-Monists will want to mushroom into great Monists and, though they claim to disdain overturning that Council—because they are, after all, free spirits, having freed themselves of all spirit—they will seek to allow certain usages and customs to become normalized. It will come about—do not take this to be a joke!—that the soul will be eliminated. In addition to all the physical medicines that exist today, a whole raft of others will be added to treat those who talk of things as fantastical as spirits and souls: they will be remediated and will be medicated against all talk of spirits or souls. Spirit could just be discarded; soul will only be driven out of people by medically treating the body. Though this may appear monstrous today, the thrust of certain objectives will arrive at the point of inventing medicines to vaccinate children with all sorts of agents whereby their physical organism is so debilitated as to allow materialistic attitudes to thrive rather well in them, when it will no longer be a matter of treating the ancient idea of soul and spirit as anything other than something people once believed in olden days and which can be consigned to smug amusement.

Saying things of this nature may seem like madness to some; but if we don't muster the courage to admit them to ourselves, we will never find the energy to unfold and kindle spiritual-scientific spirituality in our souls. This is why, in addition to the tendency just mentioned, which wishes to dispense with the soul because it will be viewed as a pathology, there must be another: that of energetically re-substantiating that, in addition to a body, the human being bears within them both a soul and a spirit. To effect knowledge of the spirit, you will need to ensure that spiritual science becomes truly embedded, that people understand which elements actually belong to their being once they traverse the portal of death. Among the old folk maxims—which so often convey benign outlooks into the modern world—is this: In death all are equal; because then everyone becomes a spirit and because the idea of equality is one which corresponds with spirit. Equality among spirits! Equality to spirits! The three ideals of Freedom, Fraternity and Equality can no longer be mixed and muddled together, but one needs to know—in concrete terms of reality—what human beings are and that they are to be free in their souls, fraternal as regards their bodies and that people must be equal in the realm of their spirits. Because inequality among people does exist—a specialization occasioned by the spirit having to be specialized in body and soul. Pneumatology—spiritual doctrine, spiritual perspective or view—is the foundation of the concept of equality. Thus we have before us the remarkable phenomenon of chaotic expressions bursting forth across the world at the end of the eighteenth century crying: Fraternity, Freedom and Equality! However, we will eventually need to understand that the only means of realizing the ideals of Brotherliness, Freedom and Equality will be once we are in a condition to add to them knowledge of the threefold nature of the human being as body, soul and spirit.

This was the basis upon which I attempted so energetically in my *Theosophy* to stratify the human being into body, soul and spirit. This organization is a challenge for our times and for the near future. It is *only* by transforming these concepts into practice and in learning to perceive human beings practically in terms of body, soul and spirit that one is able to evolve beyond the age of twenty-seven. Otherwise one *will* remain stuck at the age of twenty-seven. Think of the prospects: a sixth and seventh cultural epoch will follow our fifth age. In the sixth epoch, humanity as a whole will attain the equivalent of what is individually reached between the ages of fourteen and twenty-one. In the external world, however clever the people leading education may be, you will not absorb any more than corresponds with what an individual attains by the age of twenty-one. You will not grow more in maturity than twenty-one, though you may live well beyond that. In the seventh post-Atlantean epoch, you will not mature beyond the individual equivalent of fourteen. If you fail to grow older by means of kindling inner fire, humankind will suffer an epidemic of youthful feeblemindedness. Whoever has eyes to see and ears to hear—and whoever doesn't just live their life thoughtlessly—will, armed with knowledge such as this, be in a position to correctly evaluate phenomena already appearing today!

To take just one area: where has our era progressed in terms of its view of Christ's impetus? How many people remain close to Barrès' opinion that the generous world outlook of the Redeemer is best served by the Church, that this is precisely the reason one can so easily get along with the Church? Who makes the effort—certainly individuals may still, but in general?—who really exerts themselves to allow what is contained in the Gospels to be resurrected in them?—how Christ contrasted what others stood for and, above all, what He had to oppose? The most meaningful, the most profound aspects of Christianity: how are they fathomed today? I will just remind you of a central tenet of Christianity: the coming of the Kingdoms of Heaven. Even Blavatsky[80] mocked the prediction that the Kingdoms of Heaven would come; that in the time they were to have come, wheat had not grown more prolifically than before, grapes had not become larger, in short, the Kingdom of Heaven had not arrived on Earth.

People think themselves very clever; but such cleverness yields nothing more than opinions of this sort. Cleverness fails to ask: Could Christ have meant something different? Christ is recognized today, but only to the extent to which people wish that their own ideas—and the way they themselves conceive of them—also live in Christ. The socialist makes of Christ a good socialist, the liberal an exemplary liberal, the Protestant unionist a representative of liberal unionism and so on. A modern scholastic theologian such as Professor Harnack[81] construes Him one way and people listen to how Professor Harnack speaks about the most important ideas around Christ Jesus. It so happened that I was to hold a lecture in an association, whose chairman was a man well versed in the Bible and theology. During the course of that lecture I said that the good Professor Harnack actually had a remarkable grasp of the Resurrection, because in his paper 'The Essence of Christianity' there appeared the extraordinary sentence: 'Whatever may have gone on in the

Garden of Gethsemane can no longer be judged because it transcends human knowledge and because it also goes beyond the justified demands of belief. Yet the belief in resurrection originates in the Garden of Gethsemane and this has proved especially valuable to humanity.' Whether it is true that Christ was somehow resurrected doesn't concern him! One should just believe that the belief in the Resurrection originated in the Garden of Gethsemane—that is Harnack's doctrine. The man who was chairman of that association said: 'You must be mistaken, because that would virtually make Harnack a Catholic'—the man in question felt himself to be a superior Protestant—'That would be tantamount to Catholicism, which maintains that, no matter where the scrap of material purporting to be the cassock of Trier originates—nor whence comes the tiny bone they worship—what matters is only that faith has spread and that they are tokens originating from a particular saint. That is Catholic,' opined that man, 'and we can obviously not believe in that.' And that made it all of no consequence; whether Harnack thought it was neither here nor there whether it was true that Christ was resurrected or not, but just that one believed the belief to have originated in the Garden of Gethsemane. So he told me that I was mistaken. I replied: 'But you know, he wrote that in "The Essence of Christianity".' 'No,' came the riposte, 'that cannot be so. Have you read it?' 'Yes, often,' I said. 'I will send you a postcard with chapter and verse from "The Essence of Christianity" where that is stated.'

The man who was so well versed in theology and was so Bible-knowledgeable was not able to read closely enough to know what that book contained. But the book contains what I reported. That's the state of modern thinking. Modern thinking has a strange propensity—in all areas, but especially where efforts have been made—to popularize things.

It is not only theologians who prove to be sinful; natural scientists can be equally so. There is a booklet called *The Mechanics of Spiritual Life*—I don't know if there's also a booklet on The Iron Qualities of Wood! The author—whom I value, as I do all those whom I tackle—bears the name *Verworn*.[82] In this booklet he deals with dreams and states that, while dreaming, brain activity is 'tuned down' and 'numbed down' and is only partially active. If someone taps lightly on the window with a pin, says Verworn, we might dream that cannon are firing a volley of shots—that's a well-known dream and he starts with that statement. Further claims intervene, and at the end of that page he states: Dreams bear their strange nature because brain activity is tuned down. Just think of the ingenuity: when we are in possession of our full brain function, we hear the faint tapping of a pin on the window. When the brain is 'tuned down' and less active, we hear cannon fire. This explanation is accepted—and applauded—as is much of Freud,[83] just because a few lines separate those statements.

This sort of thing is fundamental in our time: the will to really follow up on the thoughts we encounter is very rare nowadays. It is therefore not hard to understand why one would not, without further ado, want to comprehend an imponderable such as the coming of the 'Kingdoms of Heaven' because quite something is entailed. Until the time of the Mystery of Golgotha, the Kingdoms of Heaven drew near to human beings in dreamlike manner. Before the Atlantean cataclysm, they were even absorbed during digestion. But now they had to descend. They did indeed descend, but in such a way that human beings had to exert their spirits to encompass the Kingdoms of Heaven. The grapes growing larger, the ears of wheat being more fulsome is not what is meant, but instead that the Kingdom exists in our very midst and it is we who must fortify our own spirits in order to find it.

What I have just sketched briefly is what underlies the magnificent conception of Christ Jesus. It is, however, a concept that requires our soul's energy if we wish to find our way into it. Many Christian concepts are like this; with them Christ Jesus stood up to the Roman Empire, the Imperium Romanum, which had taken shape in a way completely divergent from that of Christianity. This Roman Empire, which had swelled into tyrannous Caesarism had, in exercising its power, placed the ancient Mysteries under its dominion. Augustus[84] was the first Caesar who, on account of his external power, had to be initiated into the Mysteries. His successors, Tiberius, Caligula and others, were also initiated into the Mysteries.

They only applied their Mystery knowledge to the Kingdom of the outer world and did not, in the way of Egyptian temple priests, take the Kingdom of the Spirit out into the worldly realm. Commodus[85] even had himself made an initiator and, when initiating an acolyte, was meant to strike him symbolically, but did so with such force that he is said to have slain him.

Here two mighty contradictions come face to face: the Roman Empire and Christianity. This antithesis had to find its resolution. To this day it has not yet found any such equilibrium. We have to become capable of recognizing the spirit and also of bringing it into life. I will say only this much, because what entered us largely persists—in our thinking, as in our feelings—in the form of logic: the manner of thinking and feeling prevalent in the Roman Empire. Our grammar school students first learnt Latin and with it the mode of thinking inherited from the Roman Empire, which has been self-perpetuating. We no longer know how much has to be attributed to this inner 'root nerve', this innervating foundation of our lives, nor do we yet know how rightly to seek the spirit path leading to Christ. Such a path can only be one that includes *will for thinking*—something that has degenerated in our times—in fact, one could actually call it *intelligence.* Our age, which is so proud of intelligence, has actually divested itself of intelligence because it dispenses with conscientiousness based on thinking.

A widely read booklet on the subject of 'Christianity in the Battle between Present World Views'[86] reproduces lectures given to thousands and thousands of people by a leading contemporary figure, who has obviously studied 'Law, medicine, philosophy' and even—alas—'theology'. There, ideas are elaborated which could drive you to climb the walls! And at the end of it you even have to traipse through the lovely words, which Goethe is purported to have said:

No created spirit penetrates
Into Nature's inner core.[87]
Happy he, to whom she even shows
Her outer shell!

These are the lengths to which we have to go in acknowledging such a thought! The lecturer knows his Goethe so well that he cites a Hallerian quotation as being one of Goethe's, even though Goethe had responded to that very verse by saying:

> I curse [88] at it, but furtively.
> Nature has neither core nor shell,
> She is everything all at once.
> Test yourself, as is mostly all you do,
> Whether you be core or shell.

This is how people are fobbed off with a world view purported to be that of Goethe, who himself retorted: 'I curse at it'! Yet people listen only too willingly and that reflects the general state of thinking today. There is no point in looking aloft salaciously at certain ideas issuing from spiritual science. These ideas need to completely settle into your soul life. Then that other stream—the spiritual stream, which prevents the present mode of thinking from engulfing humankind through allowing the individual to self-evolve—will enable what already exists to flow out into evolution as a whole. Much will have to happen before such things are rightly taken hold of in concrete terms, terms under which they are grasped so thoroughly that reality-supporting thinking can reach humanity.

A good book has come out called *The State as a Form of Life* by Kjellén,[89] the well-known Swedish state sociologist. I only mention this because he has shown great goodwill towards our issue, towards my issue, such that you should not think I bear him any grudge or rancour. Just for this reason I may use him as an example of certain ways of living.

Kjellén attempts to formulate ideas about the state which, due to their assorted errors, could well become widespread. He obviously comes back to the idea of the state as an organism. He is ahead of *Wilson.*[90] Wilson in his time was sharply critical of people of Newton's time who had not had independent ideas about the state but had allowed themselves to be so influenced by the theory of gravity that they judged the various impulses in human thinking in abstract terms of gravity. The state was to be conceived of as an organism. In saying this, he failed to notice that people were thinking in Newtonian terms while he was thinking like a Darwinian. Kjellén also considers the state to be an organism, with individuals representing its cells. Well, certainly, you can compare an entity containing signs of life with an organism and its cells. You can actually compare anything with anything if the ideas are unwilling to plunge down into reality; ultimately you can even compare a lizard with a penknife. Everything is comparable. Only when you have engendered a sense of reality does a comparison lead, of itself, to a correct inference. This comparison would have led Kjellén to conceive of one state being an organism and the second as bordering it adjacently. Whoever thinks in accordance with reality will find it impossible to think of human beings as cells. A valid comparison might involve thinking of a totality of states with single states as cells; however, the human being doesn't figure at all in this scenario of a state; in which case, only the entirety of social life across the globe would be comparable with an organism. If one then wanted to add people, it would look like this: let's imagine an organism. Cells would need to protrude from it, much like a strange sort of hedgehog. Only were it to be an organism like this—one out of which living entities protruded—would it be an organism with which one could compare all social life on Earth.

What this means is: all human life cannot be subsumed into the state. It must project outwards into the spiritual from what the state is able to encompass. That is something all too easily forgotten in all areas of practical life. You could bring in example after example to illustrate how one forgets this, and how one forgets—alongside all things external, as modelled upon the Roman Empire—the Realm of the Spirit, which Christ sought to bring to the Earth. We need to dignify that thought in all its seriousness.

You know, whenever things start to become concrete, thinking does not usually reach far enough to plumb it. Just think how everything has recently conspired to suppress the autonomy of academic education, so that everything dependent on centres of learning is forced into forms subservient to state policies. Today, in order for a doctor to become a doctor at all, they are first required to have passed the state's civil service exam, after which they are entitled to use the title doctor almost as a kind of decoration. The autonomy of spiritual or intellectual institutions as such has been completely set back and suppressed. We could cite many examples of instances where there is great enthusiasm for moving in that direction. People cannot do enough to make all titles state-compliant. Engineer was synonymous with 'ingenium' or talent, and now people no longer aim to *be* one such, but just aim for the diploma. If it states on the diploma that you are an engineer, then you are allowed to call yourself one; otherwise no amount of 'ingenium' will come to your aid. All this detracts from a spiritual conception of the world. But people don't think about that. Quite the opposite; they are enthused by this battle, across the board, against all things spiritual. To bring this to our notice—because people are so fond of wordage—one ought perhaps to invent a new word and say: People are not en-thused but 'en-bodied'[91] about de-spiritualization. Then perhaps the odd individual might start to take notice of the direction of travel being pursued! Not taking notice is proof of the thoughtlessness of life, of the hatred levelled against any will to think.

So you see how necessary it is to introduce spiritual science into the most everyday details of daily life. Spiritual science is a serious matter. That is why, in addition to the remarkable figures of yesterday, aspects of the immediate present had to be mentioned; because the nature of spiritual science cannot be compromised by being made philistine or cliquish; nor can obstacle after obstacle be raised—via the Anthroposophical Society—to hinder what spiritual science is intended to be. Among sensible people you will always find understanding for the fact that it is precisely those who are somehow at a point of divergence in their lives—sometimes to the extent of having lost their equilibrium—who join us. The question always arises: Should we move towards these people or harden our attitude? People such as this may change, may further lose their inner stability, or they may change their stories later in the way we have seen, intending to harm a sacred matter, to relegate it to the rubbish heap, to betray or to denigrate it. If what I said yesterday is unfounded—basically, that what I say is heeded little—then this would be within the rights of an individual. I spoke of some non-members speaking ill of adherents and their blind faith. One doesn't need blind faith for any teaching because it can be tested. Only for matters pertaining to arrangements is trust sometimes required. The opposite of what I intended often happens precisely in such cases. That's why what I said yesterday about the imposition of necessary measures could be felt as unfair. Yet these measures will be upheld and so, on the other hand, will care be taken of those genuinely undertaking robust esoteric development. Let us give this time. Who knows what will come about through activities in the Anthroposophical Society, what may transpire through misunderstanding or through betrayal to the world! People who know full well how much time has been devoted to matters will convince themselves that books have appeared—or are about to appear—once these measures have been in place for a certain amount of time. At that time, I was forced to approve the publication of cycles over which I have no control. It was not my will but that of other people, who wanted to read them. Certainly, one is not obliged to resist others' will, and I gave way; but you can read the accusations that were made: it was thought to be a trick, the lecture cycles were in a style inviting criticism—ultimately, everything can be construed as wrong through ill will. But, my dear friends, if spiritual science is to be rightly related to the Anthroposophical Society, then the Society must feel itself to be bound to the life of spiritual science itself. And yet how many only feel bound up with their own personal lives!

In the Anthroposophical Society there really are—and there have always been—numerous people who have expressed, in one form or another, that they only joined the Anthroposophical Society in order to discuss some esoteric matter or other with me and who refuse to extend any trust towards people whom I myself trust. This is a particularly distressing experience. It is to no avail that I extend trust towards one friend or another in the Society. Those people are not welcomed and people try to circumvent them. Well, such things originate in so much of a *personal* nature being brought into the Anthroposophical Society. Do you know which word I most frequently encountered in those so-called esoteric consultations? Don't imagine I heard most frequently about issues such as freedom, equality, human evolution and so on. The word I heard most often from every single person was: I! People would arrive with their most personal concerns. I would have gladly made allowance for this, had it progressed beyond that point, but it simply never does so, for the reasons given yesterday. And that needs to be understood.

I know that this will best be understood primarily by those who work with real devotion towards anthroposophy's progress, by those who are able to see in developing anthroposophy a task concerning humanity as a whole, those same people who do not merely seek an easing of their family situations—or whatever other personal issues—in their joining the Anthroposophical Society; and this includes all those who seek a legally-permitted little medical back door because they would continually retreat, were it a case of publicly combatting materialistic medicine—people looking for a handy little back door to being cured without standing up to materialistic medicine! It is in no other way possible to continue dealing with everything that harms society from also harming the Anthroposophical Society except by imposing the measures of which I spoke yesterday and from which—at least in the near future—there will be no deviating. Only in this way will it be possible to eradicate what has so terribly *nested* in our midst. In doing this, the Anthroposophical Society will be able to thrive ever better. Likewise esoteric life—I will take care that this happens—will be able to thrive. The fabrications mentioned yesterday—much depends on this—may to some extent have the rug pulled from under their feet once the two-part measures mentioned yesterday are energetically put in place. Do understand this, because in doing so you are signalling your agreement with the unique nature of the task of the anthroposophical movement. There are enough people in the world at large who do not feel they are capable of fighting anthroposophy—in the sense it is here intended. It is too uncomfortable and entails getting to know something about anthroposophy—a discomfort to some wishing to oppose it. But turning a blind eye to betrayal and denigration—even spreading it—provides a means of opposing anthroposophy without understanding it. Our contemporaries are very susceptible to betrayal and vilification—nothing is more newsworthy. Let us seriously take hold of anthroposophy's task; let us take to heart the seriousness of the situation, and then all will be well with regard to those measures. This is the mood in which we wish to close. I hope that we continue—in deploying our forces appropriately—to work together.

# Lecture 9

## 14 FEBRUARY 1918, MUNICH

Before I move on to address the main subject of today's considerations, I have a heartfelt need to express—both personally and in the name of our shared enterprise—how pleased I am that—in the space[92] in which we are meeting today, here in Munich—we serve a common goal, common work and intentions, which promise to be exceptionally blessed in their fulfilment, which have already begun and of which we must believe that they are capable of sending vital impulses into the spiritual life of the present time.

Now moving on to the subject of our deliberations, I would not like to fail in taking this opportunity—particularly at this time—to mention those close to us who are taking a heartfelt interest in our anthroposophically-orientated spiritual science during these times of humanity's hardest trials; and to reflect on the connection between the fact that—from this point early in the twentieth century—this spiritual-scientific movement has been trying to embed its stimuli into human evolution—to connect this with the other fact: that present humanity—precisely through its other pursuits—has admittedly led humankind into many catastrophic events. Just how catastrophic is humanity's situation is beyond the sufficiently serious and concerned comprehension of large numbers of people. The wish to live without spirit is widely accepted. This implies living superficially, which in turn involves sleeping through events surrounding us and affecting us so incisively. It has to be said that people nowadays are extremely prone to sleeping through many events. It is a minority who seek an adequate idea of the difficulty and poignancy of present events; most people living from one day to the next. And if one makes so bold as to speak of times that could come in future, people—often those very people on whom much depends—reject it in the strongest terms. If spiritual science is to achieve one thing among its many tasks, it will be to stir souls to be a bit more energetic—to encourage them to be slightly more wakeful—then it will have done something fundamentally important for our times. Spiritual-scientific ideas demand greater exertion in thinking, greater intensity in feeling and sensing, than do other conceptual areas, particularly than the ways of thought actually governing today.

Most especially, it is not unimportant that you familiarize yourselves with the ideas garnered from spiritual science, which can both direct and lead you to an understanding of the present in its widest sense. Today I would like to take you through some fundamental ideas, upon which we can build at the next meeting of this Branch—ideas which are useful for the purpose of shining a light on some crucial facets of the present. Today I will start from more general thoughts—from ideas involving more of a personal human angle—but which, from a certain point of view, can offer us a basis for our later spiritual-scientific considerations.

Over the course of spiritual-scientific considerations, it has to be emphasized again and again how our lives undergo changes of consciousness between birth—or conception—and death: by alternating between waking and sleeping. People know about sleeping and waking in broad terms; their true, more delicate nuances can only be appreciated when brought before the soul by a spiritual-scientific outlook. Normally, we think that we just sleep between falling asleep and waking up and one is awake between waking up and falling asleep again. This is only the crudest understanding. In truth, the border we demarcate between sleeping and waking is a false one. The condition of dull consciousness—which, in many respects, is no real consciousness at all and is one we undergo during sleep—extends into our daytime life and we remain within it with a portion of our being even between waking and falling asleep. Between waking and falling asleep we are by no means awake with our entire being, but are only awake with part of it while another part continues to sleep even when we consider ourselves awake. In one respect we are permanently sleeping beings. We are only really awake in respect of our perceiving and imagining. In that we perceive the outer world through our senses, in that we see and hear and so on, we are awake during that seeing and hearing; in short, in our perceptions. In this we are completely awake. We are also awake—though to a lesser degree—in that we imagine. When we form thoughts, when concepts elapse within us, when memories are dredged up from the dark substrata of our souls, then we are awake in respect of the processes we are experiencing, that is, in relation to the processes of having-perceived, of perception and of imagining.

You know, however, that our life of soul also contains feeling and willing apart from perceiving and imagining. Regarding feeling, we are not awake even when we think ourselves to be; what we know of all that goes on in our feelings is no more than we know about dreaming while asleep. The degree and intensity of consciousness of which we are aware while feeling equals the degree and intensity of consciousness while we are dreaming. Just as dreams arise as images from unconscious soul depths, so do forces of feeling arise as feelings. We are no more wakeful in feeling than we are in dreaming; only that we bring dreams into our normal waking, imagining consciousness and, after sleep, distinguish dream from waking in that we can remember the dream, whilst feeling is instantaneous. Feeling itself is dreamed by us, but we accompany our feeling with concepts. In conceptualizing, we are devoid of feeling but regard feeling from the perspective of concepts in the same way as we look at a dream after waking. It is just that in feeling we are doing this simultaneously, which is why we are not conscious of the fact that we retain in our consciousness only the concept of feeling. Feeling is down in dream regions, just as dreams themselves are.

You can recognize will purely externally. Do you know what actually happens when you decide to take hold of a book and your hand then grasps it? Do you know what takes place between the concept you alone have in your consciousness—'I want to take hold of that book'—and all the mysterious processes that unfold within your entire organism? We know what we think about willing but, for our normal consciousness, we know nothing about willing itself.

Whilst we dream through feeling, we sleep away the actual content of willing. Inasmuch as we are perceptive beings who imagine, we are awake; inasmuch as we feel and will during waking we are actually dreaming and sleeping respectively. Thus, in feeling and willing does a state of sleep extend into our waking consciousness. We therefore need to say: The condition in which we exist between falling asleep and waking up—in terms of our entire being—also empowers us with regard to feeling and willing while we are awake.

Through perceiving and imagining we learn to recognize a world around us which we designate a physical-sense world; yet through feeling and willing we do not learn to recognize the world in which we exist as feeling and willing beings. We are continually in a supra-sensible world. Our feeling and willing—as regards their *forces*—originate in this extrasensory world, just as our perceiving and imagining originate in the physical-sense world. We have no organs for feeling and willing but for perceiving and conceptualizing we do have organs. That some physiologists believe we have organs for feeling and willing—some more thoughtful physiologists do not, however—is only a result of not knowing what they are talking about, talking anyway about something they'd like to know a bit about—and yet do not!

What I have just described is by and large the state we legitimately inhabit between birth and death: we wake in terms of our perceiving and conceiving or imagining, we sleep in relation to our feeling and our willing.

It is a different matter between death and a new birth. In a certain sense it is the reverse: there we begin to awaken in our feeling and willing. And there our perceptions and imagination fall asleep, although sleep is a different condition in the world in which our souls then live. But from what I have just said you will be able to appreciate that the so-called dead can almost only be distinguished from the so-called living in that the so-called living sleep through that in which the so-called dead actually exist. Those supposedly alive sleep through the feeling and willing perpetually streaming through their being; the deceased exist within that very feeling and willing. It will not be hard for you to understand that, in the same world in which we exist as so-called living people, the dead are also present. We are separated from them in no other way than that we do not perceive the world in which they live and weave. Those beings who have died are continually around us, living and weaving without entering into physical incarnation. We just do not perceive them. You only need to imagine a person asleep in a room; objects surround them yet they do not perceive them. That something is not perceived is no proof that it isn't there and says absolutely nothing as to whether it is around us or not. In actual fact, as regards the realm of the dead, we are in the same position as we are in relation to physical beings when we are asleep. We live in the same world as do the dead, the same world in which the exalted beings of the higher hierarchies also exist; they are here among us and it is only our means of perceiving that separates us from them.

And yet the issue is such that human beings only perceive part of that reality, only conceive of a fragment of the reality in which they are actually living. Were they to encompass the whole reality, then their knowledge would obviously look quite different from the way it is presently configured: within that knowing there would co-exist not only the forces issuing from the realms of nature well known to us, but this knowledge would also encompass the forces of higher spiritual beings as well as those from the realm of the so-called dead. For the large majority of today's humanity, this remains an outlandish prospect. For even greater numbers—especially for those who interest themselves in the evolution and onward progress of human life—it needs to become a subject infused with thoughtful reason. Because, in times that still extend into the present, human beings have been led by relatively dark and unknown forces in relation to what they cannot perceive in their surroundings. This being led by dark and unknown forces—about which we will speak again in future Branch meetings—has now largely ceased. Human beings now have to place themselves into conscious affiliation with forces issuing from realms that project into ours, realms in which the so-called dead also tarry. Bringing to humankind a level of consciousness—consciousness open to accepting what is true and real instead of the fantastical inadequacies swirling about and shaping life so catastrophically— will not be without its difficulties. To this effect, I will mention just one point by way of introducing you to the subject.

Amongst many a topic presented as 'scientific' are some historical themes. History, for instance, is taught and learnt in schools. Yet what is this history? A science of history is—as the expert knows—not much older than a century. Whoever is familiar with older literature knows that what is now termed historical science or science of history is not much older. I don't intend to go into this further. However, what now constitutes history will be considered by people, established by people with the same conceptions, with the same definitions, as those conventionally used in external life, with those same notions that can be used in observing nature. Yet nobody asks themselves whether it is appropriate to set about observing historical life in the same way as external nature is observed. It is clearly not applicable. For in the historical life of humanity reign stimuli that cannot be encompassed with the concepts we have in our waking consciousness. But whoever can really observe history knows that in history we are governed by such impulsions as are only accessible for normal consciousness in dream states—at most in a state of dreaming. What flows by as history is dreamed by humanity. In just the same way as humanity dreams away its life of feeling does it likewise dream through what are historical forces of impetus. Should one wish to observe human historical life with the same conceptual tools as are well suited to observing nature, it cannot be captured. It only allows of being observed on a superficial level. What is being taught and learnt in schools as history? It is no more related to real, actual history than were you to describe a living human by demonstrating this on a corpse. Today's conventional history consists in observing corpses. History needs to be most radically transformed. And what actually holds sway in history will in future only be encompassed through Inspiration, through inspired concepts. That will result in true history. Then you will know what holds sway in humanity, and you will also know what works into social life from out of history.

What I am saying here is of profound importance. People think they understand socio-historical life. They do not understand it because they only wish to conceive of it within the conventional conceptual parameters of their waking life. This is not apparent in written history because, there, nothing much depends on it being correct. Many an obvious example would illustrate that very little depends on accuracy, and I will bring one such here: you will normally learn in conventional history books that America was discovered in 1492. That is the case. From what literature states you educe that before that date America was completely unknown, however far back you search. But that is not so. America was only unknown for a few centuries. In the twelfth and thirteenth centuries there was still lively traffic between Iceland, Ireland and America. Particularly remedial herbs and suchlike were traded into Europe. For reasons connected with the inner karma of Europe and with the role Ireland had played in earlier ages, it turns out that Rome did everything possible to close Europe off from America and to render America forgotten. What took place at the instigation of Rome was not actually unfavourable to European relations; it was well intentioned towards Europe. With this example I just wish to show that a fact need not necessarily be a historical fact; that one can still remain quite ignorant of important historical matters.

Now, on the other hand, whether you are historically knowledgeable or ignorant is important as regards the social and societal life of humanity in general. That is of moment. How often do we hear people today saying: You need to think about this or that event in such and such a way because history teaches us this or that ...Just look at today's exoteric publications and you will see how often the phrase crops up: History teaches us this or that. People partially sleep through historical events they have experienced, yet they still form judgements or allow themselves to be inoculated with opinions about those events. You will frequently hear that phrase: History teaches us. Men of consequence at the start of this war told us what history had taught them: it was at the time the honest conviction of seemingly clever people that this war would last at most four to six months, in line with general social and economic conditions across the globe. Many predicted that it would only last four to six months! This turned out exactly as did the other predictions of a far greater person, who declared them historical prophecy. Yet these were only based on the ordinary concepts of ordinary consciousness, which cannot capture history because history is usually slept through, which can at most be dreamed and only grasped within the widest terms of reference. Schiller, on taking up his Jena professorship, held his renowned speech on studying history; it dates to shortly before the outbreak of the French Revolution. Schiller, truly no insignificant figure, drawing on his deeply-researched view—a view deeply-researched only with ordinary historical concepts—says, not literally, but something along the lines of: History teaches us that in days of yore there was much strife and warfare among people; from all that contributed to this we can deduce that in future Europeans may have disharmony among their number, yet they will always feel themselves to be members of a large family and will not therefore mutually tear each other to pieces. That, according to Friedrich Schiller! There followed the French Revolution and all that overwhelmed the family of peoples in the nineteenth century and all this demolished Schiller's so-called historical assessment.

History will only teach us when we can penetrate it with inspired concepts. Because it is not only the living who play into humanity's historical life but the souls of the so-called dead, the spirits, with whom the so-called dead live much as we live with the beings of the animal, plant and mineral kingdoms. Today this is largely construed as a mere saying. But humanity will have to break radically from its habit of according no more verity to sayings than it presently does. We will only succeed in this once we have acquired concepts or ideas that are truly drenched in reality. One such particularly important idea is that which tells our awareness that we are separated from the so-called dead by nothing but our own consciousness. This consciousness—as regards the world in which the dead are around us—is sleep consciousness, as far as our feeling and willing are concerned, in just the same way as sleep consciousness relates to objects in our vicinity while we are asleep. Clairvoyant consciousness corroborates in every detail what I have just characterized more generally.

The question might, however, arise: How can human beings know so little about the world in which they are immersed, the world through which they wander with every step they take? Well, you see, it is precisely the *ways and means* by which clairvoyant consciousness explains in concrete terms what we must call interrelating with the so-called dead which form living proof of the fact that, for everyday consciousness, the realm in which the dead live must initially remain unknown. I need only outline a few traits of such inter-communicating with the apparently dead—admittedly at a somewhat enhanced level of clairvoyance, of *sighted* consciousness—and you will see why in normal life one knows nothing of the interchange with those who have died. It is entirely possible—though it can have dubious aspects—that people awaken their consciousness to a point where the realm of the dead is open to them, that they are able to perceive this realm of the so-called dead and are in a position to, as it were, commune with departed individuals. In order to understand the dead reliably, they need to learn to behave quite differently in their consciousness. This needs to be quite different from that in everyday use in the physical world. Let me give you a couple of features.

You see, when you communicate with another person in the physical world, you rely on certain habits. When I talk with someone, I am used—when asking them questions or conveying something—to speaking, being conscious that speech issues from my soul via my organs of speech to the other person. I am conscious that I am speaking, conscious also as regards outer perception. In answering or telling me something, the words of the other person—here on the physical plane—resonate towards me.

It is not like this in fully conscious converse with the dead—though in semi-conscious converse it again varies. It is the exact opposite. If I can express it thus in a realm such as this, it differs completely from expectation. When I face a deceased person, they speak in their soul what I am asking or what I wish to tell them; I receive it as being said by the other. What they tell me sounds upwards from my own soul.

If the person can face their thoughts so objectively that they appear to swarm around them, the dead can understand those thoughts. People are connected with the dead in normal consciousness but are unaware of this because they are not in a position to discern the factual process just outlined.

In order to gain insight into it, we need to focus on the fact that we have important states of consciousness other than sleeping, waking and dreaming. We have two other extraordinarily vital states of consciousness, which we also ignore in normal life. We ignore them for a reason which will immediately make sense once I name them: we also experience the processes of falling asleep and waking up. They do not last long but pass so swiftly that people do not notice them as to their content. At the very moments of falling asleep and waking up the most important occurrences take place. If one learns to recognize their essential nature when falling asleep and awakening then, from a certain point of view, one is able to receive true ideas about the relationship of the human being with the world, a world in which the dead also exist alongside us.

I said that human beings are continuously connected with the realm of the dead. This relationship is especially active at the moments of falling asleep and waking up. Clairvoyant sight confirms that the moment of falling asleep renders one particularly suited to asking questions of the deceased, to bringing them news and so on, in short: turning to the dead. The moment of awakening equips one especially for receiving news and tidings from the dead. These tidings arrive swiftly just before one is wide awake. What is so quickly delivered is immediately overlaid with tumultuous wakefulness. This was known and implicit among atavistic conditions and populations not so long ago, conditions that are being gradually lost to our materialistic culture, even among remoter ethnicities. Those having grown up among older people in remote agricultural areas know that a fundamental rule pertained: that one should remain quiet for a moment on waking up before looking out of brightly lit windows, because the lingering after-echo of what was experienced in sleep was not to be drowned out by turbulent wakefulness. Indigenous folk appreciated lying for a spell in semi-darkness on waking instead of focusing on bright daylight.

Something else comes into consideration, though it is not too difficult to perceive that the moments of awaking and falling asleep contain something special. To be able to take proper note of such moments demands, if I may say, a certain alertness in thinking, a capacity which has never been in such short supply as now. Grotesque examples could be cited as to the present state of 'wakeful thought'; banal examples running throughout daily life can be found on every street corner. Here is one such banal example.

A few days ago my eye fell on an announcement about an eighth of a newspaper page in size. I saw that it was a widely distributed advertisement extolling a famous method of memory training: Pöhlmann—something like that. Among myriad adverts, this one claimed that one could not gain influence over other people without taking advantage of the Pöhlmann method. I am not now commenting on the legality, rights or wrongs of gaining influence over other people—that doesn't concern us here—but am only referring to what the advertisement claimed. It continued in this vein: some people claim—by cultivating their personal magnetism and by strengthening who knows what other attributes in the human arsenal—to exert influence over other people. It's easy to prove to such people that they are not telling the truth because it only takes one person to come clean as to whether they have attained the personal wealth of a Rothschild or that some other wealthy person has left them millions. As this has patently not happened—despite it having been tried—there is ample proof that this method does not make you capable of influencing others, because influence is only attained through science and education. Then the Pöhlmann method is described. We know that a whole number of people will be convinced by it: other chaps don't have the option to cultivate qualities that influence others because it's quite clear, isn't it, that they have no such influence as compels, say, a Rothschild, to part with millions. Ask yourself: How many who read this advertisement will query: Might Pöhlmann really have so many students who have relieved millionaires of their cash? Just ask yourself how many will make this thought association!

That's a trivial example, but it shows how thought processes are not awake to what has been read. I chose it, firstly, because of its everyday character and, secondly, because there are obviously none here present who would not have had the thought that Pöhlmann himself did not succeed in making millions. Obviously, all those who were gullible enough to be taken in by the advertisement are elsewhere and, out of politeness, I am not using an example into which those present might have fallen! What I do wish to say is that, from morning till night, people read assertions of this kind. They claim not to take any notice of them. They don't notice them. I once read in a speech a sentence like this: 'Our connection with a certain empire is the key that must in future give direction to our politics.' Just imagine thinking constructed in this way: a connection is a key, which will become a direction! Someone who thinks like this is in a position to take action and to do all manner of things in life. We just don't notice how many correlations there are between such stunted thinking and public life.

Today we do need to respond to the non-wakefulness of thinking that is such a feature of our times and to beware of this non-wakeful thinking. *Executable thoughts* are a first requirement for anyone wanting to be capable of taking note of the revelations at the moment of falling asleep and waking up.

I once took part in a lecture by a very famous literary historian. It was his inauguration speech and he had put much effort into it. He had formulated all manner of literary-historical questions, at the end of which he said: So, ladies and gentlemen, I have led you into a forest of question marks! At the time, I imagined a forest of question marks—just think: a forest of question marks!

Whoever is used to putting into practice concepts formed within themselves, anyone developing wakefulness in their thinking, they alone are prepared to also notice moments such as those of awakening and falling asleep. What is not perceived is still present, though, including communion with the departed, which is particularly active at the moments of falling asleep and waking up. Basically, every person poses countless questions and conveys countless tidings to those loved ones who have died, also receiving messages and answers from the deceased at the moment of waking up. This communion with the dead can, to some extent, be cultivated. We have discussed various ways of nurturing this dialogue, but I'd like to say the following.

There is a difference as to whether or not a thought, which has connected us with someone who has died, leads us to being able to turn to them when we fall asleep. It is a distinct difference.

Anyone for whom life is not solely a matter of putting themselves first in an egotistical or sensual way will—due to their healthy sensibilities—feel a need not to interrupt a conversation with people with whom karma has brought them into contact and who may have gone through the gate of death either recently or longer ago; they will often join thoughts with such personalities. It is entirely possible that the thoughts we connect with an image of a departed individual may give rise to proper exchanges, even if we do not personally know them, even if we are not able to pay sufficient attention to the processes unfolding at the moment of falling asleep. Some thoughts are more favourable for such exchanges, others less auspicious. Abstract thoughts, thoughts containing a certain indifference, perhaps thoughts we harbour only out of a sense of duty are less conducive to moving towards a person on falling asleep. By contrast, thoughts and concepts issuing from a feeling of an especial interest, or which may have associated us with the person during life, are well suited to linking with the deceased. Let us remember the dead in such a way that we think of them not just in abstract thoughts or cold concepts but by calling up a moment in our souls when we were warmed at their side, when what they said was not just factual but something lovely, dearly remembered; let us think back to moments we spent with the deceased when we shared in communal feelings and joint impulses of will; let us remember when we undertook combined ventures or decided on something of value to us both, something that led to shared work, in short whatever made our hearts chime in unison; let us enliven and bring to life this harmony of hearts, and it will colour thoughts of the departed such that these thoughts can stream across to them when we next fall asleep. Whether you have these thoughts at nine o'clock, twelve o'clock or two o'clock, the whole day offers us the time to have such thoughts; they remain, they persist, and flow across to the deceased at the moment of our falling asleep.

At the moment of waking up we may receive communications, news or answers. These may not immediately surface in our souls at a time when we can pay attention to them, but may arise throughout the course of the day in the form of some inkling or notion—if we believe in such possibilities at all. Here again, some attitudes are more enabling than others and the dead find certain conditions easier for speaking into our souls so that it actually resounds in them; other conditions are less favourable to this. Especially conducive are circumstances in which we have acquired a clear and strong image of the being of the deceased—generating lively interest in them—that their being arises in great reality before the eyes of our soul. You may ask: Why is he saying that? If a person has been close to me, then of course I will have an impression of their being! My dear friends, I do not believe this to be so, especially nowadays! Today people pass each other by and know each other very, very little. This may not estrange you much here in the physical world. It does, however, estrange you greatly in the world which the dead are experiencing. You see, here and for this physical world, numerous unconscious or subconscious forces and impulsions bring human beings towards each other, even if they do not wish to get to know each other. It can happen in life—as some of you may have read—that one can have been married for decades and yet hardly have really got to know the other person. But there are other stimuli that bring people together which do not depend on them being mutually acquainted. Life everywhere is saturated with unconscious and subconscious incitement. As just mentioned, these subconscious impactions bind us here, but they do not bind us to the beings who have gone ahead of us through death. For that we need to have really absorbed into our souls something whereby the other being can vitally dwell in us. The more spiritedly they can live in us, the more easily can they gain access to our souls and the better can they make themselves understood to us.

This is what I wanted to characterize for you about communion of the so-called living with the so-called dead, which endures and is ever and ever again present. Each one of us communicates endlessly with the dead and just because we do not realize it is only a result of not being to a sufficient degree alert in observing the moments of falling asleep and waking up. I say this to give you more concrete contours to co-existing with the supra-sensible world in which the dead live. It will become all the more firmly concrete if we bring a few other circumstances into consideration.

Young people are dying; older people are dying. And yet the deaths of young people who pass on are, for those remaining behind, something different in nature when compared with the deaths of old people who expire. It is only really possible to talk about such issues if one is able to focus on individual, concrete examples. What I am depicting definitely does not originate in general science, but I am just summarizing what has taken place in concrete individual instances. If one follows with visionary consciousness what happens when children leave their parents in death, when young people take leave of those to whom they belong and go through the gate of death, and when one learns to recognize how these souls live onwards, then this knowledge presents itself in the following words, with which I wish to summarize it. One has to say: In the consciousness of those younger people who have traversed the portal of death, lives what can be outlined by saying: They are not actually lost to the living; they remain there, they stay in their vicinity, they endure within the very beings of those outliving them. As younger people, they are not separated from those left behind but remain for long spells within their orbit, within their sphere. About older people dying—such as parents leaving their children—one has to say something different, something best said epigrammatically. Of older souls dying it can be said that their souls do not—for their part—lose the souls of those they leave behind. So, while those left behind do not lose their younger departed souls, the older people, having gone through the portal of death, do not lose their contact with the souls of those left behind, despite the latter remaining here. They to some extent draw with them what they want of us; they can more easily acquire everything from souls remaining here, something the younger souls can only obtain if they stay where they are. This is what younger souls do, remaining more or less within the sphere of those left behind.

These relationships can be studied in a specific way, so that what I have just said can become a certainty—they need of course to be studied with visionary consciousness. With this *seeing* consciousness, one can observe the sorrow of mourning, the pain of separation. Grief and separation pain are actually two differing conditions. People don't know this, but if one observes the grief and pain over a departed child, it is quite different from the grief and pain observable over the death of an older person. Though people are unaware of this, they are two fundamentally differing states, when determined within the soul as an inner condition.

A remarkable aspect is this: when, let's say, parents mourn their early-departed children, this is actually a grief which—as far as its actual content and its deeper impetus are concerned—is only a reflex, a reflection of what the child remaining nearby radiates into the souls of those left behind. The child has lingered and, remaining nearby, it feels all manner of sensations, which percolate into the souls of those left behind and there awaken a response. It is a pain of compassion, a feeling of shared pain-in-common, which is actually the pain or sorrow of the child itself—this is the pain one feels. One may naturally ascribe this pain to oneself but it is a pain of co-empathy. You must not misunderstand me: we need to take these expressions sensibly and definitely without any negative or extraneous connotations. One could say: When a younger loved one dies, one is *beset* with the pain of one's own soul life—if only obsessed to a normal degree—so that it does no harm; they live on in us and what is interpreted as pain is their life continuing in us.

It is another matter in relation to an older person who has departed from us. Pain is caused, but not now as a reflection of what lives in the deceased, because they can really receive upwards what is in our soul; for their part, we are not lost to them. We cannot become obsessed with their pain—nor in any way beset by their feelings—because they have no longing to radiate into us with their feelings; and again: because they draw us along with them. They do not lose us. That is why this sort of mourning is an egotistical grief. That is not to apportion any blame and is certainly justified, but we do need quite fundamentally to differentiate between these two sorts of grief.

The matter becomes critical once one moves on to observe descriptions of pain or co-existing with the departed, as regards the deceased themselves. Given that the relationship with a younger person who has died is quite different from that with an older departed person, it will be equally understandable that, for the tending of remembrance and memories in relation to the departed in each of the two scenarios, it will have to differ. In relation to a young person, we will find the right service and memorial if we take account of the fact that the child or youth remains living with us, participating particularly in what we might have enabled the child to do, had it remained here. Experience shows that what such children or youths particularly long for—in their hindsight memory, in all that we can bring towards them after their death—is to find universal human relationships. In the funeral service, too, this includes everything that offers more of generalized, universal focus than anything to do with specialized interests. For children and the early departed, the Catholic[93] funeral service is more suitable, where rites are universal, where the service offers something to all in equal measure. A departed child longs for a ritual that is pan-human; one not especially for them individually, but one encompassing everyone.

For an older person, a Protestant funeral service is preferable, one which goes into the life and specific circumstances of the deceased and includes a eulogy. If one wishes to care for their memory, in remembrance of an older departed it will be especially propitious to think about the details in their life, what was unique to them, all that was specific in their biography and there to seek the thoughts with which one wants to celebrate the passing of one such older person.

You see from this that, rightly viewed, spiritual science cannot remain mere theory. It can show us a great deal about world conditions and circumstances, from which we remain closed off only because we dream away our feelings and sleep through our impulses of will. Spiritual science speaks of worlds in which our feeling and willing are immersed. If we grasp spiritual-scientific ideas with sufficient intensity and robust energy, they do not remain concepts but work affectively upon feeling and willing. Just think how abundantly and effectively these spiritual-scientific ideas can affect life! Priests performing funerals may find the right approach, the right insight, to lead these celebrations in a changed way instead of adhering to mere abstract theology.

All this is really no wonder, because the world of which spiritual science speaks is the real world, the genuine world in which our feelings and our incentives of will live, so that what that world is able to bequeath in turn plays into feeling and willing. It radiates into our feelings—as into all else—when we, for instance, nurture our feelings towards those who have died. But the spiritual world also rays into our impulses of will—something that we ought especially to take into consideration today. For if you were to pursue the promptings of will that spur people today, you would not come up against any profound depths in the human soul. It is a peculiarity of our times that human beings need to find spiritual incentives for their will. That is also its tragic aspect: that so far there has been no decision to seek them. Salvation or redemption will only emerge out of present confusion and trouble if people evince a widespread will to seek spirit-inspired impetus for external life. As I have outlined this evening, this is still being rejected in the most widespread human circles. Yet they will have to learn about it because this time—which has cut a swathe through humankind itself—will be by far the greater teacher than it has hitherto been.

Next Sunday morning, let us continue today's contribution—which explored some of the more personal aspects of the individual—and speak about present circumstances, but in an appropriately spiritual-scientific way.

# LECTURE 10

## 17 FEBRUARY 1918, MUNICH

TODAY it will be my task to move on from the fundamental principles of a spiritual method of observing—recently nurtured here—to spiritual processes, which in one sense lie immediately behind our times and speak so fatefully to our souls.

As you can imagine, it is in the context of what spiritual science calls co-existing with forces streaming from the so-called dead into the realm in which we ourselves live during our incarnation—it is in this shared existence that we can observe in all its dynamism precisely what spiritually underlies these gruelling times. However, present-day people barely look for the spiritual background to existence. This *non-seeking* for the spiritual background to existence is far more closely intertwined than you may think with the baleful cataclysm that has engulfed humanity. I have drawn attention to the time that can be designated the last third of the nineteenth century during which, in contrast with earlier times spans, humankind as a whole underwent mighty, all-encompassing changes in its evolution. I have often referred to the end of the 1870s as a decisive incision into human evolution. You have to admit that only very few among present-day people realize how fundamentally different spiritual life has been since the end of the eighteen-seventies compared with all that went before it. I'd like to say: Humanity has secured far too little distance to be in a position to notice this. You can only really see something of this kind if you can discern its differences—its distinct differentiations—once you are not in the middle of it but have gained a certain distance from it. If humanity is not to have even greater woes in prospect, that distance must be achieved as quickly as possible. Because at present—seen spiritually—there is a remarkable and very active contradiction. In the way I am about to portray that contradiction, it may strike you as surprisingly bizarre: there have been no other times in historically-traceable human evolution that are more spiritual than the times in which we have been living since the end of the 1870s. Observed historically, we live in the most spiritual times there have ever been. And yet we live in such a way—this is undeniable—that multitudes of people who certainly deem themselves spiritual believe the present to be extremely materialistic. You see, as far as life is concerned, our age is not materialistic. According to what many people believe—and in line with all that flows from that belief—our times are certainly materialistic. So what is actually meant by saying our time is spiritual?

Well, firstly, a natural-scientific world view prevails: in face of this natural-scientific world view, all previous natural-scientific world views were materialistic! You see, we have a natural-scientific world outlook that has set itself up to be among the finest, most spiritually-pervaded models. The person best able to perceive this is one who can see beyond immediate physical existence.

As for most of today's concepts—which, spiritually speaking, are well-intentioned—the supposedly dead have exceptionally few—they have very few. Yet of present natural-scientific concepts—when impartially reflected upon—they have extraordinarily many. It is also interesting that ostensibly materialistic Darwinism is grasped and applied in highly spiritual form in the realm of the dead. Matters transpire in life quite differently from the way in which they transpire in the belief—the often very mistaken belief—that is a result of what people experience when physically embodied here. What do I actually mean by referring first of all to what is natural-scientifically spiritual? Well, you see, in order to form concepts such as these—in order to soar aloft to thoughts such as those presently held about evolution and so on—requires a spirituality that was not available in earlier times. It is much easier to see ghosts and think them to be spiritual than it is to form finely-chiselled ideas about what appears to be merely material. This has had the effect that people form the most spiritually-suffused ideas in their souls' life—and then deny or disown those same spiritually-suffused ideas. They compact those spiritually-suffused ideas together so that they are allowed solely to express aspects of materiality. The materialistic interpretation of our natural-scientific world outlook is nothing other than a denial of the real nature of the natural-scientific world view. It originates in a bias that is basically cowardice! People cannot manage to make their living feelings and their delicate, spiritually-permeated ideas co-exist, nor can they take hold of spirituality itself in the rarified dilution—if I may put it like that—in which it has to be grasped if one is to form pure concepts about nature. People do not dare to admit that they live in what is spiritual, in spirit itself, when they have such spiritually-rarified, dilute concepts and so they lie to themselves, saying: These ideas only represent what is material—something untrue and just self-delusion. It is also the case in other areas of life. One could mention, for example—as I did the day before yesterday—that, for instance, many an artistic creation has benefitted from these refined spiritual sensitivities coming to light in the present, advantages that were not available to earlier epochs of art evolution. It is absolutely without doubt that today, in the realm of artistic creativity, much is coming to light for which one would seek in vain in Raphael or Michelangelo's art. The about-turn in spiritual life has been brought about by a specific spiritual event. It is this spiritual event that I would like to characterize for you from certain perspectives.

Just before the middle of the nineteenth century—that is, at the start of the 1840s—a certain spiritual being—names do not add much, but so as to relate to a name, we can call this being by the name borrowed from Christian theology: the Archangel Michaël—so, Michaël was gradually preparing to become a Time Spirit, having been an Archangel, aiming to attain an evolution of this kind so as to act in human life not only from the standpoint of the supra-sensible but directly from out of earthly life. The Archangel Michaël was preparing to descend to Earth, in a certain sense following the great deed of Christ Jesus Himself, in a way re-enacting that great event: he was preparing to take up his inaugural point on Earth for his onward task, now from a terrestrial perspective. It was therefore necessary that, from the 1840s forward till the 1870s, preparations were made by and on behalf of this spiritual being. One can therefore observe how the years between the '40s and the '70s of the nineteenth century represent a crucial battle in the super-sensible region adjoining the Earth. The spiritual being we can call the Archangel Michaël fought a hard and mighty battle against certain opposing, adversarial spirits. We need to look at these opposing spirits a bit if we are to understand what was actually taking place.

The spiritual beings to be opposed by the being evolving from Archangel to Time Spirit—the Archangel Michaël—have always intervened in human life and evolution. In the millennia before the middle of the nineteenth century, those beings had the task of severing humanity from the spiritual world. Spiritual beings, proximate followers of Archangels, cherished the aim, in a sense, of leading humanity back to being a single human group soul, to pour forth unity over all humankind. This would not have succeeded had they worked only on humanity. Humankind would have dissolved into something of an un-differentiable unit, would only have imagined as a single group—much as do the animals—only at a slightly higher level. The spiritual beings engaged in fighting Michaëlic principles are those tasked with bringing differentiation into humankind, splitting a unified humanity into races, into peoples, into all manner of distinctions connected with blood, nerves, temperament and so on. This had to take place. One can call the spiritual beings who had to effect such differentiation in humankind ahrimanic beings; call them this by all means, but you need to be quite clear that the intervention of the ahrimanic principle was essential for the whole course of human evolution.

Now the time approached, an important moment in human evolution with regard to what I have just related. The time beginning with the 1840s now arrived, and with it the ancient differentiations were to vanish: the time when differentiated humankind was to be amalgamated into a single unified humanity.

Cosmopolitan views—some of which were certainly expanded into cosmopolitan phraseology in the eighteenth and the first half of the nineteenth centuries—are just a reflection of what was taking place in spiritual worlds. Human beings were already tending towards extinguishing the many and varied distinctions based around nervous disposition, blood and temperament. It is in fact not an inclination of the spiritual world to further differentiate humankind, but the direction of travel, as it were, in spiritual worlds is rather to cascade cosmopolitan values into humanity as a whole. However little understanding there is for this under the pressures of present catastrophic times, it is nevertheless so and the verity of this fact has to be acknowledged. This fact, which is mirrored in earthly events, leads one to see—when viewed in their spiritual context—how the spirits of races, those folk spirits differentiating humankind, were being fought from the 1840s onwards specifically by that Spirit who was to become Time Spirit for the new age. What has always been depicted in the form of a momentous symbol was in fact being fulfilled, if at a different level. That symbol is also applicable to other stages of evolution, because events tend to be repeated on various levels, and what I am now talking about is just one such repetition, at a specific stage, of other spiritual events that have taken place. It is what is symbolically portrayed as Michaël's conquest over the dragon. This victory over the dragon by Michaël signifies that opposing forces have been banished from the realm inhabited by Michaël, and this has been fulfilled in some areas since the beginning of the 1840s onwards. Certain spiritual beings, whose task in spiritual worlds had until then been to separate humanity into peoples and races, they were—if I may express it like this—cast from Heaven to Earth. Those same spiritual beings who, until the 1840s had been differentiating humanity into groupings, no longer exert their power today in the realm adjoining the Earth. They were thrust amongst humankind on Earth, bringing with them all they could. This is what in spiritual science we know as the victory of the Archangel Michaël over forces of opposition, which was established at the end of the 1870s: the casting down to Earth of spirits combatting him.

What exists since the end of the 1870s is therefore twofold. On the one hand, for those of goodwill—here understood in a conditional sense—since 1879 there is the earthly sovereignty of the Time Spirit, Michaël, who enables us to grasp spiritualized concepts and to lead a spiritualized inner life. Also to be found here on Earth are the opposing forces, forces that tempt us to negate and deny the spirituality of the present. In fighting the materialism of our times, you always need to be aware that you should not fight what benefits our times but should be fighting against the lie of our age. For it is essentially spirits of untruth that were cast out of Heaven onto Earth which, presently working as spirits of obstruction, hinder spirituality from being sought in time-compatible conceptions of existence. If you come to know people who descended from spiritual worlds into earthly incarnation after 1841, and who have since died, I would say that you can indeed see how things are thought of from yonder side; you are then able to correct much of what is so difficult to access with understanding from the physical world.

It gradually began to emerge—at the start of the nineteenth century—how essential it was to point to the various realms of the spirit in life; those who did so were essentially people who—since 1848, or in fact since 1840—had joined the bitterly-fought battle being led by the Archangel Michaël in the spiritual world, the battle which culminated in 1879 in the antithetical spirits being cast down onto Earth, where they continue to exist among human beings. Basically, all opposition to these beings, all attempts to expel them from the field, entails fighting on the side of the Archangel Michaël.

Now, my dear friends, there is a certain law. Implicit in this law is that every point of time in evolution can be pursued in both a forwards and a backwards direction. When focusing on any point in humanity's historical development, one can say: Here is a point in time, this or that is taking place; now time flows onwards and one can observe subsequent events. One can also observe time in a retrograde direction. One can move from 1879 to 1878, to 1877, back to 1860, 1850 and so on further back in time, and one can then observe how in the spiritual world things can be followed in a reverse direction. The following can then be seen: one sees during such observation—embedded in the deeper structure of events and also during its progress—what lies in and as the background *being repeated.* Sometimes when something of enormity is said simply, it may sound trivial. Yet I will just say it.

If you focus on the point in time of 1879, you can go forwards to 1880 or back to 1878. If you go ahead to 1880, you will notice—in deeper spiritual-structural layers—that what happened in 1878 in a certain way co-works in concert with it, works with it such that, behind the events of 1880, the event of 1878 co-re-runs *as a force*. It is, the further back one goes, as if the line of time were to loop back on itself so that the events lying further back relate to a given time-point and events ahead of it by lying or running alongside them in the background. If you can grasp processes such as this, you will be understanding a great deal.

Now I ask you to recall that I have been speaking about the year 1879 for many years, not just since 1914 when it became commonplace. That's important, my dear friends, and I'd ask you now to carry out a simple calculation. Work backwards from 1879 to a year I have often designated as another threshold; I have always said that the battle of which I am now speaking began at the start of the '40s: around 1840 or 1841. Now calculate backwards: 1879, 1869, 1859, 1849 plus another eight or nine years, which makes 38 or 39 years. Now calculate forwards: 1879, 1889, 1899, 1909, 1914 and onwards until today, which gives us about the same: some 38 or 39 years. Were you to focus on the year 1917, you would come to a surprising conclusion. You would realize what deep significance is entailed when an occultist says: If you proceed from an incisive historical event, the preceding spiritual event finds a certain repetition in the subsequent.

Behind the events of the present day, here on a physical level, stand those spiritual events which began in the 1840s and which can be designated as the battle by the Archangel Michaël against spirits of opposition. They form the backdrop. We see a recapitulation of what took place at the start of the 1840s. You can imagine how differently present events would be viewed were we to return to this lawful principle. Perhaps then what will otherwise pass tonelessly by the human ear without reaching the human soul will be more profoundly understood. It could then be reflected how the Archangel Michaël's battle with antagonistic forces has in some respects returned to its point of origin.

By and large, it is always difficult to speak of such profound connections with people of today because they reject so vehemently just what would help them to understand their times rightly and hence to take appropriate action. Our time really does make it essential to let go of old prejudices and preconceptions, makes it vital to make this understandable, to bring it to consciousness. Things sometimes happen here in the immediate physical which are, in their way, far more spiritual than many another happening. This is actually connected with the descent of the Archangel Michaël into our earthly realm. Many speak of this Michaëlic descent into our earthly domain. But when this fact—in all the significance of its true background—actually comes to it, people don't want to align themselves with it, they just don't want to take it up! Yet it is enormously important that, in ever widening circles, a spiritual understanding of the most important impulses of our lifetimes takes hold. That is why what has been continuing in our Branch meetings for years on end has been absolutely indispensable in drawing attention to the fact that the stream of events so strongly influenced by the Spirit in our times should not be slept through. This sleeping through events is such a feature of our times. People pass events by as if comatose. It could even be stated that the more trenchantly decisive the event on the physical plane—the deeper and greater its significant—the more soundly will people sleep through it.

If I may just hint at something in concrete terms: March 1917[94] was one such momentous period as regards its potential—one that will have consequences of which humanity can barely dream today—and it is positively appalling how little people understand the imperative that almost every opinion and judgement be revised. Almost everything that people ever believed before 1914 needs to undergo complete revision.

This may be the occasion to draw attention to the fact that, in 1910 in Kristiania,[95] I held a series of lectures about European Folk Souls. In the first of these you can read that in the near future humanity would be called upon to have some understanding of the relationships between European Folk Souls. It was repeatedly emphasized in those lectures that our gaze ought to be directed towards the immediate East, that what emanates from that area is of importance for human evolution. How often was this said! Everyone present can attest to it. And again, in the lecture cycle in Vienna in spring 1914,[96] I dared to suggest that the social life of the present can, in a very real sense, be compared with a form of illness—with a carcinoma—and that a cancer-like sickness was creeping throughout social life. Obviously, such things cannot, under our present circumstances, be described any differently, but they must be understood.

World events are not turning out to be that fabled progression of which historians dream: that the subsequent always evolves out of the previous, this from that, and so on. To assume that the subsequent will emerge as quietly as possible of its own accord—or at least that it ought to—can be left to people with less grasp of reality than the thinking anthroposophist ought to have developed. If I am to hint at something concrete, this assumption can largely be left to politicians of the old school—as indeed to those of the present—for as long as humanity wants to. In reality, it is a matter of something quite different. It is a case of the course of events being like the beam of a set of scales in full alternating tilt, where now this pan, now the other, sinks downward. That is why one can characterize the period since the 1840s something like this: there would have been opportunities, in the period between the years of 1840 and 1914—a time span bisected by the year 1879—had there been appropriate and timely attempts to prepare for the spiritualizing of humanity, which is the aim of the Archangel Michaël; had there been attempts on a larger scale to introduce spiritual concepts, spiritual ideas, to humanity. If free human will neglects to do this—because freedom has to hold sway among modern human beings—then the scales will dip to the opposite side. Then what could have been achieved by spiritual means will be discharged through blood. It will then be discharged by what I'd like to call supra-physical means. What we are experiencing in these catastrophic times is only the rebalancing of the scales. Humanity—having refused spiritualization—will then be compelled into spiritualization. This may be achieved by means of physical catastrophes.

You can confirm this idea for yourselves, if you are firmly grounded, as in what follows: we live here, in this physical world, but we are awake only as far as our perceptions and conceptions are concerned, as I recently explained. Here we dream with our feelings and are fast asleep as regards our will, something natural for human beings. However, if you find your way into yonder world through Imagination, Intuition and Inspiration—into the spiritual world surrounding us, just as air surrounds us here, and in which the seemingly dead and their incentives of will exist in community with us—then you will perceive how our lives in the physical are interwoven with those of the apparently deceased. Those dead can absorb from our human hearts only the spiritual element among our conceptual images.

Remember what I said three days ago: Seen spiritually, when a younger person dies, they have not taken leave of those belonging to them. They remain; they are in reality there. Yet for the deceased it is quite different from just being there—I beg you to take this very seriously—for the deceased it is a matter of bearing that existence, being able to encompass it. If the deceased is present in a family which is materialistically minded and not given to spiritual ideas, though they remain within that family, the deceased will be continuously burdened and oppressed. The family is for them like a nightmare, where excessively inhaling air can cause nightmares. Only spiritual ideas can banish these nightmares for the deceased and make co-existing with those near to whom they remain bearably possible.

I also said to you earlier: When an older person is torn from those belonging to them, they to some extent take the souls of their adherents with them. They draw them along with themselves; they draw them in train. And here, too, if people are not suffused with spiritual ideas, it is like a nightmare for the deceased.

Let us now consider something else. You can learn an enormous amount if you observe when a person dies very suddenly, whether caused by external agency or abnormal inner states. Let us imagine that a person is hit or shot. A death such as this is quite different from one ending a long illness or other natural processes. Imagine someone aged thirty-five is shot, their life annihilated by external agency. Had the bullet not hit them—this is certainly connected with their karma, but the following nevertheless applies—the person concerned may well have lived a further thirty-five years according to their constitution. You see, their constitution might have granted them a further thirty-five years, and this has a specific effect.

If someone dies violently, while they still contain markedly vigorous life forces, they experience a tremendous amount at that very moment. Compressed into one moment, they experience what would otherwise have stretched ahead over a long time span. What they might have experienced over that further period of, say, thirty-five years—whatever life would have been apportioned to them over that time—is compressed into a single moment. This is because the most important realization one comes to in the hour of death is to view one's corporeality from outside, how it makes the transition from being ruled by forces it previously possessed—when their soul still inhabited their body—to the present situation, where their soul becomes a being of nature and is given over to the forces of nature, to external physical forces. That is the most tremendously significant aspect of the moment of dying, when the human being looks back on how their organism is delivered up to physical forces of nature. When someone undergoes a violent death, they are not only surrendered to normal natural forces but due, for instance, to the sudden bullet wound, are treated like an inorganic and inert object, totally transposed into the realm of the inorganic. There is a huge difference whether one sickens and dies or whether one experiences death by being abruptly dispatched, in which case the universe intervenes externally in the organism, be it in the form of a bullet or other means. Then what happens is an instant illumination, a blaze of infinite spirituality. It is the flaring-over of a spiritual aura that takes place. The person who has gone through the gate of death looks back at this flaring up, at a blazing forth that is very similar to what only comes about when human beings devote themselves in thought to spiritual concepts. These phenomena are mutually interchangeable. From the other side, from the perspective of the deceased, it is incredibly interesting to see how similar are the thoughts—those feeling, felt, sentient thoughts—of someone looking at, enjoying or creating a work of art or a painting that is born out of spiritual insight, with those experienced when—without it going via human consciousness—let's say, an arm is injured or pain arises in a person. There is an extraordinary kinship between both these phenomena, such that each can stand in for the other.

Now you will understand the karmic connection existing between two events. As the 1840s approached, of course, a large number of people knew what I might call the 'state of the stars', which is just a technical term among occultists wishing to denote an event such as the battle of the Archangel Michaël with the dragon with the expression: 'That is the state of the stars'. Anyway, there were a whole number of people who knew at that time that a process as vital as this was taking place. There were also people who cared, who wanted to take positive pre-emptive measures; it was just that the pans of the scales, as it were, had been too heavily weighted against them, that is, the materialistic bent of people was too strong. Instead, people reached for the most false sources possible at the time. It was realized that spiritual life needed to enter human existence. Had this spiritual life entered humanity in the early 1840s, humankind would have been spared many disasters. Despite this, what took place would anyway have come about, just in a different manner; because whatever is karmically necessary will take place, but can do so by a variety of means. You must always bear this firmly in mind.

I will express myself even more clearly: if a person today thinks about what should happen in the social arena, or indeed anywhere else, they can do this in one of two ways. They can set up a programme, create programmatic concepts, think up ways the world ought to work in a given field. All this can be turned into pleasant-sounding wordage. You can swear by this wordage as if it were dogma, but nothing—absolutely nothing—will result! You can have the nicest ideas about how things should work out: nothing can result. Nothing actually needs to come of many a nice idea. Thought-out, thought-up programmes are the most—the very most—useless things in life. Alternatively, you can do something else—and some people manage this without added clairvoyance: you can ask yourself—quite naively, with just an intuitive grasp of the conditions of the time—'What will in any event happen in the next twenty or thirty years? What exists in our time that longs to be actualized?' Once you have identified this, you will be able to tell what will anyway happen. Now you have a choice: either you will use reason to direct progress in the direction it will anyway take—then things will turn out well. Or you ignore this and fail to do anything, letting the matter depend on what presently exists; you sleep, you do not awake and the issue is resolved through catastrophes or revolutions, cataclysms, disasters or similar will then follow. No statistics, no pre-fabricated programme, however cleverly thought out, will then be of any use. The only thing of value will be observing what lies in the lap of the times. This is what has to be taken up, what needs to be fathomed; this is what must govern the intentions of the present.

In the 1840s most people were of the programming ilk and outweighed those who understood what I have just described. Because of this, all sorts of measures were used to spiritualize humanity: for instance spiritualism, which is just an attempt to spiritualize people by improper means, to reform them by materialistic means, by trying to manifest the spiritual world in lifelike forms. One can be very materialistic in one's thinking. One is materialistic if one maintains: This or that section of humanity is in the right—so why doesn't the spiritual world step in on the side of righteousness? How often have we heard that nowadays? Why don't these spiritual powers intervene? I replied in slightly abstract mien recently: Humanity is grounded in freedom today. Those who continue to ask why spiritual powers don't intervene proceed from the belief that ghosts ought to run politics instead of human beings. It would indeed make for easy progress were ghosts instead of humans to bring in reforms; that would make a real difference. They cannot of course do this because people are grounded in freedom. Waiting for ghosts is what confuses people most and it diverts them from what actually needs to happen. So it is precisely the time for people, in accordance with their lives, to work their way into the refined spiritual ideas that live so clearly in some, yet on the other hand it is also a time in which people are susceptible to the most powerful materialistic temptations. People simply cannot distinguish between refined, spiritualized concepts and the tempting impressions that approach them, undermining their perception of the spirituality they contain, of what has been spiritualized, of what itself constitutes genuine spirituality. Because, at the crucial time, people failed to grasp how evolution had to progress, it has necessarily resulted in the catastrophically bitter age in which we now find ourselves. In the absence of this terribly disastrous present, humanity would have sunk even deeper into disbelief in itself. All the more would it have reached a point where spirituality would albeit have developed but been all the more strongly rejected.

Such is some background to history in the making. I would so much like to throw light on what lies in the foreground but, for reasons easily understood, that cannot be done, particularly at the moment. It must be left to each individual to illuminate the foreground—what is living in their immediate present—on the basis of these backgrounds.

That somnolence, that sleeping-through-events, which I described earlier, conditions us to prefer to overlook life's sharper corners and contours, and this includes inwardly. Ignoring life's sharp corners and contours involves compromise. Now, there can be times when compromise is called for. What went on in the '40s of the nineteenth century was one such instance to which compromise would have been well suited; but our present time is not. It sets us the task of seeing things as they really are, complete with their sharpest corners and contours. Yet it also implants in human nature the urge to close our eyes sleepily to the sharp corners and contours that exist in life. Particularly in face of the greatest, most significant events in human evolution can what I have just described be observed.

In face of the greatest event in world history, human evolution has brought humanity to these harsh corners and contours, especially that very greatest event in world history: the Mystery of Golgotha. We know what theological developments of the nineteenth century have contributed. From the time when Lessing[97] spoke about the Mystery of Golgotha to that of the philosopher Drews,[98] all sorts of perspectives have been discussed. One could say: The whole theological debate of the nineteenth century offers the most fulsome proof that we have totally *unlearnt* even the most initial understanding of the Mystery of Golgotha. Yet there are some very interesting publications[99] about Christ Jesus. For instance, a Danish one, written completely from the standpoint of a modern natural-scientific thinker. This person says of his point of view: I am a psychologist, a physiologist, a psychiatrist and I view the Gospels from this perspective. What did he conclude? In line with current psychiatric thinking and constructs, the man concluded: The image which the Gospels create of Christ Jesus is one of pathology. One can only encompass Christ Jesus in terms of a being constituted of mania, epilepsy, pathological visions and so forth. All the symptoms of an acutely mentally ill person are present. When I read out parts of this book recently, people were horrified.[100] That is understandable. If people are faced with what they hold sacred being described in terms of pathological symptoms, they are outraged. But what is this actually? What is being presented is that, among large numbers of disingenuous concession-granters, one has raised their head above the parapet who stands full-square within the natural-scientific mode of thinking, one who no longer makes compromises but instead says: I am utterly a natural scientist. And because that is what I am, I have to say things as I do because it is fact.

Were people to be honest enough to put themselves into the standpoint occupied by natural science, they would have to acquire perspectives such as these. Here there are sharp corners and contours and one cannot do otherwise. Nor can one do other than: either vacate the natural-scientific standpoint and migrate to spiritual science—one would then be remaining honest—or one can remain honestly within the natural-scientific mindset, in which case one must be uncompromising and only view things as does this hidebound man who is honest in his field; he is at least thoroughly hidebound and does not whitewash his bigotry, is narrow-minded but consistently so. You have to put yourself in their position. Were people nowadays to appreciate what certain nuances necessitate—when they arise illuminatingly—only then would they begin to see life without compromise.

An interesting pamphlet was recently passed to me. I knew about the book mentioned in it but do not have it with me, so I can only read the leaflet. It was slipped to me to illustrate what is possible today.

'Whoever has burdened the benches of a grammar school will be unable to forget the hours spent "enjoying" the Platonic conversations between Socrates and his friends; unforgettable for the fabulous boredom those discussions engendered. Maybe one remembers that one found those Socratic conversations wholeheartedly stupid; but of course one never dared to express that view because, after all, the man in question was "the greatest philosopher" Socrates.'—With this quite unjustified overestimation of the worthy Athenian, the book *Socrates the Idiot* by Alexander Moszkowski[101] is quite properly tidied up and rounded off. In this small and entertaining work, the polyhistor Moszkowsky undertakes nothing less than stripping Socrates almost entirely of his philosophic virtue. The title 'Socrates the Idiot' is intended literally. You will not go astray in assuming that scientific debate will ensue in connection with this book.

You may find it awful that things of this sort are written, isn't that so? But I don't find it awful at all. I think it obvious and honest of Moszkowsky. Because, according to his concepts and percepts, he can, if he is consistent, call Socrates an idiot; that is clear. In doing so he is more honest than countless others who ought—in line with their views—also to call Socrates an idiot but who do not do so out of sheer equivocation. Needless to say, I trust that it would not be spread abroad—through the porous walls of the Munich Branch—that I have declared myself in agreement with Moszkowsky when he calls Socrates an idiot. I would hope you understand what I actually mean.

However, I must also acknowledge that nowadays some opinions only percolate into human sensitivities because dishonest compromises are made. One cannot simultaneously think about mental illness—in the way modern psychiatry thinks—and not write a book such as the Dane wrote about Christ Jesus. It cannot be done. One is not being honest if one either fails to reject such concepts and replace them with spiritual concepts, or aligns oneself squarely with the view that Christ Jesus was mentally ill. Nor can one, knowing all this—if one knows Alexander Moszkowsky's idiosyncratic views on radiation or quantum theory; one just has to be conversant with such people and remain abreast of their views on remote concepts, on the entire fabric of the universe—avoid calling Socrates and Plato idiots, that is, if one is to be thoroughly consistent and consequential.

Motivation exceptionally useful to humankind includes above all this: that we reject compromise, that we do not make compromises, at least—and for a start—not in our minds. It is important, extremely important, to see this as an obligation of our time. Because it is among the most vital impulses of the Time Spirit, Michaël, to cascade clarity—unconditional clarity—into human souls. If one wants to follow the Archangel Michaël, then it is essential to inundate human souls with clarity, with lucidity, in order to overcome all sleepiness. Drowsiness can arise in other fields, too. But it is an absolutely prime requirement to make clear the consequences of any given issue. This was different in times gone by. In previous ages, before the age of Michaël, when European humanity was essentially governed by Gabriel, it was the case that what people here considered compromise was already being weakened by spiritual worlds. Michaël is the Spirit who—in the most pre-eminent sense—works with human freedom. Michaël therefore does what is right. You must not believe that Michaël does not do what is right; he absolutely does do what is right. In the unconscious regions of every human soul today those sharp corners and contours of spiritual life can be found. They are already there. Even those individuals who have the slightest—and be it only the very slightest—facility to raise to surface consciousness what exists in the subterranean recesses of soul life by way of latent vision, know how much discrepancy and disparate non-cohesion prevails there. They know that a materialistic psychiatry that does not shy away from seeing in them epileptics—even from diagnosing Christ Jesus as such—can co-exist cheek by jowl in souls. They know that. If things rise to consciousness even a little—if someone only has a slight ability to raise things to consciousness—then they will be aware how matters stand. It would be interesting to see how a modern painter with a sense of present predicaments might paint 'Christ from the perspective of a psychiatrist', how what is happening today might be brought to expression. It would be really interesting if a painter had some understanding of what presently goes on in those subterranean recesses of soul life.

You see, you have to dig deep in our times to understand what is taking place on the surface of existence. On the other hand, people are recognizably overcome by a certain cowardice—a lack of courage—when trying to approach what has just been described. And that is the other quality required in the present: courage, even a degree of audacity in one's outlook, in one's way of thinking, the sort of audacity that doesn't blunt concepts but instead tends to make them as *pointedly acute* as possible. I have said all this so that—inasmuch as they are spiritually accessible—anyone can themselves observe them. It is quite possible to observe these traits yourself if you really wish to examine spiritual life in the present. Everything that has had to be said today can be confirmed by outer events; the spiritual researcher will merely present it more precisely because they can see its corresponding spiritual background. And if you receive from the spiritual researcher background facts such as these, you will be all the more able to see the veracity proved of what has, for example, been indicated today.

A few people asked me today what they should actually do. What they ought to do lies immediately to hand. One would like to say: Just open your eyes, albeit your spiritual eyes! The will for action will follow from opening your eyes. Will often depends on the location in which you are placed. It's not always possible to do what is right in accordance with your karma in the place in which you find yourself, but you should try to open your eyes spiritually. Nowadays it is often the case that, when trying to introduce something in the form of words—something essential for the present—people tend to rapidly close their eyes before equally rapidly turning away from the thrust of what is being said. Such is just the weighting of the scales towards the other extremity.

Speaking in this way could easily be taken as criticism of the times. That is never my intention. What I intend is to draw wakeful attention to the impulses flowing from the spiritual world into human souls, to what has to flow into human feelings if we want to emerge from the catastrophic times in which we find ourselves. As I said, it is unfortunately not possible to go into concrete details. Everyone can do this for themselves.

# Lecture 11

2 MAY 1918, MUNICH

TODAY—on the first day of our Branch reflections, and as befits conditions of the time—we will set out to consider what light can be thrown by the intentions and efforts of our spiritual science on all that confronts and interrogates people at present, filling each person with the challenge to fulfil at least such tasks as the spirit of the times most urgently sets them. It is upon each individual recognizing their task that the destiny of humanity may potentially depend. Starting with something that may be close to us: you will have noticed that for some time now there has been a change in the attitude of the world at large towards our anthroposophically-orientated spiritual science, a change of mood that amounts to it being viewed in some places with greater antipathy. Only someone unfamiliar with the history of spiritual movements and who doesn't accord them due respect can be surprised at such a change of attitude and mood having set in; this will occur more intensely in future. As long as a movement such as this contains within its core aims any sectarian modalities, as long as—in this town or that—a few people get together in their front or back rooms to hold sect-like meetings, any striving movement will be regarded with a certain benign indulgence, but with an attitude that can easily turn into something quite different. Things may continue for the moment, while people do not consider us worth serious investigation, because movements such as these usually vanish again and those front or back rooms revert to more domestic use. Attitudes of this kind have been prevalent for many years in relation to our movement, and what there was of antipathy only arose in isolated cases. Things have improved slightly because—in some quarters, at least—there have been increased efforts to slough off any sectarian elements. Yet—particularly from among the ranks of our Society itself—there has been repeated opposition to ridding ourselves of every vestige of sectarianism, opposition to uniting with contemporary culture. Strenuous efforts have to be made to challenge such opposition, to challenge such obstinacy, and to align ourselves with the aims of present culture. We will not be able to continue reading lectures in cosy comfort and so forth—though that can of course be a pleasantly familiar undertaking—as it will be essential to engage with what people long for in their various locations, so that—precisely through mutual exchange with potentially differing or opposing movements in the world at large—we find out what is presently needed and also what is found in anthroposophically-orientated spiritual science.

It will be our friends' most important task to unfold the requisite mobility of spirit entailed in taking leave of comfortable, safe, warm familiarity. It is essential, but its inevitability is not yet being felt everywhere. This leads directly to us asking ourselves: How will anyone in future—based on what originates in our spiritual movement—be able to get to grips with old-inherited or new issues—even if they be armed with the belief that ours *is indeed* something new—how will what issues from us converse in mutual exchange with other movements? How will this interchange take shape?

Well, above all—and despite apparent agreement arising sporadically—opposition will become particularly virulent from the quarter of official representatives of religious, denominational world outlooks. Of these representatives of religious or confessional views—among whose ranks exemplary people who agree with our movement will certainly be found—the majority will nevertheless always insist on what they can read up in terms of their own inherited assets. Though populations profess not to believe in authority, they acquiesce to every authority and with what religious representatives claim will find widespread resonance among the population. It will become especially difficult to introduce spiritual-scientific content to *one* particular attitude and this attitude rests—in the exceptionally convenient manner to which human souls have become accustomed—on finding its relationship with spiritual worlds. How many people are there at present who say: Oh, here comes one of those spiritual researchers who construct an entire stratified world of hierarchies! First one has to go up through hierarchies of Angeloi, Archangeloi and so on to the highest divinity. People find all this too 'intellectual' to accompany and they point to what they call the only simple, naïve relationship through which the soul can attain to God or Christ or suchlike: through strong inner experience. That is what one hears again and again from those of better intention: Direct experience of the highest divinity! Why would a person need so-and-so many strata of hierarchical intermediaries in order to attain spiritual knowledge when they can—with childlike simplicity—have an experience of union with the loftiest divinity?

We do, however, need to ask ourselves: What takes place in the souls of those who—with a real, if comfortable, degree of honesty—describe their striving as being one of experiencing the divine? There are indeed people who have experienced a certain landslide or sea change in their life of soul such that everything they call divine or spiritual now appears differently to them from the way in which it appeared previously. Some call this evangelisation, others use different terms, but that is neither here nor there. It is their belief that they have found—by naïve, childlike means—access to the highest Divinity. People imagine quite simply that they have experienced Christ inwardly. What are they really experiencing?

Now, my starting point is the assumption that the experiences in question here are honest and genuine and that people really have experienced a change in their soul lives. I am also proceeding from a completely honest conviction and a certain judgement-free open-mindedness as regards inherited denominational directions of faith. What these people experience is, at most, the closest experience a person can have with what is spiritual. And what is this closest spiritual that is experienced? The closest spiritual experience is of a being from the hierarchy of the Angeloi, a being assigned to each human being for their guidance, a being one can call whatever one will: Christ, the highest Godhead—it matters not what we call this, it matters only what it really is to which the soul draws near when experiencing this honestly, when it is a real experience: it is an Angel, an Angelos, and we see this being only as the highest God. We are too comfortable to stride onwards to something else, and the first, closest being one encounters one calls God and one constructs for oneself—yes, what does one actually construct?—the most egotistical religion it is possible to construct! The fact that all people are in agreement—in uniformly naming their encounter—is not the crucial factor because—as long as people only want to experience what has been indicated—each one only experiences their Angel, each one prays exclusively to their Angel. And though legions of preachers may speak of the one-and-only God—of the seemingly monotheistic God—in truth they are only speaking of millions of Angels, to whom people pray, and whom they give the same name, thus herding people into the confused idea that these millions of Angel beings are all *one* being. That is the reality. It points to the illusion to which one submits if one wants to unite with the egotistical God.

There is even an external indicator of what I have just described. Try to take refuge in the learned resources used in cases when something exceptional is experienced; turn to the most enlightened of these helpful aids and try to find out the origin of a most useful, most used word. You will find just *one* word, of which all scholars within German-speaking regions will say: The origin of this word cannot be fathomed. That is the word God and its adjective, divine. Look in any German dictionary [102] and the word Spirit is also described very unsatisfactorily, but still slightly better than the word God. You only get as far as knowing that the word God is of unknown origin. There are all manner of hypotheses, but it remains unknown. Is one still going to be shocked in face of such a learned result and the assertion that so many people speak of God and the Divine and have no idea what they are talking about? Of course, because they are using a word of unknown origin to describe, well, whatever they happen to wish to describe. The matter is more serious than they want to admit. But people don't want their usages to die out and don't know how strongly they live by phrases nor how happy they feel to be able to live in those phrases. That is one thing. But others can also be found.

If one tackles what is real in what people experience today when they—even transcending their denominations—speak of their God, the God they experience inwardly, whether they name it mystically or theosophically, one finds in countless instances that people say: Everything depends only on experiencing God within, on becoming one with God! With what is one actually becoming one? If one investigates what it is with which people become one, albeit without realizing it, it is nothing but their own soul, as it was before it entered physical existence pre-natally or, rather, before conception—how this soul lived between its last death and its present birth. Today people pray—even if they want to be upstandingly religious—either to their Angel or to their own I as it was before their birth or conception. They call it God, designating it with a word of unknown origin; yet what they feel looming upwards from their unconscious is actually their own self. And the curious aspect that comes to light for anyone who can see through to reality is that, from every pulpit, there is endless talk of predestination but—since this is unthinkable without repeated earthly lives—this is in fact talk of earthly life—that is, of one's own self, which goes through this life—while denying the fact of repeated earthly lives. In truth, there is talk of nothing other than what anthroposophy wants to bring to conscious human knowledge.

Now people find it necessary to give this a name of unknown origin. They are actually talking about something that looms upwards out of their unconscious and can be experienced mystically. They call it the Union of Man with God. In reality it is the union of Man with themselves, with their own self, as it was before their birth. In calling it God, people are being challenged to worship themselves. What is celebrated as religion nowadays is largely idolatry, idolatrous worship of the self. It is important to address this today because it represents the entire seriousness of reality. Yet it is simultaneously uncomfortable because it points to the enormous, deep-running deception pervading our lives.

What led to this deceitful lie about life is something to which I have often referred: that in the year 869, at the general Ecumenical Council of Constantinople, the spirit was abolished. I also mentioned that those philosophically judgement-free people basing themselves on prejudice-free science today speak of human beings consisting of body and soul. In truth, the human being consists of body, soul and spirit. But talk of spirit was proscribed in the year 869. And nothing—nothing at all—was as proscribed by Christian philosophers of medieval times as talk of the so-called trichotomy, which included the spirit. No sooner had this trichotomy been abandoned—out of which, for example, Dionysios the Areopagite[103] proceeded in writings that were copied as late as the sixth century, and which still speak of the higher hierarchies—as soon as leave was taken of what is still disputed today—of the ancient Gnosis, which has to confront us today but which was, in its time, something immensely lofty—no sooner does one take leave of all this and take intellectual comfort into account, one is also gradually pre-condemned to speaking of something that led to a terrible deception in life. Because spiritual science has to speak the truth in these matters, it is no wonder that the most vehement opposition is aroused. Nowadays there is a large-scale lack of commitment to what human beings wish to bring to expression in their inner lives and it is really the case that most people have totally forgotten how to listen with their souls.

Often, crass manifestations of this surface. It no longer matters to people what is actually being said: everything depends on what they themselves have to say, quite regardless of its appropriateness. This is no isolated phenomenon; it is typical and it occurs at every turn. I could mention not hundreds but thousands of examples. It occurs in literature and across the board worldwide.

Things of this kind, spiritual conceptions in present times, are closely connected with impulsions driving the present, with what the present is carrying out and what has ultimately led to this catastrophe. One has to return to this time and again. There are always people today who feel compelled to speak of loving their neighbours, of committing to others lovingly and with understanding. But in reality this is not accurate; in reality the underlying mood is that which Fritz Mauthner[104] expresses in the case of Boll,[105] with whom you are acquainted, where he roundly upbraids someone who actually agrees with him.

These are instances which express—in typically characteristic form—what we need to focus on clearly and sharply at present. Only when we have developed the will to forge ahead into such matters will we find the perspective necessary to make progress and to make sense of where karma places us within human evolution.

Above all, we will need to recognize the following today: it will be absolutely vital to observe what has been evolving in a person's essential being between their last death and present birth. We will not be able to continue duping ourselves nor creating illusions through self-deification or self-worship, by calling what we find within us 'God', which is in truth our own genuine I. We will no longer be able to succumb to such self-deception, but will have to look to our legacy from spiritual worlds, which each individual brings with them through their birth into physical existence. Where is that actually? Yes, my dear friends, we bring it all with us, we bring immense wisdom with us and inherit spiritual treasure for our birth into physical life. But where is this wisdom? By being born, we are all so wise that we cannot believe how wise we are. But where does this wisdom reside? On the one hand it dwells, enchanted, having united with our bodily nature and its disposition and, on the other, in our destiny. It longs to be released from this. The potential lies within the present cycle of human time to release this legacy by free human activity, to raise it upwards through higher I-knowledge and release from enchantment what lies dormant in our destiny. We can gain some insight into this by making clear to ourselves that the present human being lives quite differently from the human being of bygone cultural epochs.

I want to remind you of something previously mentioned.[106] I said that, in the first cultural epoch of post-Atlantean times, human beings existed quite differently from today's humanity. As regards their soul-spiritual life, they participated in the processes taking place in their physical bodies. Just as we as children experienced the change of teeth as a special turning point, sexual maturity as a soul change, the human being of the first post-Atlantean age experienced their physical maturing right into their fifties. There then followed a time in which this experience of evolving ended in humans' forties and, later still, ended in their thirties. We are now only conscious of our maturing into our twenties. It is only into our twenties that we experience what is maturing physically-corporeally in our bodies; thereafter we are to some extent liberated. We can no longer experience the quality we did during our descending, incarnating years; we now have to experience it by allowing ourselves to be fired by what is spiritual. Spiritual science has to give the impulsion to release and to redeem whatever lies *enthralled* in our bodies and our destinies. Modern education is very far from reaching any such insight—let alone pressing ahead with it. We will have to forge insight into this: that the motivation has to be laid in early youth to learn how to grow old. People nowadays do not know how to grow old. At most they notice that their hair turns grey or—how often!—that their hair is receding, or other signs of ageing, but this is not the essential feature that can be present: the expectation, the hopeful expectation, of each new year in the certainty that we can learn something new with each passing year that could not have been learnt any earlier. Each year brings something new, each year brings new revelations, if only we understand how to put them to use.

The mood must surely dawn in human beings by which they reflect: I'm going to be twenty. The thirty-to-forty-year-old has something I cannot yet access. I will have to wait until that 'something' is revealed to me. Just think—in every detail—what this would mean: if education were to lay the foundations for awaiting—with hopeful anticipation—all that lies ahead in life. The very opposite mood is fostered nowadays. People want to be elected to parliaments and assemblies in the first flush of youth because they believe they are optimal in every respect and are fully furnished personalities. What you now find is young whippersnappers, both male and female, who proclaim at every opportunity: That's my view! Everyone has their own point of view nowadays, from earliest youth onwards. People do not have any idea whatsoever about waiting in hopeful anticipation of something, that life contains mysteries which are only unveiled in stages. It would be quite something if this came into education. Then one would have the will gradually to release and redeem what has been enchanted and lies enthralled in our bodies and our destinies.

Anyway, we will have to view culture, as it gradually unfolds, in a quite particular light if we want some clarity in these issues. You will have to ask yourselves: Where does one find the right standpoint, the right perspective, to release and redeem what lies enchanted within us? Yes, indeed, you may want to frame the question slightly differently: Why should one want to redeem what is captivated under a spell within? Isn't it more comfortable to leave all that to our blood, nerves and flesh? Then it could just stay there until one died, went over into the other world, where it could eke out its existence. Just leave destiny to the nerves and muscles in which it is captivated. Why does it need redeeming? One should—and one must—redeem it because the ways of the spirit are subject to their own specific laws. What has been bequeathed to us as a gift of legacy from spiritual realms wants to be redeemed, longs to be freed from captivity. And this begins with being brought to consciousness. What lies in body and destiny longs to migrate aloft into consciousness. Its rightful refuge is within our consciousness. It ought to live in our consciousness and not remain under enchantment in our nervous system, in our circulation, in our muscles or our bones. For if it does remain in nerves, muscles, bones or amidst an indeterminate, undefined destiny that is merely borne, then this spiritual element is transformed into something quite different: into impoverished forces. It is predetermined to be taken up by consciousness and carried into life. If it remains outwith consciousness yet still united with the person, it is transformed into either luciferic or ahrimanic forces, and is gradually given over to Lucifer or Ahriman.

Luciferic forces have long been reckoned with in our Western cultural evolution, and it is now resigned—due to a particularly well-regarded spiritual stream—to dealing with ahrimanic forces and to onward life with them. People are to be installed in life, to find their allotted place in life: that is the aim of their upbringing. Certain motivational impulses, certain sensations, certain feelings are nurtured. Which of these impulses, these feelings, are put to use? Look around you in the world; it is now on the decrease and will soon be of little meaning, but it has meant a great deal for centuries: Orders, badges of honour, titles, virtues. But what lies behind all this? Feelings and sensations that grant consent to strive for them, compulsions and desires that amplify luciferic tendencies among humanity. Just think how much luciferic striving existed, was cultivated in human nature, in order to put human beings—diverted via this luciferic tendency—into positions they were intended to occupy. That was the luciferic period. It is now on the ebb. It is hardly worth talking about any more, because what happens in this respect is on the wane. Even if people don't believe the extent to which this is happening, they will soon notice it. It is talk of a direction on the wane if one is talking about actual luciferic cultural influences.

Yet ahrimanic forces are menacingly on the rise. An example of this would be: at the moment people—how would one put it?—go through the 'academic jungle' in German and other cultures, vaingloriously introducing what promises so vastly much by way of advancing humankind in the future: intelligence testing, talent screening. Within academia some very peculiar plants have recently sprung up: every hue of psychologist and soul researcher, conducting experimental psychologies, investigating human beings, probing psyches, who have lately also been pitching into young people, considering them fair game. Because people can no longer deal with old examinations and the social order of yesteryear, young people are next in line for intelligence testing, so that—in language already widespread in rarified circles—'the right person for the right job' can be identified. Obviously, children will have to start being tested so as to identify 'the right sort of person'. Concept-capability is tested and all manner of tests are constructed: how quickly a child can guess this or that, whether it can work out the function of a baffling item. Intelligence and memory are tested; intelligence, for example, by showing the child or young person two unconnected words—mirror and robber—and expecting them to meaningfully link them, using some concept. One child saying that even a thief looking in a mirror is seeing himself, will possibly be considered the least intelligent. Another will think: the one from whom the thief is stealing—or even being killed by—has a mirror, sees the thief coming from afar and can save himself—that girl or boy might be thought the brighter one.

Some magazines are running brain-teasing, hair-tearing ways of testing intelligence; they are being developed as a particularly successful means of statistical analysis, putting memory and brainpower to the test. Those able to say most—be it about, say, thieves and mirrors—will earn two or more marks—rather like on the census—with the one collecting the most such marks, making the most connections, being designated the brainiest. These are the young women and men who will be given access to specialist colleges and will be supported by all manner of means. What is typical of these achievements so praised by humanity—and the boldest pedagogues set great store by astuteness testing—is that they come absolutely no closer to *soul elements*, but only test in people what is ahrimanically dependent on their bodies. Thus the only thing being tested is how strongly Ahriman can ripen in a given young person. What is being introduced into human culture are ahrimanic impulsions. Yet today people simply succumb to these delusions and deceptions.

The most important aspect of our spiritual science is that its seriousness be recognized. Certainly, one can gather in small conventicles and, as I said, read cosy lectures among family-like friends. That does no harm nor, by extension, does what may ensue from without. But as soon as spiritual science starts to become more widespread, so must our seriousness increase, a seriousness which can only consist in committing unconditionally to what needs to be taken up in the context of everything evolving around us. It is essential that we understand this as deeply as possible; essential also that we nurture mobility of spirit, which will enable us to emerge from sectarianism into a worldly-wise, cultured conception of what our spiritual-scientific movement should exemplify. For diverse initiatives need to arise out of spiritual science—healthy initiatives in contrast to the widespread emergence of decadent and degenerate impulsions. Above all, freedom and self-reliance of spirit are essential for what longs to enter this spiritual-scientific movement.

Belief in authority does not in the least align with us; only does acquiring free and independent discernment. For nothing said about spiritual science can be generalized nor universalized; everything applies individually, everything is concretely valid for each specific case. It is a certain indolence that prompts people to generalize, but this cannot happen once one enters spiritual realms. Today we need—we really need—to commit to knowledge that doesn't merely remain in abstract or mystical generalities but which proceeds from a grasp of spirituality and penetrates into reality. Some may believe themselves to be great mystics, making their solitary way through the world, undisturbed by world events, believing God to be experienced within. But that is 'thin' spirituality, so thin that it fails to penetrate the reality existing in the world. Mystics of this kind are not called for by the present. Loners can claim mysticism because it lulls them into the comforting belief that their elevated souls are experiencing loftiness. But the present demands strong spirituality which acts incisively in immediate reality. It demands not only talk of higher hierarchies but such probing awareness of the higher hierarchies that, proceeding from such recognition, insight into what surrounds us on Earth can be won. Because the time is now beginning when order will no longer be found in human affairs unless genuine insight into the essence of what is evolving here on Earth is won—even if that proves uncomfortable.

Read the lecture cycle I gave in Kristiania[107] quite some time before the war in order to prepare for today; it concerned the connection and structure of individual Folk Souls. There you will see that you can take seriously what the higher hierarchies recognize and can apply it to the configuration of the Earth. Knowledge of this kind is essential for the present time, because knowledge has to provide the practical foundation for what needs to be undertaken in future. You will have to recognize what needs to be done, not on the basis of rhetorical scribblings and chatter—such as today expounds on issues of European populations and ethnicity, based on purported observation—but you will really have to delve trenchantly into the impulses active on Earth that issue from spiritual worlds.

Admittedly, people today think they have something to say in every circumstance because they have experienced something. Do you really think someone living a simple life in a remote Provence village between 1789 and 1800 has anything very enlightening to say about the French Revolution? They experienced it; they are not required to comment extensively! Similarly, countless people go to America or to Italy and can, as they like to put it, give you chapter and verse on the country and its people. Yet what they say doesn't need to be of enormous value when assessing what is needed there. This latter involves having the opportunity to delve into the substrata of existence. For this we need, as far as I'm concerned, neither to embrace nor to reject materialism, nor indeed embrace nor reject spiritualism. No, for the researcher into reality, for the spiritual researcher in our case, it must be a matter of indifference whether their starting point is materialism or spiritualism. We don't need to despise materialism in every situation—that is not the crux of the matter, because it is of no consequence whether you start from materialism or spiritualism—if we are just going from A to B! Whoever really observes matter to its bitter end will find—in all that happens materially around us—spirit! And whoever wants the support of the spiritual and continually cries 'spirit, spirit, spirit' ought above all to find a way from an abstract concept of spirit to a concrete conception of what takes place materially. Because what takes place materially is a manifestation of spirit, though you have to develop the correct belief in what is spiritual. Those who do not have a life filled with anticipation—with the expectant hope that with each new year new mysteries may radiate into us through our growing older—they actually believe, however much they speak of God and spirit, in neither God nor spirit. For they believe, at the ripe age of twenty-five, to be totally discernment-competent. The rest of their lives—as regards their souls—will then be of little use or value; the Godhead will then reveal nothing further.

You have to forge ahead with spirit right into the material and grasp it. What is spiritual has to be so condensed that it can find materiality. If we conceive of the material phenomena generally existing in the external world only in terms of what is within us, we would need to say: There is an abyss between the outer world and what occurs within us. Spiritual science alone is capable of bringing externality closer to us and bringing us closer to externality so that the two meet. We can do this for individual human beings and we can do this for Earth evolution. Issues of this kind have to be grasped. Natural science, as I indicated yesterday,[108] is the very least equipped to grasp that the head is to be understood as being in regression while the extremities are over-developed. It is particularly important that we understand such concepts. How does one get hold of them?

They can be grasped by going beyond conventional ideas, beyond abstraction, by creating an imaginative view of our own imagination. One cannot view one's own imagining without simultaneously nearing what goes on materially in our heads during the process of imagining. In habitually imagining habitual consciousness, one doesn't notice what goes on in one's head. That can only be observed once one has ascended to Imaginative thinking; then one can participate in experiencing the material process.

And do you know what goes on in our heads while we are developing normal consciousness? A process of hunger is taking place. Wakeful imaginative life consists in our head being hungry. Those faux ascetics and mystics knew this instinctively, which is why they allowed their entire body to starve. It is not normal, however, for spiritual experiences to arise by starving the body. That is always wrong. The fasting ascetic, hoping for mystical entrancement, is exercising an unhealthy one-sidedness. The state of equilibrium in our bodies is normally disposed such that, from morning to evening, from external awakening until falling asleep, our heads—not our entire bodies—are in a constant state of hunger. Our heads are chronically under-nourished, something inherent in regression, in regressive development. Due to the under-nourishment of our heads we are in a state that makes way for imaginative spiritual life. Those who learn to know imaginative spiritual life through Imagination are aware of what others only know in its baser manifestation as the rumbling of their stomachs: that from morning till falling asleep at night, our heads suffer rumbling pangs of hunger. This shows what we could describe as the spiritual advancing on the material in our own lives. One-sided mysticism is a comforting immersion in our interiors, where little more is experienced than a slightly denser version of what we usually encounter. True spiritual development involves strengthening spiritual life such that, when applied to our own experience, we come to know ourselves more accurately, far more accurately. We also come to know physical corporeality better, because this is brought closer to us, so that corporeality is raised towards spirituality, bridging the abyss that is otherwise always present between what is spiritual and what is physical.

This is how the abyss between spirit and physical can be bridged, also in the life of peoples. We ought to look at European Folk Souls, at least at some of them. You know—from the lecture cycle about the Folk Souls—about the connection between leading beings of the higher hierarchies and peoples. They are beings from the hierarchy of Archangels, the Archangeloi. But how do they work? Initially expressed in abstraction: an Archangel is the leader of one nation or another. In saying this, we are no further than talking about the human soul which, between birth and death, can only exist here because it has a material base from which to evolve, namely our bodies. Likewise an Archangel who, in leading a people, is connected with external materiality. The connection between the purely spiritual being of an Archangel and that of a people is a material one, even if this is not so distinctively outlined nor sharply contoured as our bodies. We ask, for example: How is this the case with the population of the Apennine Peninsula—those Romans of old, a once-Germanic people who are now Italians? Basically, the majority of the population in that area are transformed Germanic peoples, yet they owe their configuration, their folk-determinacy, to something else: in their breathing process—in the air they breathe—their Archangel is, as it were, 'aired in'—one cannot quite call this inhaling incarnating. In breathing in—and with—air, the inhabitants of the Italian peninsula connect with their Archangel. Whoever wants to study this in depth, so that they come to a real recognition of what is actually at work here, will have to make the idiosyncratic connection between the population of the Italian peninsula—the Iberian peninsula likewise, but to a lesser degree—with breathing and with air. They will have to find out how air and this particular breathing process are co-mingled within human inner life.

It is different with the population presently inhabiting France. Here the Archangel casts a different bridging connection, one which works through all that develops the human organism through liquid. French people widely drink in the folk character with their wines and also with the other fluid elements that feature in their organism. You see, in this way you arrive not merely at an abstract depiction of the connection between the spiritual world and the physical. Here is an outline, which similarly only hints at the Archangel, while, down below, human beings go about their lives and are guided by their Archangel. Spiritual science can elucidate processes such as these so that they can be grasped in all their concrete reality.

The inhabitants of the British Isles[109] receive what their Archangel bestows with the solidity evolving in their bodies. They absorb it by forming solid components in their bodies that connect with their solid structure. Obviously only applicable in a restricted sense—and here radically expressed—yet this is not just a mordant truth but a spiritual-scientific verity: the Archangel affects the British through their eating of beefsteaks. This is obviously not meant in any chauvinistic sense, because every single individual is an exception in themselves; it is only applicable to one aspect of the human being, yet inasmuch as each also belongs to their people, this principle is active in them. It will only be possible to learn about the world as a whole if future generations are not afraid to research such things further. People have an incurable fear of the truth, because from truth uncomfortable issues naturally ensue. Yet as soon as you take truth seriously, it is essential not to shrink back in horror in face of your discomfort.

Let us turn to America: purely from their external configuration, it is clear how dependent human beings are on what radiates from the ground! In Italy, it is from out of the air, in France from water, in Britain from what defines solidity entering the body or causing it to be solid. It is quite different in America.

You will find in every quarter that spiritual science finds its confirmation in reality. It is just that this confirmation is not yet being sought. In a lecture, I once posited[110] that the evolution of the consciousness soul—which particularly emphasizes the human ego or egotism—is externally, materially exaggerated by sugar. I indicated at the time how vastly greater sugar consumption is in the British Isles than, for example, among the selfless Russian people, where sugar consumption is far, far less. But when I describe how it is only around the fifteenth century that the consciousness soul is in the ascendant, one need only observe the increase in sugar production, which also begins in the fifteenth century. Where does sugar production actually originate? From the fifteenth century onwards, people start to become dependent on sugar. Everything genuinely educed from spiritual worlds by spiritual science is fully substantiated precisely when it evolves spiritually to such a strong degree that it is able to plunge into materiality, where it then exists and has to be recognized. As soon as one transits to America one finds—not just externally—that Europeans who have emigrated evolve different arms and legs over the course of time; their limbs then resemble more closely those of original, first nation 'Indian' populations, who have been so depleted. This also applies to the configuration of facial forms, even though it may arise quietly in third and fourth generations. Obviously, we are not imagining that, within the span of several generations, smug British worthies come to resemble original ethnicities, yet certain faint resemblances can sometimes be detected facially. Subtle phenomena of this kind need to be faced, because it is only through knowledge that genuine, true love can develop across the world. Love can only be engendered by finding one's way towards other human beings. For this one needs to grow to know them. Their Folk Spirit works upwards into American folk from the substrata of the Earth, through magnetic and electrical forces slumbering in the Earth. It is the subterranean that radiates upwards, endowing America with the means whereby the Folk Spirit can guide people native there.

Turning now to Central Europe: here it is a good idea to allow people to reflect for themselves. However, a few things can be mentioned. Actually, there are intensely limber, unstable and highly personal elements connected with the material manifestation and ramifications of the Folk Spirit. These are primarily the effects of warmth upon warmth. The differentiation that arises between being warm externally and inner warmth, warmth in winter, the warmth of spring, of summer, in short everything expressed through varying states of warmth: that is the medium through which the Folk Spirit works in Central Europe. Everything originating in differentiations of warmth on the blood circulation and breathing is the indirect route whereby the Folk Spirit is affective here. You can also follow this at a soul level. We still have the opportunity—unlike Fritz Mauthner—to sense, in elements of speech, the after-effects of what

I might call the warmed-through quality of feeling. If one has not been abandoned by all the good spirits of speech, one is still able—in German, for instance—to feel one's way into language—not just abstractly, not just stopping short at the abstract stage—but by sensing the spirit of the language, because physical warmth is related to soul warmth. Nothing is more physically interrelated with the soul than soul warmth; likewise its opposite, cold. What lives in the sentient soul is more alien to air; what lives in the intellectual or mind soul is far more alien to the element of water; and indeed what lives in the consciousness soul is alien to beefsteaks or, rather, to Earth. And most terribly alien to the human soul is what comes to expression in magnetic or electrical forces radiating from the subterranean into human evolution in the American folk character. This is one reason why so much in an American's folk character looks as though it were obsessed with what it is doing, in contrast with a Central European, who has to be present in soul, accompanying on a soul level everything they are doing, hence also able to generate mystical warmth. By contrast, Americans may easily evolve a psychic-spiritualistic frame of mind; may become possessed by elements that do not directly stream into human beings—such as air, water, earth—but primarily by subterranean forces working upwards and forming the very structures of populations.

In the Russian character, in what is being prepared in the East, the Folk Spirit works through light—though it will only be called upon to play its unique role through its people in future. We will return to this the day after tomorrow. It works through light, though not directly through the light raying down from the Sun but through light first absorbed by vegetation and the Earth itself, and then radiated back again. These Sun forces—this sunlight, rayed back from the ground, from Earth and vegetation—is the medium used by the Russian Folk Spirit to effect and create folk structures and folk dispositions.

If you observe this in all its detail—we shall return to it the day after tomorrow—you will see how the present and the near future do not require vague, nebulous mysticism full of empty phrases, but such a strongly spiritual recognition of spirit that it can plunge down, can penetrate, the material existence with which we have to live. So that material existence, in its relationship with the spirit, is not viewed as something to be got rid of nor, as it were, purged from under one's skin in order to reach the spirit—as has been the mistaken case in the past—but that material be seen as a revelation of spirit.

Those unable to see that what is physical is in truth a manifestation of the spirit do not yet have the right attitude towards the spirit. Everything surrounding us is a body of the spirit. Only if we are able to conceive of spirit such that we see nature as a body of the spirit, only then are we in a position to gain real spirit knowledge. This is concrete spiritual knowledge, and we need to aim for knowledge such as this. Aren't these precisely the issues—once one has approached them with the requisite deep seriousness—which modern people find so uncomfortable; truths they do not love at all, and instead of which they would most prefer to hear: Human beings across the world ought to love one another! Yes, definitely, but they must first grow to recognize each other. Love has to become independent of what approaches you in knowledge; and yet love can only become independent if it approaches us in knowledge. Everything I have described, including everything I characterized around the Folk Souls, you know this, your nerves, your blood, your muscles know this: this is where it lies, enchanted, captivated, and it is from here that it needs salvaging. If it is not retrieved in the near future, it will rumble and fester in nerves, muscle and blood, spreading throughout the world as disharmony, as compulsions to strife and war. Preventing this from coming about can only be achieved by the spirit—which is otherwise distorted into its luciferic or ahrimanic counter-image—being released, redeemed from nerves, muscles and blood and brought to consciousness, because it is only in consciousness that spirit longs to live here on Earth. Only in consciousness is spirit in its rightful environs. Only there can spirit guide humanity towards what it must attain in future. Spirit cannot be allowed to remain abandoned in luciferic and ahrimanic domains because, if it cannot find its rightful place, it distorts. Spirit's capacity to transform itself needs to be understood, because in recognizing this lie the tasks of the future. You cannot frivolously elevate yourself to the state demanded of humanity for the future; instead it is vital to delve deeply, with knowledge, to resolve the tasks of the future. For this you need to overcome certain discomforts. And because humans do not want to overcome discomfort, they will increasingly become enemies of a spiritual evolution. You will have to reckon with this, especially once spiritual science becomes more widespread. You will have to reckon with it all the more, the stronger anthroposophy becomes and the more you all take up the challenge of moving forwards, away from comfortable sectarianism towards world-citizen perspectives, working on a worldwide scale, spreading spiritual science abroad; out of those nice front- and back-parlours to all the places where you best believe you need to affect—and deal with—the concerns of humanity.

That is what I wanted to speak about today. We'll continue the day after tomorrow.

# Lecture 12

4 MAY 1918, MUNICH

FROM the considerations of the day before yesterday—and in the wider context of recent public lectures[111]—it will be apparent that there is a particular urgency for humanity to develop spiritual-scientific interests at the present time. For spiritual science, among its other tasks, is in a position to provide humanity—and in a more focused way, each individual—with clarity in respect of mind, soul disposition and life's essentials; clarity for issues with which modern human beings absolutely have to engage. It was precisely from this perspective that I drew attention to the urgent need for seriousness in those wishing to approach and focus on spiritual science while allowing it to work upon individual souls. There is a need to attempt to investigate, in the most diverse areas, how humanity has come to be in such a catastrophic situation. The significance of this catastrophic situation is still not being seen in its full seriousness and depth by many people. However, the time will come when events—the facts themselves—will manifest seriousness by means quite different from those of today. Especially from a standpoint of spiritual science, it ought to be clear that it is not enough simply to wait until the last moment to grasp what needs to be understood in face of the deeply-founded demands of this time. Above all, it is essential to acknowledge that certain truths vital to humankind—both at present and in the near future—are extremely uncomfortable, and that it is far more comfortable to go along with all the songs in praise of the great cultural and scientific achievements, which have brought us thus far, than to focus on what lives and works in human relationships across the whole world, on what to some extent lives and works in conditioning present humanity. Present-day human beings are being challenged in many ways and are necessarily being led into understanding a thing or two; but some things that need to be understood are simply difficult and demand of us an absence of tentativeness and a prejudice-free discernment in regarding our own human nature.

In evolution, certain tendencies persist through time. Hypothetically, one could say: It might well be possible to continue seeing as great what I mentioned yesterday: aptitude or intelligence testing. Some educationalists propagate this view, considering it hugely progressive while the rest of the population avoids forming an opinion, finding it hard not to sleep through the ahrimanic tendencies being introduced by way of testing intelligence and much else. If such efforts and ideals—after all, they too are ideals—persist in gaining the upper hand, they will have a profound influence on the entire evolution of the human soul and above all a specifically-configured influence on the fundamental forces of the human soul: on thinking, feeling and willing. You cannot even ask hypothetically, as this should not arise in the first place; because the matter should be helpfully deflected by those who subscribe to an anthroposophical world view. Yet you can ask yourself a hypothetical question to ascertain what you have to do about it: What sort of configuration would the main soul forces of thinking, feeling and willing display if the present materialistic-ahrimanic tendency *alone* were to seize control? If no spiritual striving, no spiritual willing were to counteract it? So enormously powerful are these effects in the field of technology—fed in turn by natural science and related fields of natural-scientific endeavour—that human imagination and human thinking in particular will gradually and increasingly become imprinted with narrow-minded, bigoted characteristics. This cannot be described in any other way and I would say that the beginnings of such bigotry and narrow-mindedness are already widely visible in our surroundings. It will consist in ever increasingly transgressing against what was mentioned yesterday in my public lecture: transgressing against opening up our souls to the entire world. People will increasingly restrict themselves to hearing only in theoretical and intellectual terms what their ideas, concepts and imagination are telling them. I want to state publicly that two people may say exactly the same words and yet we are not justified in assuming that what those two people say *is* in fact exactly the same.

Today we are living in an age of programmes. The age of programmes is one of intellectualism. What do people like to do best today when offering themselves in the cause of humanity's wellbeing? They found associations for everything imaginable and set up programmes and ideals. These can of course be very sage, well-intentioned and plausible; but for the evolution of humanity they need not be worth a tinker's cuss. But then you ask yourself: What does the person concerned want? And when that person says—let's take an abstract example; everyone loves abstraction—I'd like to cultivate universal human love, then you think: What could be more beautiful? Obviously, I need to join an association like that! Yet we live at a time when, due to culture having reached a certain surfeit, it is easy to set up the nicest programmes with the nicest ideas. In the process you can become—in terms of interest in the general wellbeing of humanity and its true situation—a very narrow, limited person. Nowadays, I'd say, you may sometimes be right—in a refined cultural sense—in matters about which, in the view of many people, you may be completely mistaken. For instance, you might find yourself valuing poetic stammering—which could possibly betoken inner strength of soul in reality—more highly than perfect verse, which simply arises as such because, as regards poetry's outer configuration—language itself—the spirit of language writes verse today and only uses the human soul for this purpose. Someone can still write brilliant verse within old formats though they lack strong soul forces. Things of this kind need to be taken into account at a time such as this when great—vastly great—questions are facing human evolution.

It has to be said: human beings must learn to open their whole soul to every other whole soul. They need to learn to place ever less value on the content of what is being said while gaining ever greater insight into the wisdom and power of what a person is actually able to *place into* the world. We are experiencing the most terrible world-historical drama because right across the world people bow down to fundamentalism—such as that emanating from Woodrow

Wilson[112]—because these fundamentalist principles make sense, because they cannot be refuted. Of course they make sense, of course they cannot be gainsaid, but they are as old as human thinking: thus it has ever been expressed. In all this there is nothing whatsoever to do with the real, concrete and immediate tasks in hand. Yet people find it uncomfortable to involve themselves in real, concrete and immediate tasks while developing mobility in their thinking. For this mobility in thinking involves engaging with the immediate, concrete tasks in hand. It may admittedly take quite a while to find your way into such concreteness; but it is important to understand such things now and to insert yourself a little into the course of human evolution.

There is a town peopled by a South German population. Here, in the eighteenth century, an important person was born: Johann Heinrich Lambert.[113] Johann Heinrich Lambert's contemporary, Kant, called him the greatest genius of his century; for had Lambert's ideas only replaced those of the so-called Kant-Laplace theory, something really significant would have emerged. Lambert grew up in a town in southern Germany, the son of a tailor and showed exceptional gifts at the age of fourteen. His father sought financial support from the sage Municipal Councillor who, after much deliberation, was moved to grant the gifted youngster forty francs on condition that he never again ask for support. A hundred years were to elapse before, in the nineteenth century, the town would fund a memorial to the man they hounded out of town as a fourteen-year-old. He had had to leave the town and, through exceptional circumstances, attained greatness in Berlin. Now there is a fine monument in his honour on which the globe of the world is set on high, indicating that this genius, capable of spanning the globe, was nurtured and flourished thanks to the very ground of that great, powerful city!

Sometimes it may take more than a century to appreciate the talent swilling around, something that may have persisted into—or may still persist in—our times. How often has it been emphasized among us that time has been edging onwards and human beings need to wake up to free consciousness, consciousness that is dependent only on itself, consciousness in which people can no longer be allowed to sleep through all that is going on around them. That time has been approaching in giant strides and people need to learn to open their souls so that they can see what is actually there. Because, as has been said, due to the peculiar configuration of materialistic culture, thinking and imagination are under threat from restrictive pettiness and chauvinism. Spiritual science provides ideas and concepts that do not allow you to become narrow-minded in your thinking. We are continually being challenged—precisely by spiritual-scientific concepts—to view everything from various angles. This is what annoys some people among the ranks of anthroposophists when they hear: Here comes another lecture cycle, which will approach the subject from a completely different angle. It is unavoidable that issues are grappled with from several perspectives, so that you ultimately emerge with something I'd like to call 'rendering discernment absolute'.[114] Truth captured in spirit is not easy to render in sharp contour because spirit is mobile. So spiritual science works against bigotry at a thinking level. It is difficult to say this at present, of course, but it is necessary.

The second element which can be observed in the soul is feeling. In respect of feeling—the realm of feeling—what is the influence emanating from materialistic culture which aspires to affect human beings? One can say: In this area, especially, a great degree of success has been met with. Within feeling, materialistic culture causes pettiness and philistinism. Philistinism aims to grow to gigantic proportions and materialistic culture is heavily predisposed towards enabling this. Petty meanness of interest! People want to close themselves off in smaller and smaller circles. But today human beings are not called to close themselves off in small circles; they are called to recognize that they are tones in the great cosmic symphony.

Let us once again turn our attention to what is meant here, to what has been mentioned here, and view it from a comprehensive perspective. I would like to say: One can calculate—and calculating is much admired nowadays—how wonderfully the human being is integrated into the cosmos. In every minute, the number of breaths we take is around eighteen. Multiplied by sixty and twenty-four, this gives us within every day: 25,920 breaths. Within twenty-four hours: 25,920 breaths! Work out the following: you know that every year the vernal equinox—the point at which the Sun rises in spring [115]—moves forward [sic] onward by a fraction around the dome of Heaven. Going back to remote ages: at the start of spring, the Sun used to rise in Taurus, further back and it rose a little further back in Taurus, still further back until the Sun rose in Aries and continuing further and further back, thus did the Sun course through the Heavens, seemingly naturally. How many years does the Sun require to progress, little by little, until it arrives at the same point once again? Making such small precessional movements, the Sun takes 25,920 years to complete a round of the zodiac—as many years as we breathe in one day. Just think, what marvellously consonant harmony! We breathe 25,920 times a day while the Sun moves forwards [sic] onwards and, when it has done this 25,920 times—as we move inwardly with each breath—it has completed a circuit of the cosmos, of the zodiac. In this way our breathing is an image of the macrocosm.

And it continues: the average lifespan—which of course can be longer, though others die earlier—is some seventy to seventy-one years. What in fact is this human life? It, too, is a sum of breaths, but these are different breaths. During normal physical breathing we suck air in and force it out again. Over the course of twenty-four hours—if we are ordinary upright folk and our nights aren't *wasted*—our ego and astral body make a great inhalation on waking and exhale ego and astral again on falling asleep; that is also one entire breath. Every day, one breath of our physical and ether bodies encounters our ego and astral body. How often does this take place over the course of a lifetime of some seventy or seventy-one years? Work out how many days a human being lives: 25,920 days! This means that not only do we reflect with our breaths over one day the course of the Sun as it goes its cosmic round—by breathing as many times in a day as the Sun takes years to return to the same point in the cosmos—but we take the same number of greater breaths—breathing in our I and astral body into our ether and physical bodies and exhaling these again—as we make in seventy to seventy-one years: 25,920. This demonstrates how our human life is integrated—number-wise and otherwise—into the great harmony of the universe. However many examples we might find, they would be no less astonishing, no less encouraging than rightly feeling what I have just described. There is a great deal concealed in the correlations between human and cosmos, but what is unknown has profound effects because it is actually identical with what was encapsulated in ancient times as the Harmony of the Spheres.

This awakens our interest in the whole world. We gradually begin to understand that we know nothing of ourselves as human beings if we restrict our interests in philistine fashion to our immediate surroundings. However, such is ever increasingly the hallmark of modern times: Philistinism! Boorish ignorance! Yes, philistinism especially has become the prevailing mood of the religious world view; an underlying tenor of philistinism has radiated into the minds of many. If you go back to the first centuries of Christianity, there were teachings which were magnificent. They were appropriate for those times. Today they need to be complemented by spiritual-scientific perspective because differing times pose differing challenges for humanity; but in days gone by those teachings, the Gnosis, were mighty. Just look in which wonderful ways æons of research and enquiry into the various spiritual hierarchies the thinking of these Gnostics revealed, how this small Earth is aligned within cosmic evolution with its countless beings, yet within whose ranks the human being has been placed. Mobility of thinking and a quantity of goodwill is required to cultivate their concepts without allowing them to calcify or silt up, as is the way today if one tries to elevate oneself to Gnosis. What then followed was—not Christianity—but Christian denominationalism. Today you can ask around what it is that the majority of official representatives of Christianity hate most of all: Gnosis. Anthroposophy is blackened mainly because they themselves don't engage with anthroposophy at all, being too smugly comfortable, and yet they have—if they dip into one book or another—a dark inkling or notion that, for Heaven's sake, this might be one such Gnosis! 'We'd have to absorb some new concepts; we'd have to make our spirits agile! Having finally led people to simplicity in their thinking, especially on the religious front, who can guess', they muse, 'what might ensue next if one starts raising oneself up to such heights!' They claim: 'Human beings can reach those heights and attain to divinity with the simplest of minds. There is no need to exert oneself; the simplest, childlike mind can reach the loftiest divinity at any moment.'

Yes, you do need to see through such claims! It is a matter of really seeing through issues such as this—everything depends upon it. Because it is from this source that the fundamental mood radiates outwards into modern times, spreading parochial bourgeois philistinism. This is why the religious mood in the various denominations has become so narrow-minded: it is due to the underlying qualities just outlined. They flatter modern-day people who claim to be humble and self-effacing but who are basically anything but humble, because self-aggrandisement and megalomania are also underlying characteristics of our time. Everything is judged, no matter how hard the experience nor whether its hardness is engraved on one's brow; it will be judged, also by those who know perfectly well that they have not exerted themselves to gain wide experience, but have only bestirred themselves to arrive at the obvious: that they should not make much effort to recognize God, but that God will be revealed to their simple, childlike natures, should He wish, at any moment. So you must see that, above all, this parochialism has to be resisted by spiritual science. This boorish, narrow-minded bigotry still lies in a different quarter from that which might widely be expected, and many of those who think they have gone beyond philistinism are trapped in it to a depth well over their heads. Many–isms and other modernisms, which have made themselves into programmes specifically purporting not to contain any bourgeois attitudes, are nothing more than parochialism in a mask. That is the second thing. In the realm of thinking and conceptualizing, such encroaching petty-mindedness and bigotry—and on a feeling level the encroaching parochialism and *philistrosity*—have to be withstood. Instead, open-heartedness and interest have to seize their territory together with the will to really look into what is taking place on the great tableau of earthly evolution.

Yesterday we tried to portray in concrete form some effects of Folk Spirits. These are Archangels. From this you could gather that these Folk Spirits are connected with the regions in which certain peoples evolve on Earth. The Folk Spirit in Italy works through air, while it is through everything liquid that the Folk Spirit works in territories now in modern France, and so on in the ways I characterized. But of course much overlaps with sundry other aspects and one needs to be aware that, though people live cheek by jowl with each other on Earth, certain evolutionary phases may lag behind in one region or another. In some places people will move forwards, whereas other areas may be brought into decline. Now, something important can be observed. If we view the whole Earth as one great organism and ask ourselves: What is taking place across the globe? We can identify various regions of Asia or the Asiatic East, as some call it. In this Asiatic East many souls are incarnating today who, through their karma, through what they have brought with them from earlier incarnations, remain in some respects within the idiosyncrasies of earlier times: souls seeking bodies on which they are able to remain dependent on their corporeal-physical development into relatively old ages. It is the norm nowadays to be dependent on one's physical body only until one's twenty-seventh year. This is very significant in our time. Many phenomena can be understood if one focuses on such facts. I referred to one such earlier.

I once asked myself: How would a modern person, one supposed to be typical as to all their work and activities, find their way into contemporary life? They would to some extent need to shut out everything that would normally approach them from outside, influencing them to rely only upon themselves until the age of twenty-seven. This would necessarily create what we know as the self-made man. They would need to remain untouched by what normally and typically riddles our lives and, until the age of twenty-seven, would have to evolve in complete isolation and self-reliance. Straight after they had self-actuated what a modern person ought to be, they would, for instance, be elected to parliament. Doesn't being elected to parliament represent a certain pinnacle of achievement nowadays? For if, having been voted in, they were to become, say, a cabinet minister after a couple of years, they would in some respects be stigmatized, because people would notice if they subsequently came unstuck, took a tumble to left or right or suffered some misfortune. What happens then? How would they continue? They cannot evolve further; they remain a contemporary type, a thoroughgoing representative of their time. Such people are rife; something I said here not long ago: one such person is Lloyd George.[116] There is nobody who more typically, more characteristically, expresses the traits of this age than Lloyd George who, until the age of twenty-seven, manifested everything a person can possibly extract from their physical-corporeal existence. He was an autodidact, a self-taught person, early in life involved in socialism and learnt early on that he, obviously, belonged in parliament at twenty-seven. He was elected and soon became one of the most feared speakers and even—don't they call it that?—quite a blinker or squinter, always sitting there and glaring when others were speaking. Lloyd George was known for having something peculiar in his glance. Then there was the premiership of Campbell-Bannerman.[117] People said: What shall we do about Lloyd George? He's a menace. Best we make him a minister—and so they brought him into the cabinet. Yes, but into which ministerial post shall we put him? He's very talented! Let's put him in a job about which he knows nothing. That's where he'll be most useful and be least troublesome! He was made minster for railways and shipbuilding. Within a few months he had acquired the knowledge he needed and made the most brilliant reforms, among other great works.

The present personality type cannot be better portrayed than by describing Lloyd George. He is like a concentrated extract of the prevailing materialism and much can be understood about the present situation by enquiring into matters such as this. This is how things stand in a 'central world position', if I may put it like that, a place between the Asiatic East and the American West. It is particularly in European culture that one can—before the age of twenty-seven—extract from a physical-corporeal level what can also be meaningful for soul-spiritual purposes. A soul-spiritual impetus then has to be awakened in the soul if one wishes to progress and what is physical-corporeal no longer delivers support. That is why, in a person like Lloyd George, everything is sourced from what the present, by its very nature, offers and he possesses nothing whatsoever of what ought to be achieved by free effort. Naturally, the present provides much geniality, much gifted talent but nothing spiritual of its own accord. That has to be seized in freedom. But in Asia there is still wide opportunity to find bodies—beyond age twenty-seven or twenty-eight—that allow for soul-spiritual development to proceed in parallel. That is why souls incarnate in those regions who wish to extract forces from the physical-corporeal beyond those ages. That is also why there is still a naturally self-evident spiritual culture there, a culture that still maintains that our surroundings need to be viewed spiritually, that what is spiritual be recognized in the world. There is, however, a similarly great decadence gaining ground in parallel, decadence that is due to the spread of a materialism most unsuited to that culture, hence the correspondingly deep decadence. But in leading personalities one can see that this self-evident spirituality is present. They inwardly despise materialistic European culture, albeit in the most general way. People such as Rabindranath Tagore,[118] who recently gave a talk on the spirit of Japan, and who said: We in the East naturally embrace European achievements as far as external technological culture is concerned; but we keep it in our depots and warehouses and do not allow it—that is, European culture—into our living rooms. This is because spirituality is natural to him. We need to be aware of this sort of thing because it typifies the forces underlying what is taking place across the world and upon which world events depend.

You will say: In Central European culture we actually have the firm beginnings of a spirituality founded on clear, bright ideas! We do indeed, and we can talk about that spirituality—as I tried to do in my book *Riddles of Humanity*—about a forgotten stream in German spiritual life. To imbue ourselves with a spirituality that would really go beyond what the Oriental spirituality has ever achieved, we only need to fill ourselves with the wondrous Imaginations that we find, for example, in Herder[119] and in Goethe. Oriental culture has not produced anything of the magnitude of Herder, who sees with every sunrise an image of renewed world creation and describes this magnificently. Those who do not want to be philistines today prove nevertheless to be just such philistines, who say: We can't be bothered with that old stuff any more; and if one asks people about Herder, he has long since been forgotten. An Oriental person judging conditions is naturally judging what lives in the current external stream of Central European culture.

Just read the astute Chinese writer Ku Hung-Ming,[120] who has sympathetically described the culture of Central Europe, or read the lecture Rabindranath Tagore recently gave, and you will see how people are querying: What stance is this Europe taking in humanity's global progress? They have an inkling that Central Europe might be called upon to take the lead in going beyond what spiritualism could provide for them. But then they check as to whether Europe has failed to nurture the great beginnings, the great germs of potential, which exist and are contained in Europe. People there had a Goethe, they say; yes, but those worthy, materialistic Germans don't know what to make of a Goethe! When his last grandchild died, there was another opportunity to bring Goetheanism into German spiritual life. Under the incomparably excellent aegis of a German princess, the Goethe-Schiller Archive was founded. This was given a great boost in the [eighteen] eighties. A Goethe Society was also founded but was consistently too embarrassed to appoint anyone to head it who had had really engaged with Goethe's spirituality. This was thought to be unworthy and at the last vote nobody conversant with Goethe's spirituality was appointed as head of the Goethe Society; instead a former finance minister was appointed. In the wake of such proceedings, the world may well judge what is going on in Central Europe! Goethe's legacy is being managed by a former finance minister, one bearing the symptomatic family name of 'Crossturnthee'.[121] But I don't know—should the symptomatic nature of that name ever be fulfilled—whether anyone better might occupy the post.

Such issues could only be changed if mean-hearted, petty interests were to be replaced by broader interests and if one were to observe how spurs of incentive actually spread across the entire world; how the bodies of the East, one might say, make possible a slightly lagging spirituality for souls who wish to incarnate into bodies experiencing this delayed spirituality, bodies that allow for an extension of what is physical-corporeal for souls over the age of twenty-seven. In the East there is a tendency to remain at earlier phases in human evolution, lingering in phases other sections of humanity have already undergone. Here, near the centre, we are in a position where a reversal has to take place, one in which, until the age of twenty-seven—this age was twenty-eight in the middle of the fifteenth century—what is needed by today can be extracted from what is physical-corporeal. But for the onward development of the human soul—and if one doesn't wish to grow old prematurely and retain nothing of one's youth—a free soul-spiritual impetus is needed in place of an unfree Eastern spiritual impetus.

Moving further West to America: humanity is fashioned such that it is delayed in reaching this stature. In the East humanity is in some respects delayed at earlier phases, in the centre you encounter that 'normal' average age, whereas in the West, in America—as I characterized yesterday—earthly and subterranean forces are at work. These affect spirits like Woodrow Wilson such that they become obsessed with their own words and principles. They are as if prematurely aged—but here in a slightly different sense: more like prematurely old children who have not yet reached the full unfolding of what can be worked upon before the age of twenty-seven. If one could only see through what today makes such an impression on people, the question might occur: How is it possible that a spirit such as Woodrow Wilson, who despite his age has never absorbed more than would normally be absorbed by the age of twenty-seven, could yet become the global schoolmaster? The breadth of interest that enables a true evaluation of such things in one's soul is simply not present. There is no will to transcend *philistrosity*!

That remarkable trait in the evolution of humankind can be characterized as follows: going from East to West, from the retention of something earlier, through a normative centre to Western decadence—all this obviously applies to the evolutions of populations and the Earth and not to individuals themselves. An interest in all this needs to be cultivated in order to discover what impulses are at work across the world—and how one is to value them. Here in the middle zone, the decisive traits have over long centuries come from the South, so that influences from the Græco–Roman world have saturated Central European culture. A conservative quality accompanied this. Today we are at a turning point. A particularly progressive element from the North needs to permeate populations in Central Europe. I would call this particularity a beneficial impetus from ancient Hyperborean times, and it needs to suffuse our souls. It is this of which we need to take account. Otherwise—if human beings don't open their eyes and their souls to these great evolutionary spurs in human advancement—the Earth will proceed in a false evolutionary direction, one not constituting healthy loam for cosmic growth and ascendant world construction. Everything representing the final phase in Earth evolution will then have to be taken up by another planet.

Enormous interests are at stake. It is essential to work your way out of parochial, bigoted, bourgeois *philistrosity* and to evolve upwards to greater, wider interests. Only when you have acquired such broader interests are you able to correctly evaluate certain phenomena in our present. It can clearly be seen that human natures are now diverging. This is in its infancy today, yet humanity is beginning to diverge in two directions. One direction manifests natures in whom to some extent the physical-corporeal element is being hardened. In this element they develop a certain hardness up to the age of twenty-seven then remain at a standstill, rejecting everything of a soul-spiritual nature. If they are not continually stimulated to incite humanity, to lead humanity towards disaster—as Lloyd George—then they congeal, they stagnate sourly, they turn to extreme philistinism and become dulled. People become stunted in this divergent direction. Those in the other direction submit—until the age of twenty-seven—to the drives and forces pulsating from their physical-corporeal nature, extracting all spirituality from it. Much lies in this physical-corporeal nature. Do not forget that we all arrive in this world as immensely wise beings; we would only need to transform this wisdom into consciousness, transform all the latent wisdom existing in our corporeality. Spiritual science tries—in a harmonious and spiritually-suffused way—to retrieve all that lives in blood, nerves and muscle and raise it upwards into consciousness. Spiritual science is rejected not only by stunted individuals but also widely by those—and there will be more and more of them—who feel buoyantly what lives, pulsates, boils and seethes as ingenuity and resourcefulness down among their nerves, blood and muscles, until sexual maturity and as far as the age of twenty-seven. These overheated natures who to some extent burn up human life are becoming more and more numerous. They already crop up sporadically and ever more frequently in considerable numbers. Mental institutions and similar facilities are peopled with them. Yet any insight into the fact that anthroposophically-orientated spiritual science represents a real source of healing is absent.

One such nature typical of recent times, who achieved world fame, is the philosopher Otto Weininger.[122] Otto Weininger was a person who, in the most chaotic, unreconstructed and disharmonious way, retrieved what lay in nerve, blood and muscle and then wrote the world-famous book *Sex and Character* for which the people who fall for everything also fell. So those philistines fell for it, not realizing that, despite all its repellent nonsense, it represented an idea, a manifestation of an element comprising blood, muscle and nerves. Such people are faced with an elemental phenomenon—it confronts them from out of their own humanity—and spiritual science wishes to develop this, but in a harmonious and orderly manner. Because they have not learned it from spiritual science, where they could properly have done so, such people need—because their nerves, blood and muscles demand it—to ask themselves the very question, which humanity as a whole urgently needs to ask. Without this question, humanity cannot progress any further. The question is this: How can I, by being in the physical world since birth or conception, be the *continuer*, creating continuity for my soul-spiritual existence between my last death and this current birth? This and similar questions—as thrown up in spiritual science and viewed as fundamental questions in progressive spiritual culture—need to be brought to light and will be brought to light by those who allow to seethe upwards what exists in nerve, blood and muscle.

You see, one chapter in Otto Weininger is extraordinarily interesting. He asked himself: Why did I actually enter into terrestrial existence? He asked this question on the basis of what I have just characterized—out of the wisdom slumbering in nerves, blood and muscle—and in his own way he answered his question, but in a way that consumes and burns the human being. He asked: Why have I been drawn from the spirit-soul realm—in which I used to dwell—into life on Earth? He found no other answer other than this: Because I was cowardly, because I didn't want to stay alone in the soul-spiritual world and hence I sought connection with other people. I didn't have the courage to remain alone and sought refuge in my mother's body. These were, to him, entirely honest answers that he was giving himself. Why do we have no memories, he asked, of the time that flowed past before birth? Because that is how we became at birth! He said literally: Because we have sunk so low that we have lost consciousness of it. Had human beings not lost themselves at birth, they would not need to seek and re-find themselves.

These are typical phenomena; they still arise sporadically nowadays. It is people such as these who in their youth extract from blood, nerve and muscle what can only become digestible, over the course of the entire process of being human, once it is purified and made harmonious by what spiritual science should be offering. But for this to happen, the breadth and magnitude of interests throughout human life have to be vastly expanded. All bourgeois pettiness—all *philistrosity*—has to recede. People being sealed off in narrow interest huddles has to be systematically combatted. Certain questions have to be framed quite differently than has so far been the case. How did religious evolution of the past millennia itself frame the question that still connects a few people with the spiritual? A materialistically-educated, witty modern man occupying a prestigious position in certain circles once said to me: If you compare the state with the Church, you arrive at the view that the Church has an easier ride than the state. Now, I don't wish to comment on the relative value of such an opinion, but that man meant that the Church has an easier time of it than does the state, because the state governs life whereas the Church, as it were, reigns over death. People being more afraid of death than they are of life, the Church has an easier job. He obviously considered this to be nonsense because he was of dyed-in-the-wool materialistic outlook.

But this topic, too, has been driven into fairly egotistical channels. Basically, people today ask: What happens in my soul-spiritual life when I have gone through the gate of death? Therein lie many egotistical impulsions. Particularly the question of immortality would take on a very different guise under the influence of spiritual science. In future, people would not only ask: To what extent is soul-spiritual life after death a continuation of life here on Earth? Instead they would ask: To what extent is life here on Earth a continuation of the life I spent earlier in soul-spiritual worlds? In the latter case we would be able to look at the following.

When a human being goes through the gate of death, Imaginative conceptualizing is initially very strongly established: a compendious pictorial world is imaginatively rolled out before them. I'd like to call this the unfurling of an image-filled world. The second third of life between death and a new birth is primarily filled with Inspiration. Inspirations arise in this second third of life between death and a new birth. And it is Intuitions that predominate in the last third. Now, Intuitions consist in human beings transposing themselves—with self and soul—into other beings, and the ultimate Intuitive transposition consists in transiting into a physical body. This transposing of one's self into a physical body through birth is just the continuation of a primarily Intuitive life in the final third between death and a new birth. And what must actually arise when a human being steps into physical existence must show up in a child as a particularly characteristic trait: this transposition into a different life. The child has to do what others do—not what originates in their own self—but by imitating and mimicking what others do.

Why did I have to describe—when talking about 'The Education of the Child from the Perspective of Spiritual Science' [123]—how children in the first seven years of their lives are primarily imitators? Because imitating—that transposing-yourself-into-others—is a continuation of the Intuitive world of the last third of existence between death and a new birth. You can still see—streaming into and illuminating their lives—that existence between death and rebirth if you observe children's lives in a meaningful way. It is therefore around this fact that the question of immortality will have to be framed, thus: To what extent is life here on Earth a continuation of life between death and a new birth? You will then learn to take this life on Earth especially seriously, but not in an egotistical sense. Above all, it will be a matter of holding onto a feeling of responsibility, felt in such a way that you reflect: I have to continue here what I was enjoined to do, in that I have brought with me a legacy from soul-spiritual worlds. It will represent an enormous about-turn in people's conceptions once they speak from this other perspective. Because what the soul experiences between death and a new birth—this vast spiritual vista experienced in Imagination, Inspiration and Intuition—is for that realm the here-and-now. And what we experience here is for that realm the yonder. And wanting to understand this yonder—wanting to revere and recognize it—will become part of the newly-framed question about immortality, which will intervene in spiritual evolution in a less egotistical way than did the question of immortality so widely throughout the evolution of religions in past millennia.

I wanted to describe these things in order to show how humanity can break free of petty philistine bigotry and to illustrate what it is not to be a philistine. You are not a philistine if you can go beyond those narrowest of interests, if you can evince an interest in the fact that here on Earth you breathe 25,950 times a day, which equates both with the number of days in a lifetime and also with the number of shifts made by the Sun as it completes its circumnavigation of cosmic ellipses. Broadening your interest to include what led to there being a forgotten stream within German spiritual life, broadening your interest to encompass what is being configured in the spiritual life of the entire world, what the underlying gestures of Eastern, Central and Western spiritual evolution are; how Asiatic spiritual evolution depends to some extent on an Eastern stream which became decadent in the West, how the central stream, once dependent on a Southern cultural influx, will in future become dependent on the North. Interests such as these can lead us out into the great scheme of human evolution, to overcoming *philistrosity*, to rightly disposing feeling towards human evolution and to teaching us genuinely to empathize with impulses alive throughout humanity.

And as for willing: willing also evolves in a specific way under the influences of materialism. It evolves such that human beings become ever less adroit, ever clumsier, that is, in the great classical sense of less adept and more inept. What can human beings do today? The most restricted work for which they are trained sets them within small groupings. Whatever spiritual science develops in terms of concepts, feeling and impulsions of will enters right down into limbs. When a person lives into spiritual science, they become adept, nimble, they can adapt to their environments; they learn over the course of their lives skills for which one might have said, when they were quite small, that they had not the slightest talent. When spiritual science is properly grasped, it makes individuals increasingly deft. Nowadays people are less handy, even on the most modest scale. You meet people who do not have a handle on the smallest tasks; you meet men who cannot even sew on a button that has ripped off, let alone anything else. Much depends on people becoming more versatile once more; that they become capable of adapting to their environments, that the limitations are overcome of being enclosed within constricted circles and hence becoming inept for the world.

However odd it may sound, humanity has this threefold task for the present and the near future in relation to thinking, feeling and willing: that petty narrow-mindedness be overcome and that mobility in finding your way into world circumstances gains ground; that philistinism is conquered and open-hearted interest takes hold of human hearts; that clumsy ineptitude is remedied and people once more become skilled, that people are educated to dexterity in the most varied areas of life. And learning to understand the world in the widest possible areas of life! Today the opposite of all this is of course being perpetrated. People are being corralled into dyspraxia, into narrow-minded *philistrosity*, and these are the predictable consequences of a materialistic mindset. Of course, not everyone who has broken their leg can learn how to reset it themselves; but clumsiness need not extend to people having no sense as to how to help themselves in the simplest of illnesses, and suchlike. Dexterous, smart understanding, so as to be equal to dealing with the most diverse of situations in life: crucially, that is what it depends on.

Haven't we seen—in the way this recent time has come about—how things have been developing? To anyone with eyes that could see events of recent decades—and to those who asked around—it was clear that actually having the sense to develop a world view, having the sense to make the impetus behind world views the focus of their observation, that only those with lively enough motivation of will to develop purely materialist interest in world views were those active in the area of socialism. Basically, it was only among those who wanted to reform the world in a socialist direction and who had observed social conditions that any question about world views arose at all. Once you went beyond the socialist deluge there was a lack of interest or, at best, a few narrow niche interests, clinging onto old handed-down ideas or, if anything new was being conceptualized, it was the abstract wordage that anticipated Wilsonism, as it raged particularly rampantly among so-called liberal parties in the second half of the nineteenth century. Any will to actively enter into the spiritual-divine impulses of the world—in the way socialism wanted to enter into all things material—will of this kind was absent. Dull obtuseness there was a-plenty among the upper echelons of the bourgeoisie, where it had begun in the first place. There are, of course, exceptions. Those present—as politeness dictates—are obviously among them.

Now, in order to place yourselves in a position facing these phenomena and asking yourselves such questions as have been raised today—as also answering them as we have tried to do—is fundamentally one and the same thing because enormous issues are at stake here. In Eastern Europe we see how something is being—as I'd like to frame it—prepared for in essence, in extract, about which Europe has terrifyingly little understanding. These seeds of Eastern European evolution have often been mentioned around our regions and today I will express it in a specific form: Eastern Europe wants to come to the understanding that all human life has meaning! When the sixth cultural epoch approaches, Eastern Europe is intended to show earthly evolution that all human life contains meaning, that we are not just to take as gospel what has been funnelled into us at school in our youth. The East is destined to demonstrate that human beings continue to develop until their death; that each year brings ever more and more new discoveries and that, when we go through the gate of death, we remain connected with the Earth, while wisdom continues to be garnered after death. What does that soul element long for, which until recently could be called Russian, and which is now temporarily heading into chaos, but which will find its way as part of Europe's cultural evolution and thence into the entire evolution of all humankind? What does this Eastern element actually want?

It wants to see an emerging sense for the fact that all human life is involved in evolving, and that the moment of death is just another such moment—albeit an exceptionally important one—in this evolution. This principle also has to find its adherents and believers in Central Europe, and will do so under the conditions here introduced. But until that principle is recognized, the belief will always prevail that the younger one is, the more one is entitled to an opinion. Those youngest of whippersnappers, both male and female, have their firmly shuttered and conclusive viewpoints and have basically no space in themselves for great expectations and hopes: that with each passing year new mysteries will be unveiled and that the instant of death will likewise reveal new mysteries. In the East, souls are evolving who—still in their unconscious—are beginning to understand that human beings are at their wisest and can be the best judges of earthly affairs and conditions precisely when they die. From among such souls living in the East there will emerge those who don't merely enquire from young whippersnappers and parliaments how to organize human affairs, but who will also ask of the dead and will learn to communicate with the dead, making this connection fruitful for earthly evolution. In future it will be a question of asking what the dead have to say in a given situation. Spiritual ways will be found of asking not only the living but also the dead when it is a matter of resolving great human conundrums here on Earth. If you deepen yourselves sufficiently through spiritual science, the spiritual means will be found to query not only the living but also the dead about the great decisions facing humanity on Earth. That is what the East wants. Never before has there been such a collision between elements so badly suited to each other as what is happening today in Eastern Europe; because what constitutes the soul of Eastern Europe is the polar opposite of the Trotskyism and Leninism of present times which—out of the purest if most self-deluding materialistic Leninism, that most bleak caricature of human cultural progress—has no sense for, nor comprehension of, real spirituality, yet which so understandably grows on the basis of the present's underlying mood. The future will learn to recognize this.

That, my dear friends, is what I wanted to say to you by way of summarizing what is intended—what ought—to kindle interest in your hearts. We need to acquire an understanding for this! We cannot be allowed to remain dull and uninterested in what, in the deepest sense, goes on in souls. That is what I wanted, during our meeting here, to lay in your souls and in your hearts.

# Notes

*Textual sources*: The lectures were taken down by several stenographers (Georg Klenk, Hedda Hummel, Helene Finckh) and transcribed into plain text. This is the basis for the published version. Only a few of the original stenographs have been preserved.

1 *Commemorate in the following words*: This verse was spoken by Rudolf Steiner at the start of all the lectures in this volume, as also before all lectures held throughout Germany during WW1. From the second lecture (3 December 1914) onwards, the words 'to those who have gone through the gate of death' were added, while 'earthly human beings' was replaced with 'beings of the spheres'.

2 . . . *these events*: The outbreak of war.

3 *Since 28 June:* date of the assassination in Sarajevo of the heirs to the thrones of Austria and Hungary, which sparked the outbreak of WW1.

4 'Christ and the Human Soul', 4 lectures held between 12 and 16 July 1914 in Norrköping, Sweden, published in vol. 155 of the Collected Works in 1960.

5 Gottlieb von Jagow, 1863–1935, 1913–1916 German Secretary of State for Foreign Affairs.

6 *Volume 2 was printed as far as page 206:* Within the Collected Works, the book *The Riddles of Philosophy* appeared in one volume (1968, vol. no.18). The corresponding place with the transition from the French philosopher Boutroux (1845–1921) and Bergson (1859–1941) to the German philosopher Wilhelm Heinrich Preuss (1843–1909) can be found on page 564.

7 The wooden building of the first Goetheanum, erected in Dornach, which was destroyed by fire on New Year's Eve 1922–23.

8 The fifth and final lecture in the cycle 'Ways to a New Style of Architecture', Collected Works vol. 286, published in 1957.

9 The declaration of war by Austria and Hungary on Serbia followed on 28 July.

10 Literally 'Wisdom is only in truth'. This saying is reproduced in 'Goethe's Natural Scientific Works, with an introduction, footnotes and notes explaining the text' volume 4, Part 2 'Prose Verses', Part 1 'Knowledge'. In the paperback version of 'Prose Verses' (Stuttgart 1967) it can be found on page 30. Rudolf Steiner chose this saying as a motto for the objectives he gave the Anthroposophical Society in 1913 (see 'The History and Conditions of the Anthroposophical Movement in Relation to the Anthroposophical Society', Collected Works 1959, vol. 258, second lecture).

11 *A respected journalist:* The identity of whom cannot be ascertained.

12 *Österreichische Rundschau* (Austrian Review), vol. 9, booklet 5 of 1 September 1914, p. 302. The quotation was read in slightly shortened form by Rudolf Steiner.

13 This teacher could not be identified.

14 The Bhagavad Gita: ancient Indian epic in which the wisdom and philosophy of the Indians is portrayed in summary. Rudolf Steiner spoke about it in detail in the lecture cycles 'The Bhagavad Gita and the Letters of Paul' in vol. 142 of the Collected Works, 1960, and in 'The Occult Foundations of the Bhagavad Gita', vol. 143 of the Collected Works 1962.

15 'The Mission of Individual Folk Souls in relation to Germanic-Scandinavian Mythology', eleven lectures held in June 1921 in Kristiania (modern and original Oslo) vol. 121 of the Collected Works, 1962.

16 Rudolf Steiner later changed the penultimate line to: 'resounding in light and power'.

17 The ruler in question is Tsar Nicholas II, who ruled Russia 1894–1917.

18 Gaius Duilius, victor in the Battle of Mylae (260 BCE) against Carthage. This marine battle took place during the First Punic War, which lasted from 264 to 241 BCE. The Carthaginians had the advantage over the Romans at sea, but the latter used boarding ramps and ladders and the battle at sea was transferred to the land, where the Romans gained the upper hand.

19 The event here referred to is the storming of the fortifications of Liège in the first days of August 1914.

20 Dr Felix Peipers, 1873–1844, anthroposophical doctor and active member of the Anthroposophical Society.

21 The lecture referred to is: 'The "Barbarian" Peoples Portrayed by Schiller and Fichte', public lecture given on 1 December 1914 in Munich. In the Collected Works this appeared with the parallel lecture of 5 November in Berlin in the volume 'In Destiny-Laden Times' vol. 64, Dornach 1959. The Munich lecture was reproduced in 'Human School' 1964, booklets 1–2.

22 See footnote xv.

23 Translator's note: In this context Steiner was almost certainly referring to Britain as a whole, to Great Britain or the British Isles, and not exclusively to England.

24 Sir Edward Grey, 1862–1933, was British Foreign Minister 1905–1916.

25 Annie Besant, 1847–1933. From 1907 President of the Theosophical Society. She declared the Indian boy, Jiddu Krishnamurti, to be the bearer of an impending reincarnation of Christ on Earth and in this connection founded the Order of the Star of the East. The fact that Steiner opposed this supposition led to the exclusion of the German Section, of which Steiner was President, and to the subsequent founding of the Anthroposophical Society.

26 21 March 1915, lecture entitled 'Roots and Blossoms of German Spiritual Life' and 22 March 1915 'What is Immortal in Human Beings?'. Insufficient notes of the first lecture exist; the second is contained in the Collected Works as a parallel lecture. A lecture of the same name, held on 12 March in Nuremberg, is included in the volume 'In Destiny-Laden Times', Collected Works, vol. 64, 1959.

27 Mrs Lina Grossheintz-Röhrer. The funeral oration given by Rudolf Steiner at her cremation is printed in the volume 'Our Departed', vol. 261 of the Collected Works 1963. The same applies to the two other deceased individuals mentioned in this lecture.

28 Sibyl Colazza.

29 Fritz Mitscher.

30 'The Inner Nature of the Human Being and Life between Death and a New Birth'—8 lectures held in Vienna between 6 and 14 April 1914, vol. 153 of the Collected Works 1959.

31 The lectures referred to here are the first two lectures in the present volume; similar content matter was given in other cities.

32 This example is found in a letter of 13 September 1870 from Ernest Renan (1823–1892) to David Friedrich Strauss. David Strauss, Collected Writings, Bonn 1876–78, vol. 1, p. 311 ff.

33 Sir Edward Grey (1862–1933) British Foreign Minister 1905–1916. The opinion expressed by a colleague of his is quoted in the book *The Secret Prehistory of World War 1* by Hans F. Helmolt, Leipzig 1914, see p. 38 ff.

34 In lecture 10 of 16 June 1910.

35 Vladimir Solovyov, 1853–1900, Russian philosopher and poet. Selected works by him have appeared in German, translated by Harry Köhler, 4 volumes, Stuttgart 1921–1922.

36 Wolffs Telegraphenbüro (W.T.B), founded in 1849 in Berlin by Bernhard Wolff, was at the time of WWI the most prominent German news agency.

37 The loan to human beings of their I by the Spirits of Form is described i.a. in the seminal work *Occult Science—an Outline*. See index of titles at the end of this volume.

38 Primarily in the above-quoted book, *Occult Science—an Outline* in the chapter on the course of human life.

39 'The Arena of Thoughts Resulting from German Idealism with Reference to our Destiny-laden Times', Munich, 28 November 1915. This lecture is reprinted in the volume 'In Destiny-laden Times', vol.64 of the Collected Works 1959.

40 This refers to an internal episode within the Anthroposophical Society, which was discussed in Dornach in August 1915. To the extent that notes of this discussion exist, they are intended to appear in vol. 253 of the Collected Works.

41 This refers to both the lectures held in Munich on 17 and 18 March 1916 entitled respectively: 'On the Evolution of German Thinking: A Forgotten Striving for Spiritual Science' and 'Healthy Spiritual Life and Research'. A lecture parallel to the first of these is contained in the volume 'On Central European Spiritual Life', vol. 65 of the Collected Works 1961; the second is intended for publication in vol. 71 of the Collected Works.

42 Herder elaborated this Russian i.e. Slavic trait of peaceability most extensively in the chapter on 'Slavic Folk' in the 4th section of the 16th volume of his *Ideas on the Philosophy of Human History* (see Konrad Bittner's *Herder's Historical Philosophy and the Slavs*, Reichenberg 1929, especially pp. 49 and 97–104).

43 See the essay on the 'Observing Power of Discernment', which was first printed in 1820 in the 2nd notebook of the 1st volume of *Morphology*. In Kürschner's 'German National Literature' it appeared in Goethe's

Scientific Writings as edited by Rudolf Steiner; see p. 115ff of the facsimile reproduction, Bern 1949.

44 Friedrich Wilhelm Joseph Schelling, 1775–1854, speaks of an 'intellectual outlook' in several works, e.g. in his *System of Transcendental Idealism* (Tübingen, 1800) and the essay 'Further Presentations of a System of Philosophy', Chapter 2. The works mentioned here by Steiner, 'Philosophy of Mythology' and 'Philosophy of Revelation' only appeared after his death within his 'Collected Works', Stuttgart and Augsburg 1858. 'On the Deities of Samothrace' was published in Stuttgart in 1815.

45 Francis Bacon of Verulam, 1561–1626.

46 Herbert Spencer, 1820–1903.

47 – see above. Mrs Besant travelled to Germany at the invitation of Rudolf Steiner in the autumn of 1904 and held lectures in Hamburg and other cities. See the volume of essays 'Lucifer Gnosis', p. 553 ff, vol. 34 of the Collected Works (*Gesamtausgabe*) 1960.

48 Helena Petrovna Blavatsky, 1831–1891. Rudolf Steiner speaks in some detail about her in 'The Occult Movement of the Nineteenth Century' vol. 254 of the Collected Works 1969.

49 Herbert Henry Asquith, Earl of Oxford and Asquith, 1852–1928, Cabinet Minister from 1892 and Prime Minister 1908–1916.

50 Laurence Oliphant, 3rd Lord Oliphant, 1829–1888. See his two most important books *Sympneumata* and *Scientific Religion*, which appeared in London in 1888.

51 Henry Steel Olcott, 1832–1907. In 1875 he founded the Theosophical Society with H.P. Blavatsky and remained its President until his death.

52 Alfred Percy Sinnett, whose main work, *Esoteric Buddhism*, appeared in 1883 [in German under the title 'The Esoteric Doctrine or Secret Buddhism', Leipzig 1884].

53 The person mentioned is the publisher of the *Almanach de Mme. de Thèbes.*

54 Jean Jaurès, 1859–1914, social-democrat politician, who tried to avert war. Shortly before the outbreak of war (31 July), he was assasinated by Raoul Villain a 29-year-old French nationalist.

55 August Weismann, 1834–1914, biologist. He published *Essays on Heredity* (two volumes, 1875–76) and *Lectures on the Theory of Heredity* (two volumes, 1903).

56 Alcyone: the name given to Jiddu Krishnamurti (born 1895) within the Theosophical Society.

57 Bertram Keightley, 1860-1944, founded the Indian Section of the Theosophical Society and was its first General Secretary, 1897-1901, and General Secretary of the English Section of the Theosophical Society, 1901-1905.

58 The processes mentioned are described in the book *Occult Science—an Outline* in the chapter on world evolution in relation to humanity.

59 Lorenz Oken, 1779–1851. The concept here mentioned by Rudolf Steiner can be found, for example, in volume 4 of *Universal Natural History for all Species*, which includes the beginning of his 'Natural History of Animals' in Chapter 2 on 'Values and Uses'. There it states: 'Just as one doesn't understand a complex, fully-assembled machine until one has disassembled its constituent components, so it is impossible to conceive of all the materials and forces of nature that constitute the completed human being if one only sees them at work in the body. In animals they do, however, manifest as separated and work without complex entanglement or disguise so that, in this respect, the animal kingdom can be termed a dis-membered, dispersed, laid-out human being.'

60 For instance, in Schelling's *System of Synthesised Philosophy*: 'How often does a multi-talented mother share her qualities among her children and only one of them fully inherits them all? Just so has nature shared out among the animals just one emphatically one-sided feature while all the rays of nature's activity coincide, coalescing in a single flashpoint. In this flashpoint exists the human being.'

61 This phrase could not be found in Oken's work.

62 The Mystery mentioned here is the fourth Mystery Drama '*The Soul's Awakening*' in the 6th scene.

63 The second Mystery Drama, scene 1 of '*The Soul's Probation*'.

64 Karl Christian Planck, 1819–1880. His work *Testament of a German* was published after his death by Karl Köstlin. In the Editor's Prologue the following appears: 'Often enough when, after decades of the fighters' restless activity, the most incisively striking truth—like the voice of a preacher in the wilderness—would seem to ring out, when the long-announced word of deeper, rightful rebirth ... sank, unheard, in the uninhibited pursuit of that selfish, disorderly profit-hunt, when the glorious fundamental law of all Nature, since primal time immemorial the creative law of a progressive concentration towards independent inner life [raised] towards the spirit, remained unnoticed and un-understood, in favour of paradoxical mechanistic externality and superficiality .... If all this were to remain equally ignored by a superficial, materialistic conception of history—and by a

theory which has become regressive—how often would the solitary person, in their bitter lifelong struggle, find the words of the ancient Roman springing to their lips: "Ungrateful fatherland, not even my bones shall you have".'

65 Friedrich Wilhelm Förster, 1869–1966, political ethicist and educationalist.

66 Meister Bertram, around 1345–1415. Panel from the Grabow altarpiece, painted around 1379, Hamburg Art Gallery.

67 Fyodor Mikhailovitch Dostoyevsky, 1821–1881. *The Brothers Karamazov* appeared in 1879–80 [and was translated into German in 1884].

68 Smerdyakov's natural mother has previously died.

69 Strizzi-ness. Strizzi, colloquial contemporary word indicative of eponymous dizzy light-headed or carelessly irresponsible behaviour.

70 Pyotr Alexeyevich Kropotkin, 1842–1921, Russian revolutionary and anarchist.

71 See the detailed depictions in *From the Akashic Chronicle* in the chapter on 'Our Atlantean Ancestors' and *Occult Science—an Outline* in the chapter 'World Evolution and the Human Being'.

72 Rudolf Eucken, 1846–1926. A description of his philosophy can be found in volume 2 of Steiner's *The Riddles of Philosophy* in the chapter on Modern Humans and their Worldviews. Eucken's philosophy is described elsewhere as ethical activism, focusing on educational and social issues, and maintaining that human beings have souls and exist at the juncture between nature and spirit. (Transl.)

73 Woodrow Wilson, 1856–1924, President of the USA 1913–1921, Professor of Philosophy.

74 Ludwig Deinhard, 1847–1917. Significant member of the Theosophical Society and later of the Anthroposophical Society, editor of the book *The Mystery of the Human Being in Light of Psychic Research—an Introduction to Occultism.*

75 Albrecht Wilhelm Sellin, 1841–1933, colonial official and member of the Anthroposophical Society.

76 Melchior Ernst Sachs, 1843–1917, conductor and composer; from 1881 lecturer in harmony at the Munich Academy of Music. He wrote a book on 'The Manifestations of Tone in terms of Over—and Sub-tone Formation'.

77 Maurice Barrès, 1862–1923, this reference is to the essay by André Germain: 'Farewell from the Youth Leader: Maurice Barrès' in the *International Review* [*Internationale Rundschau*], Zurich, first year of publication, booklet 3 of 20 July 1915.

78 Wilhelm Wundt, 1832–1920. His main work *Cultural Psychology, An Investigation into Developmental Laws of Language, Myth and Conduct* appeared in 10 volumes 1900–1920.

79 Quotation from Goethe's *Faust*, where Faust muses:

'*Habe nun, ach! Philosophie,*
*Juristerei and Medizin,*
*Und leider auch, Theologie,*
*Durchaus studiert* mit heissem Bemuehn.

This can be translated as:
'Law, medicine, philosophy
And even—alas—theology
I've studied *with passionate resolution.*'

80 The reference here is to Blavatsky's 'Esoterics', vol. 3 of *The Secret Doctrine*, Chapter 39 on 'Cycles and Avatars'.

81 Adolf von Harnack, 1851–1930, leading representative of Liberal Protestantism. His work *The Essence of Christianity* appeared in 1900. In the 1910 edition the passage mentioned by Steiner appears on p. 102: 'Whatever the grave and all its manifestations may have contributed, one thing is certain: from that grave there originated the unshakeable belief in the overcoming of death and a life eternal.'

82 *The Mechanics of Spiritual Life* by Max Verworn, 1863–1921, came out in 1907 as the 200th volume in the collection 'On Nature and Spiritual World'. It went through several editions. The passage mentioned appears in Chapter 4: 'Sleeping and Dreaming'.

83 Sigmund Freud, 1856–1939, founder of psychoanalysis.

84 Gaius Julius Caesar Octavianus Augustus, born 62 BCE, ruled 31 BCE until 14 AD, Tiberius 14–37 AD, Caligula 27–41 AD.

85 Commodus, son of Marcus Aurelius, ruled after 'the good Caesars' Trajan, Hadrian, Antonius Pius and Marcus Aurelius, in the years 180–192 AD.

86 A.W. Hunzinger *Christianity in the Battle between Present World Conceptions*, 2nd edition, Leipzig 1916, p. 127 ff. The phrase in quotation marks that follows this is again from the beginning of Goethe's *Faust.*

87 This phrase originates from Albrecht von Haller, 1708–1777, a Bern doctor and scientist, and is found in his didactic poem 'The Falseness of Human Virtues'. Goethe wrote his poem 'However, to the Physicist', contained in the section 'God and the World' of Goethe's poetry, as a riposte to von Haller's poem, given here by Rudolf Steiner in much abbreviated form.

88 In some versions the word 'curse' is given as 'laugh' (Transl.).

89 Rudolf Kjellén, 1864–1922, Swedish historian and statesman. *The State as a Form of Life* appeared in 1916 in Leipzig.

90 Ibid. Wilson's elaboration of the state as an organism is contained in his volume of essays *The New Freedom*, in Chapter 2 'What is Progress?', Leipzig 1913, German edition Munich 1914, translated by Hans Winand.

91 Enthused is *begeistert* or literally enspirited. A neologism for its opposite is intended here. (Transl.)

92 The space refers to the then newly-opened *Kunsthaus das Reich* [The Realm Art House] in Munich, secured through the initiative of Alexander von Bernus, 1880–1965, poet and writer and publisher of the journal *The Realm.*

93 Translator's note: Rudolf Steiner had not at this point collaborated with priests seeking new meaning in ritual who later founded The Christian Community, whose service, The Act of Consecration of Man, largely follows, in form, the Catholic Mass.

94 On 15 March 1917 the Russian Revolution began, which by November had led to the formation of the Russian Soviet Republic, and from 1922, the Soviet Union (USSR).

95 Kristiania is present-day Oslo, which was also its original name. 'Mission of the Folk Souls.'

96 'The Inner Nature of the Human Being and Life between Death and a New Birth'—8 lectures held in Vienna between 6 and 14 April 1914, vol. 153 of the Collected Works 1959.

97 Gotthold Ephraim Lessing, 1729–1781, spoke about Christianity in his theological writings and in the essay 'The Education of the Human Race'.

98 Arthur Drews, 1865–1935, denied the historicity of Jesus. His *Myth of Christ* appeared in two volumes between 1909 and 1911.

99 For instance, de Loosten (Dr Georg Lomer) *Jesus Christ from a Psychiatrist's Perspective*, Bamberg 1905. The Danish publication: Emil Rasmussen's *Jesus: A Comparative Study in Psychopathy*. German edition by Arthur Rothenburg, Leipzig 1905.

100 In the lecture of 24 December 1917, published as *Mystery Truths and Christmas Impulses*, No. 180 of the Collected Works 1966.

101 Alexander Moszkowski, 1851–1934, known primarily as a humorous writer. Since 1886 he has been Editor of *Funny Pages*. The book *Socrates the Idiot* appeared in 1917.

[102] This discussion begins with the Brothers Grimm, Jakob and Wilhelm. The word 'God' is treated of in the 1st portion of Part 5 of the 4th volume of *God.* There, i.a., it states: 'The myriad attempts to equate the German root "guda" with parallel forms among other Indo-Germanic languages ... have so far failed to reach a formally compelling or satisfactory, meaning-related outcome.'

[103] Dionysios the Areopagite, mentioned in the 17th chapter of The Acts of the Apostles, lived in Athens as a pupil of the Apostle Paul. Writings attributed to him exist entitled 'On the Heavenly Hierarchies' and 'On Church Hierarchies'.

[104] Fritz Mauthner, 1849–1923, Language Philosopher. He wrote *Dictionary of Philosophy: New Contributions towards a Critique of Language*, which appeared in 1910–1911.

[105] Franz Boll writes, in the tiny volume 628 of the collection entitled 'Nature and Spiritual Worlds' in the book *Star Belief and Star Meanings.* Mauthner wrote an article opposing these ideas in the *Berlin Daily* on 28 March 1918. In the same newspaper, Franz Boll stated (16 April 1918) that he was in complete agreement with Mauthner on the points Mauthner had criticized. A further account of this is found in 'Dying Earth and Living Cosmos', volume 181 of Steiner's Collected Works, 1967 edition, in lecture 19.

[106] In lecture 7 of this volume.

[107] See the cycle *The Mission of Folk Souls*, 11 lectures held in Christiania (Oslo), vol. 121 of the Collected Works, 1962.

[108] In the public lecture of 1 May 1918 in Munich 'The Supersensible Human Being and Questions of Freedom of Will and Immortality of Soul as Results of Spiritual Science'. Rudolf Steiner spoke in greater detail on the same subject in both lectures of 18 and 20 April in Berlin, which appear in the volume 'The Eternal Element in the Human Soul—Immortality and Freedom', published in vol. 67 of the Collected Works 1961.

[109] Rudolf Steiner here calls the British Isles the British Peninsula. (Transl.)

[110] Compare this with the cycle 'The Effects of Spiritual Development on the Sheaths and the Self' in Collected Works vol. 145, 1957, 2nd lecture.

[111] Lectures referred to here include that of 3 May 1918, which was postponed but which appears as a parallel lecture in the Collected Works under the title of 'The Human Being: The Historical and Moral Life of

Humanity according to Results of Spiritual Science'. The corresponding lecture in the above-mentioned volume of the Collected Works is that of 14 March in Berlin.

[112] What is here referred to are the 'Fourteen Points' which President Woodrow Wilson proclaimed to America's Congress in 1918 and which served as the basis for peace negotiations.

[113] Johann Heinrich Lambert, 1728–1777, physicist, astronomer and mathematician. In 1761 his *Cosmological Letters*, were published and in 1764 his main work, *New Organon*. He was born in Mulhouse, now Alsace.

[114] *Die Verabsolutierung des Urteils*. (Transl.)

[115] That is: crosses the Celestial Equator in a westerly direction. (Transl.)

[116] Lloyd George, 1863–1945, was a British Cabinet Minister 1905–08, Minister for Trade, later Chancellor of the Exchequer and Minister for War and 1916–1922 Prime Minister.

[117] Sir Henry Campbell-Bannerman, 1836–1908, leader of the English Liberals and 1905–08 Prime Minister.

[118] Rabindranath Tagore, 1861–1941, Indian poet and philosopher. The speech mentioned is 'The Spirit of Japan', which appeared in *Prussian Almanac* vol. 171, book 1, January 1918. [This was translated into German by Helene Meyer-Franck.]

[119] A description of the rising sun as an image of world creation can be found, i.a., in the poem 'The Creation—a morning song', 1773.

[120] Ku Hung-Ming, author of *The Spirit of the Chinese People and an Exit Strategy from War*, often quoted by Rudolf Steiner [and translated into German by Oskar A. H Schmitz, Jena 1916].

[121] Literally: 'Crossturnthee': Georg Kreuzwendedich von Rheinbaben, Baron and Prussian Minister of State and Finance, Supreme President of the Rhine Province.

[122] Otto Weininger, 1880–1903, philosopher. The book *Sex and Character* appeared in Vienna in 1903. The reference mentioned originates in the book *On Last Things*, published by Moritz Rappaport, Vienna, 1907. The quotation is literally: 'Remembrance of conditions before our birth is probably impossible for the reason that we have sunk so far through being born: we have lost [that] consciousness and demanded that we be born totally instinctually, without sensible resolve and without knowledge, which is why we know nothing of this past.'

[123] This lecture of 1907 was given in many cities and was then written by Rudolf Steiner in the form of an essay, which appears in the volume 'Lucifer Gnosis 1903–1908', vol. 34 of the Collected Works, Dornach, 1960; further as an individual volume, Dornach, 1969.

# Rudolf Steiner's Collected Works

The German Edition of Rudolf Steiner's Collected Works (the *Gesamtausgabe* [GA], published by Rudolf Steiner Verlag, Dornach, Switzerland) will be completed in the year 2025. The works are organized either by type of work (written, spoken, artistic creations), chronology, audience (public or other), or subject (education, art, etc.). For ease of comparison, the Collected Works in English (CW), listed below, follows the German organization and numbering.

The volumes that have so far been published in the English Collected Works edition appear *in italics with their published titles*; all other volumes, including those that have appeared in editions other than the CW, are set in Roman type with *literal translations* of the German titles. Published English titles are not necessarily the same as the German.

This list is current as of the date of this volume's publication.

## A. Written Works

### I. Writings 1884–1925

| | |
|---|---|
| CW 1 | Introductions and Selected Commentary on Goethe's Natural-scientific Writings |
| CW 1a–e | Goethe's Natural-scientific Writings |
| CW 1f | Editorial Afterwords to Goethe's Natural-scientific Writings in the Weimar Edition (1891–1896) |
| CW 2 | *Goethe's Theory of Knowledge: An Outline of the Epistemology of His Worldview* |
| CW 3 | Truth and Science |
| CW 4 | The Philosophy of Freedom |
| CW 4a | Documents to 'The Philosophy of Freedom' |
| CW 5 | Friedrich Nietzsche, A Fighter against His Own Time |
| CW 6 | Goethe's Worldview |
| CW 7 | Mysticism at the Dawn of Modern Spiritual Life and Its Relationship with Modern Worldviews |
| CW 8 | *Christianity as Mystical Fact and the Mysteries of Antiquity* |

CW 9 Theosophy: An Introduction into Supersensible World Knowledge and Human Purpose
CW 10 How Does One Attain Knowledge of Higher Worlds?
CW 11 From the Akasha-Chronicle
CW 12 Levels of Higher Knowledge
CW 13 Occult Science in Outline
CW 14 *Four Modern Mystery Dramas*
CW 15 The Spiritual Guidance of the Individual and Humanity
CW 16/17 *A Way of Self-Knowledge & The Threshold of the Spiritual World*
CW 18 The Riddles of Philosophy in Their History, Presented as an Outline
CW 18a Views of the World and of Life in the Nineteenth Century
CW 19 Thoughts during the Time of War (1915) and Further Texts on the Events of the World War (1917–1921)
CW 20 The Riddles of the Human Being: Articulated and Unarticulated in the Thinking, Views and Opinions of a Series of German and Austrian Personalities
CW 21 The Riddles of the Soul
CW 22 Goethe's Spiritual Nature and Its Revelation in 'Faust' and through the 'Fairy Tale of the Snake and the Lily'
CW 23 The Central Points of the Social Question in the Necessities of Life in the Present and the Future
CW 24 Essays Concerning the Threefold Division of the Social Organism and the Period 1915–1921
CW 25 Three Steps of Anthroposophy. Philosophy – Cosmology – Religion
CW 26 Anthroposophical Leading Thoughts
CW 27 Fundamentals for Expansion of the Art of Healing according to Spiritual-Scientific Insights
CW 28 *Autobiography: Chapters in the Course of My Life: 1861–1907*

## II. Collected Essays

CW 29 Collected Essays on Dramaturgy, 1889–1900
CW 30 Methodical Foundations of Anthroposophy: Collected Essays on Philosophy, Natural Science, Aesthetics and Psychology, 1884–1901
CW 31 Collected Essays on Culture and Current Events, 1887–1901
CW 32 Collected Essays on Literature, 1884–1902
CW 33 Biographies and Biographical Sketches, 1894–1905
CW 34 Lucifer-Gnosis: Foundational Essays on Anthroposophy and Reports from the Periodicals 'Luzifer' and 'Lucifer-Gnosis,' 1903–1908
CW 35 Philosophy and Anthroposophy: Collected Essays, 1904–1923
CW 36 The Goetheanum-Idea in the Middle of the Cultural Crisis of the Present: Collected Essays from the Periodical 'Das Goetheanum,' 1921–1925

CW 37 Writings on the History of the Anthroposophical Movement and Society 1902–1925

### III. Publications from the Literary Estate

CW 38/1 Complete Letters, Vol. 1: Weimar Period 1879–1890
CW 38/2 Complete Letters, Vol. 2: Weimar Period 1890–1897
CW 38/3 Complete Letters, Vol. 3: Early Berlin Period 1897–1905 [forthcoming]
CW 38/4 Complete Letters, Vol. 4: Activity within the Theosophical Society 1905–1912 [forthcoming]
CW 38/5 Complete Letters, Vol. 5: From the Founding of the Anthroposophical Society to the Opening of the Goetheanum 1913–1920 [forthcoming]
CW 38/6 Compelte Letters, Vol. 6: The Last Years 1920–1925 [forthcoming]
CW 40 Truth-Wrought Words
CW 40a Sayings, Poems and Mantras; Supplementary Volume
CW 41a Translations and Free Renderings from the Old and New Testaments
CW 41b Translations and Free Renderings of Various Works
CW 42 Stage Adaptations I: Dramas by Edouard Schuré
CW 43 Stage Adaptations II: The Oberufer Christmas Plays
CW 44 Sketches, Fragments and Paralipomena on the Four Mystery Dramas
CW 45 Anthroposophy: A Fragment from the Year 1910
CW 46 Posthumous Essays and Fragments 1879–1924
CW 47/48 Notebooks and Notepads (digital edition)
CW 49 Notes for and about Helmuth and Eliza von Moltke and Relatives, 1904–1924 [forthcoming]
CW 50 [Blank number]

## B. Lectures

### I. Public Lectures

CW 51 *On Philosophy, History, and Literature: Lectures at the Worker Education School and the Independent College, Berlin, 1901–1905*
CW 52 Spiritual Teachings Concerning the Soul and Observation of the World
CW 53 The Origin and Goal of the Human Being
CW 54 The Riddles of the World and Anthroposophy
CW 55 Knowledge of the Supersensible in Our Times and Its Meaning for Life Today
CW 56 Knowledge of the Soul and of the Spirit
CW 57 Where and How Does One Find the Spirit?
CW 58 The Metamorphoses of the Soul Life. Paths of Soul Experiences: Part One
CW 59 The Metamorphoses of the Soul Life. Paths of Soul Experiences: Part Two

| | |
|---|---|
| CW 60 | The Answers of Spiritual Science to the Biggest Questions of Existence |
| CW 61 | Human History in the Light of Spiritual Research |
| CW 62 | *Results of Spiritual Research* |
| CW 63 | Spiritual Science as a Treasure for Life |
| CW 64 | Out of Destiny-Burdened Times |
| CW 65 | Out of Central European Spiritual Life |
| CW 66 | Spirit and Matter, Life and Death |
| CW 67 | The Eternal in the Human Soul. Immortality and Freedom |
| CW 68a | On the Being of Christianity |
| CW 68b | The Cycle of the Human Being within the Sense-, Soul-, and Spirit-World |
| CW 68c | Goethe and the Present |
| CW 68d | The Being of Man in the Light of Spiritual Science |
| CW 69a | Truths and Errors of Spiritual Research. Spiritual Science and the Future of Mankind |
| CW 69b | Knowledge and Immortality |
| CW 69c | New Christ-Experience |
| CW 69d | Death and Immortality in the Light of Spiritual Science |
| CW 69e | Spiritual Science and the Spiritual Goals of Our Time |
| CW 70a | Human Soul, Destiny and Death |
| CW 70b | Paths to the Knowledge of the Eternal Powers of the Human Soul |
| CW 71a | Soul Immortality [forthcoming] |
| CW 71b | The Human Being as a Soul and Spirit Being |
| CW 72 | Freedom – Immortality – Social Life |
| CW 73 | The Supplementing of the Modern Sciences through Anthroposophy |
| CW 73a | Specialized Fields of Knowledge and Anthroposophy |
| CW 74 | The Philosophy of Thomas Aquinas |
| CW 75 | *Anthroposophy and the Natural Sciences: Foundations and Methods* |
| CW 76 | The Fructifying Effect of Anthroposophy on Specialized Fields |
| CW 77a | The Task of Anthroposophy in Relation to Science and Life: The Darmstadt College Course |
| CW 77b | Art and Anthroposophy. The Goetheanum-Impulse |
| CW 78 | Anthroposophy, Its Roots of Knowledge and Fruits for Life |
| CW 79 | The Reality of the Higher Worlds |
| CW 80a | The Being of Anthroposophy |
| CW 80b | The Inner Realm of Nature and the Being of the Human Soul |
| CW 80c | Anthroposophical Spiritual Science and the Great Civilizational Questions of the Present |
| CW 81 | *Reimagining Academic Studies: Science, Philosophy, Education, Social Science, Theology, Theory of Language* |
| CW 82 | *Becoming Fully Human: The Significance of Anthroposophy in Contemporary Spiritual Life* |
| CW 83 | *The Tension between East and West* |

| | |
|---|---|
| CW 84 | *The Aims of Anthroposophy and the Purpose of the Goetheanum* |
| CW 85 | Supplementary Volume: Individual Public Lectures I [forthcoming] |
| CW 86 | Supplementary Volume: Individual Public Lectures II [forthcoming] |

**II. Lectures to the Members of the Anthroposophical Society**

| | |
|---|---|
| CW 87 | Ancient Mysteries and Christianity |
| CW 88 | *Concerning the Astral World and Devachan* |
| CW 89 | Consciousness–Life–Form. Fundamental Principles of a Spiritual-Scientific Cosmology |
| CW 90a | Self-knowledge and Knowledge of the Divine, Vol. I. Theosophy, Christology, and Mythology |
| CW 90b | Self-knowledge and Knowledge of the Divine, Vol. II. Theosophy, Christology, and Mythology |
| CW 90c | Theosophy and Occultism |
| CW 91 | Cosmology and Human Evolution. Introduction to Theosophy – Theory of Colours |
| CW 92 | *The Occult Truths of Myths and Legends: Greek and Germanic Mythology: Richard Wagner in the Light of Spiritual Science* |
| CW 93 | The Temple Legend and the Golden Legend as a Symbolic Expression of Past and Future Secrets of Human Development. From the Contents of the Esoteric School |
| CW 93a | Fundamentals of Esotericism |
| CW 94 | Cosmogony. Popular Occultism. The Gospel of John. Theosophy Based on the Gospel of John |
| CW 95 | At the Gates of Theosophy |
| CW 96 | Origin-Impulses of Spiritual Science. Christian Esotericism in the Light of New Spirit-knowledge |
| CW 97 | The Christian Mystery |
| CW 98 | *Nature Beings and Spirit Beings: Their Activity in Our Visible World* |
| CW 99 | The Theosophy of the Rosicrucians |
| CW 100 | *True Knowledge of the Christ: Theosophy and Rosicucianism—The Gospel of John* |
| CW 101 | Myths and Legends. Occult Signs and Symbols |
| CW 102 | *Good and Evil Spirits and Their Influence on Humanity* |
| CW 103 | *The Gospel of John* |
| CW 104 | The Apocalypse of John |
| CW 104a | From the Picture-Script of the Apocalypse of John |
| CW 105 | *Universe, Earth, Human Being: Their Relationship to Egyptian Myths and Modern Civilization* |
| CW 106 | Egyptian Myths and Mysteries in Relation to the Active Spiritual Forces of the Present |
| CW 107 | *Disease, Karma, and Healing: Spiritual-scientific Enquiries into the Nature of the Human Being* |

CW 108 Answering the Questions of Life and the World through Anthroposophy

CW 109 The Principle of Spiritual Economy in Connection with the Question of Reincarnation. An Aspect of the Spiritual Guidance of Humanity

CW 110 *The Spiritual Hierarchies and the Physical World: Zodiac, Planets, and Cosmos*

CW 111 Introduction to the Foundations of Theosophy

CW 112 The Gospel of John in Relation to the Three Other Gospels, Especially the Gospel of Luke

CW 113 The Orient in the Light of the Occident. The Children of Lucifer and the Brothers of Christ

CW 114 The Gospel of Luke

CW 115 Anthroposophy – Psychosophy – Pneumatosophy

CW 116 *The Christ-Impulse and the Development of Ego-Consciousness*

CW 117 *Deeper Secrets of Human Evolution in Light of the Gospels*

CW 117a The Gospel of John and the Three Other Gospels

CW 118 The Event of the Christ-Appearance in the Etheric World

CW 119 *Macrocosm and Microcosm: The Greater and the Lesser World: Questions Concerning the Soul, Life and the Spirit*

CW 120 The Revelations of Karma

CW 121 *The Mission of Folk Souls*

CW 122 The Secrets of the Biblical Creation-Story. The Six-Day Work in the First Book of Moses

CW 123 The Gospel of Matthew

CW 124 *Background to the Gospel of St Mark*

CW 125 *Paths and Goals of the Spiritual Human Being: Life Questions in the Light of Spiritual Science*

CW 126 Occult History. Esoteric Observations of the Karmic Relationships of Personalities and Events of World History

CW 127 *The Mission of the New Spiritual Revelation: The Pivotal Nature of the Christ Event in Earth Evolution*

CW 128 An Occult Physiology

CW 129 *Wonders of the World: Trials of the Soul, Revelations of the Spirit*

CW 130 Esoteric Christianity and the Spiritual Guidance of Humanity

CW 131 From Jesus to Christ

CW 132 *Inner Experiences of Evolution*

CW 133 The Earthly and the Cosmic Human Being

CW 134 *The World of the Senses and the World of the Spirit*

CW 135 Reincarnation and Karma and Their Meaning for the Culture of the Present

CW 136 *Spiritual Beings in the Heavenly Bodies and in the Kingdoms of Nature*

CW 137 The Human Being in the Light of Occultism, Theosophy and Philosophy

CW 138 On Initiation. On Eternity and the Passing Moment. On the Light of the Spirit and the Darkness of Life

CW 139 The Gospel of Mark
CW 140 Occult Investigation into the Life between Death and New Birth. The Living Interaction between Life and Death
CW 141 *Between Death and Rebirth: In Relation to Cosmic Facts*
CW 142/46 *The Bhagavad Gita and the West: The Esoteric Significance of the Bhagavad Gita and Its Relation to the Epistles of Paul*
CW 143 *Three Paths to Christ: Experiencing the Supersensible*
CW 144 *The Mysteries of Initiation: From Isis to the Holy Grail*
CW 145 What Significance Does Occult Development of the Human Being Have for the Sheaths–Physical Body, Etheric Body, Astral Body, and Self?
CW 146 [See CW 142/46]
CW 147 The Secrets of the Threshold
CW 148 The Fifth Gospel
CW 149 *Christ and the Spiritual World: The Quest for the Holy Grail*
CW 150 *How the Spiritual World Projects into Physical Existence: The Influence of the Dead*
CW 151 *Human and Cosmic Thought*
CW 152 *Approaching the Mystery of Golgotha*
CW 153 The Inner Being of Man and Life Between Death and New Birth
CW 154 How Does One Gain an Understanding of the Spiritual World? The Flowing in of Spiritual Impulses from out of the World of the Deceased
CW 155 *Christ and the Human Soul: The Meaning of Life – The Spiritual Foundation of Morality – Anthroposophy and Christianity*
CW 156 *Inner Reading and Inner Hearing: And How to Achieve Existence in the World of Ideas*
CW 157 Human Destinies and the Destiny of Peoples
CW 157a The Formation of Destiny and the Life after Death
CW 158 *Our Connection with the Elemental World: Kalevala – Olaf Åsteson – the Russian People: The World as the Result of Balancing Influences*
CW 159 *The Mystery of Death: The Nature and Significance of Central Europe and the European Folk-Spirits*
CW 160 [Blank number]
CW 161 *Artistic Sensitivity as a Spiritual Approach to Knowing Life and the World*
CW 162 Questions of Art and Life in Light of Spiritual Science
CW 163 Coincidence, Necessity and Providence. Imaginative Knowledge and the Processes after Death
CW 164 *The Value of Thinking for a Cognition that Satisfies the Human Being: The Relationship between Spiritual Science and Natural Science*
CW 165 *Unifying Humanity Spiritually through the Christ Impulse*
CW 166 Necessity and Freedom in World Events and in Human Action
CW 167 *The Human Spirit Past and Present: Occult Fraternities and the Mystery of Golgotha*
CW 168 *The Connection between the Living and the Dead*
CW 169 World-being and Selfhood

CW 170 The Riddle of the Human Being. The Spiritual Background of Human History

CW 171 Inner Development-Impulses of Humanity. Goethe and the Crisis of the 19th Century.

CW 172 The Karma of the Vocation of the Human Being in Connection with Goethe's Life.

CW 173a Observations of Modern History, Vol. I: Paths to an Objective Judgment;

CW 173b Observations of Modern History, Vol. II: The Karma of Untruthfulness

CW 173c Observations of Modern History, Vol. III: The Reality of Occult Impulses

CW 174a *Europe Between East and West in Cosmic and Human History*

CW 174b *The Spiritual Background to the First World War*

CW 175 *Building Stones for an Understanding of the Mystery of Golgotha: Human Life in a Cosmic Context*

CW 176 *The Karma of Materialism: Aspects of Human Evolution*

CW 177 *The Fall of the Spirits of Darkness: The Spiritual Background to the Outer World: Spiritual Beings and Their Effects*

CW 178 Individual Spiritual Beings and Their Influence in the Soul of the Human Being

CW 179 *The Influence of the Dead on Destiny*

CW 180 Mystery Truths and Christmas Impulses. Ancient Myths and their Meaning.

CW 181 *Dying Earth and Living Cosmos: The Living Gifts of Anthroposophy: The Need for New Forms of Consciousness*

CW 182 Death as Transformation of Life

CW 183 *Human Evolution: A Spiritual-Scientific Quest*

CW 184 *Eternal and Transient Elements in Human Life: The Cosmic Past of Humanity and the Mystery of Evil*

CW 185 Historical Symptomology

CW 185a Historical-Developmental Foundations for Forming a Social Judgment

CW 186 The Fundamental Social Demands of Our Time. In Changed Times

CW 187 How Can Humanity Find the Christ Again? The Threefold Shadow-Existence of our Time and the New Christ-Light

CW 188 Goetheanism, a Transformation-Impulse and Resurrection-Thought. Science of the Human Being and Science of Sociology

CW 189 *Conscious Society: Anthroposophy and the Social Question*

CW 190 *Past and Future Impulses in Societal Events*

CW 191 *Understanding Society through Spiritual-Scientific Knowledge: Social Threefolding, Christ, Lucifer, and Ahriman*

CW 192 Spiritual-Scientific Treatment of Social and Pedagogical Questions

CW 193 *Problems of Society: An Esoteric View, from Luciferic Past to Ahrimanic Future*

| | |
|---|---|
| CW 194 | *Michael's Mission: Revealing the Essential Secrets of Human Nature* |
| CW 195 | *Cosmic New Year: Thoughts for New Year 1920* |
| CW 196 | *What Is Necessary in These Urgent Times* |
| CW 197 | *Polarities in the Evolution of Humanity: West and East – Materialism and Mysticism – Knowledge and Belief* |
| CW 198 | Healing Factors for the Social Organism |
| CW 199 | Spiritual Science as Knowledge of the Foundational Impulses of Social Formation |
| CW 200 | The New Spirituality and the Christ-Experience of the 20th Century |
| CW 201 | The Correspondences Between Microcosm and Macrocosm. The Human Being – A Hieroglyph of the Universe. |
| CW 202 | *Universal Spirituality and Human Physicality: Bridging the Divide: The Search for the New Isis and the Divine Sophia* |
| CW 203 | The Responsibility of Human Beings for the Development of the World through their Spiritual Connection with the Planet Earth and the World of the Stars. |
| CW 204 | Perspectives of the Development of Humanity. The Materialistic Knowledge-Impulse and the Task of Anthroposophy. |
| CW 205 | Human Development, World-Soul, and World-Spirit. Part One: The Human Being as a Being of Body and Soul in Relationship to the World. |
| CW 206 | Human Development, World-Soul, and World-Spirit. Part Two: The Human Being as a Spiritual Being in the Process of Historical Development |
| CW 207 | Anthroposophy as Cosmosophy. Part One: Characteristic Features of the Human Being in the Earthly and the Cosmic Realms |
| CW 208 | Anthroposophy as Cosmosophy. Part Two: The Forming of the Human Being as the Result of Cosmic Influence |
| CW 209 | *The Language of the Cosmos: Cosmic Influences and the Spiritual Task of Northern Europe* |
| CW 210 | Old and New Methods of Initiation. Drama and Poetry in the Change of Consciousness in the Modern Age |
| CW 211 | *The Sun Mystery and the Mystery of Death and Resurrection: Exoteric and Esoteric Christianity* |
| CW 212 | *Life of the Human Soul: And Its Relation to World Evolution* |
| CW 213 | Human Questions and World Answers |
| CW 214 | The Mystery of the Trinity: The Human Being in Relationship with the Spiritual World in the Course of Time |
| CW 215 | Philosophy, Cosmology, and Religion in Anthroposophy |
| CW 216 | *Supersensible Impulses in the Historical Development of Humanity* |
| CW 217 | *Becoming the Archangel Michael's Companions: Rudolf Steiner's Challenge to the Younger Generation* |
| CW 217a | *Youth and the Etheric Heart: Rudolf Steiner Speaks to the Younger Generation* |
| CW 218 | *Spirit as Sculptor of the Human Organism* |

CW 219 The Relationship of the World of the Stars to the Human Being, and of the Human Being to the World of the Stars. The Spiritual Communion of Humanity
CW 220 *Awake! For the Sake of the Future*
CW 221 Earth-Knowing and Heaven-Insight
CW 222 *The Driving Force of Spiritual Powers in World History*
CW 223 The Cycle of the Year as Breathing Process of the Earth and the Four Great Festival-Seasons. Anthroposophy and the Human Heart (*Gemüt*)
CW 224 The Human Soul and its Connection with Divine-Spiritual Individualities. The Internalization of the Festivals of the Year
CW 225 *Three Perspectives of Anthroposophy: Cultural Phenomena from the Point of View of Spiritual Science*
CW 226 Human Being, Human Destiny, and World Development
CW 227 Initiation-Knowledge
CW 228 *Initiation Science: And the Development of the Human Mind*
CW 229 The Experiencing of the Course of the Year in Four Cosmic Imaginations
CW 230 The Human Being as Harmony of the Creative, Building, and Formative World-Word
CW 231 The Supersensible Human Being, Understood Anthroposophically
CW 232 The Forming of the Mysteries
CW 233 *World History and the Mysteries in the Light of Anthroposophy*
CW 233a *Rosicrucianism and Modern Initiation: Mystery Centres of the Middle Ages: The Easter Festival and the History of the Mysteries*
CW 234 Anthroposophy. A Summary after 21 Years
CW 235 Esoteric Observations of Karmic Relationships in 6 Volumes, Vol. 1
CW 236 Esoteric Observations of Karmic Relationships in 6 Volumes, Vol. 2
CW 237 Esoteric Observations of Karmic Relationships in 6 Volumes, Vol. 3: The Karmic Relationships of the Anthroposophical Movement
CW 238 Esoteric Observations of Karmic Relationships in 6 Volumes, Vol. 4: The Spiritual Life of the Present in Relationship to the Anthroposophical Movement
CW 239 Esoteric Observations of Karmic Relationships in 6 Volumes, Vol. 5
CW 240 Esoteric Observations of Karmic Relationships in 6 Volumes, Vol. 6
CW 241 [Blank number]
CW 242 [Blank number]
CW 243 *True and False Paths of Spiritual Research*
CW 244 Answers to Questions, and Interviews
CW 245 [Blank number]
CW 246 Supplementary Volume I: Individual Members Lectures
CW 247 Supplementary Volume II: Individual Members Lectures
CW 248 [Blank number]
CW 249 [Blank number]
CW 250 On the History of the German Section of the Theosophical Society 1902–1913. Lectures, Speeches, Reports, and Minutes

| | |
|---|---|
| CW 251 | On the History of the Anthroposophical Society 1913–1922 |
| CW 252 | On the History of the Building Association and the Goetheanum Association 1911–1924 |
| CW 253 | *Sexuality, Inner Development, and Community Life: Ethical and Spiritual Dimensions of the Crisis in the Anthroposophical Society in Dornach, 1915* |
| CW 254 | The Occult Movement in the 19th Century and Its Relationship to World Culture. Significant Points from the Exoteric Cultural Life around the Middle of the 19th Century |
| CW 255b | Anthroposophy and Its Opponents |
| CW 256 | [Blank number] |
| CW 257 | Anthroposophical Community-Building |
| CW 258 | *The Anthroposophic Movement: The History and Conditions of the Anthroposophical Movement in Relation to the Anthroposophical Society: An Encouragement for Self-Examination* |
| CW 259 | The Year of Destiny 1923 in the History of the Anthroposophical Society. From the Burning of the Goetheanum to the Christmas Conference |
| CW 260 | The Christmas Conference for the Founding of the General Anthroposophical Society 1923/24 |
| CW 260a | The Constitution of the General Anthroposophical Society and the School for Spiritual Science. The Rebuilding of the Goetheanum |
| CW 261 | *Our Dead: Memorial, Funeral, and Cremation Addresses 1906–1924* |
| CW 262 | Rudolf Steiner and Marie Steiner-von Sivers: Correspondence and Documents, 1901–1925 |
| CW 263/1 | Rudolf Steiner and Edith Maryon: Correspondence: Letters, Verses, Sketches, 1912–1924 |
| CW 264 | *From the History and Contents of the First Section of the Esoteric School: Letters, Documents, and Lectures: 1904–1914* |
| CW 265 | *Freemasonry and Ritual Work: The Misraim Service* |
| CW 265a | Teaching and Instruction Lessons for Members of the Knowledge-Cultic Section of the Esoteric School 1904–1914 [forthcoming] |
| CW 266/1 | *From the Esoteric School: Esoteric Lessons 1904–1909* |
| CW 266/2 | *From the Esoteric School: Esoteric Lessons 1910–1912* |
| CW 266/3 | *From the Esoteric School: Esoteric Lessons 1913–1923* |
| CW 267 | *Soul Exercises: Word and Symbol Meditations* |
| CW 268 | *Mantric Sayings: Meditations 1903–1925* |
| CW 269 | Ritual Texts for the Celebration of the Free Christian Religious Instruction. The Collected Verses for Teachers and Students of the Waldorf School |
| CW 270 | Esoteric Instructions for the First Class of the School for Spiritual Science at the Goetheanum 1924, 4 Volumes |

## III. Lectures and Courses on Specific Realms of Life

### Lectures on Art

CW 271 *Art and Theory of Art: Foundations of a New Aesthetics*
CW 272 *Anthroposophy in the Light of Goethe's* Faust*: Volume One of Spiritual-Scientific Commentaries on Goethe's* Faust
CW 273 *Goethe's* Faust *in the Light of Anthroposophy: Volume Two of Spiritual-Scientific Commentaries on Goethe's* Faust
CW 274 Addresses for the Christmas Plays from the Old Folk Traditions
CW 275 Art in the Light of Mystery Wisdom
CW 276 *The Arts and Their Mission*
CW 277a The Origin and Development of Eurythmy 1912–1918
CW 277b The Origin and Development of Eurythmy 1918–1920
CW 277c The Origin and Development of Eurythmy 1920–1922 [forthcoming]
CW 277d The Origin and Development of Eurythmy 1923–1924 [forthcoming]
CW 278 Eurythmy as Visible Song
CW 279 *Eurythmy as Speech Made Visible: Speech Eurythmy Course*
CW 280 The Method and Nature of Speech Formation
CW 281 The Art of Recitation and Declamation
CW 282 Speech Formation and Dramatic Art
CW 283 The Nature of the Musical Element and the Experience of Tone in the Human Being
CW 284 *Rosicrucianism Renewed: The Unity of Art, Science & Religion: The Theosophical Congress of Whitsun 1907*
CW 285 [Blank number]
CW 286 Paths to a New Style of Architecture. 'And the Building Becomes Man'
CW 287 *Architecture as Peacework: The First Goetheanum, Dornach, 1914*
CW 288 *Architecture, Sculpture, and Painting of the First Goetheanum*
CW 289 The Building-Idea of the Goetheanum: Lectures with Slides from the Years 1920–1921
CW 290 *Toward a New Theory of Architecture: The First Goetheanum in Pictures* [no longer in the German GA]
CW 291 The Being of Colours
CW 291a Knowledge of Colours. Supplementary Volume to 'The Being of Colours'
CW 292 *Art History as a Reflection of Inner Spiritual Impulses*

### Lectures on Education

CW 293 General Knowledge of the Human Being as the Foundation of Pedagogy
CW 294 The Art of Education: Methodology and Didactics

**Lectures on Medicine**

**Lectures on Natural Science**

| | |
|---|---|
| CW 320 | Spiritual-Scientific Impulses for the Development of Physics 1: The First Natural-Scientific Course: Light, Colour, Tone, Mass, Electricity, Magnetism |
| CW 321 | Spiritual-Scientific Impulses for the Development of Physics 2: The Second Natural-Scientific Course: Warmth at the Border of Positive and Negative Materiality |
| CW 322 | The Borders of the Knowledge of Nature |
| CW 323 | *Interdisciplinary Astronomy: Third Scientific Course* |
| CW 324 | Nature Observation, Mathematics, and Scientific Experimentation and Results from the Viewpoint of Anthroposophy |
| CW 324a | The Fourth Dimension in Mathematics and Reality |
| CW 325 | Natural Science and the World-Historical Development of Humanity since Ancient Times |
| CW 326 | The Moment of the Coming Into Being of Natural Science in World History and Its Development Since Then |
| CW 327 | Spiritual-Scientific Foundations for Success in Farming. The Agricultural Course |

**Lectures on Social Life and the Threefold Arrangement of the Social Organism**

| | |
|---|---|
| CW 328 | The Social Question |
| CW 329 | The Liberation of the Human Being as the Foundation for a New Social Form |
| CW 330 | The Renewal of the Social Organism |
| CW 331 | Work-Council and Socialization |
| CW 332a | The Social Future |
| CW 332b | Lectures and Speeches on Social and Economic Issues |
| CW 333 | *Freedom of Thought and Societal Forces: Implementing the Demands of Modern Society* |
| CW 334 | From the Unified State to the Threefold Social Organism |
| CW 335 | The Crisis of the Present and the Path to Healthy Thinking |
| CW 336 | The Great Questions of the Times and Anthroposophical Spiritual Knowledge |
| CW 337a | Social Ideas, Social Realities, Social Practice, Vol. 1: Question-and-Answer Evenings and Study Evenings of the Alliance for the Threefold Social Organism in Stuttgart, 1919–1920 |
| CW 337b | Social Ideas, Social Realities, Social Practice, Vol. 2: Discussion Evenings of the Swiss Alliance for the Threefold Social Organism |
| CW 338 | *Communicating Anthroposophy: The Course for Speakers to Promote the Idea of Threefolding* |
| CW 339 | Anthroposophy, Threefold Social Organism, and the Art of Public Speaking |
| CW 340/41 | *Rethinking Economics: Lectures and Seminars on World Economics* |

**Lectures and Courses on Christian Religious Work**

CW 342 *First Steps in Christian Religious Renewal: Preparing the Ground for The Christian Community*
CW 343 Lectures and Courses on Christian Religious Work, Vol. 2: Spiritual Knowledge – Religious Feeling – Cultic Doing
CW 344 Lectures and Courses on Christian Religious Work, Vol. 3: Lectures at the Founding of The Christian Community
CW 345 Lectures and Courses on Christian Religious Work, Vol. 4: Concerning the Nature of the Working Word
CW 346 Lectures and Courses on Christian Religious Work, Vol. 5: The Apocalypse and the Work of the Priest

**Lectures for Workers at the Goetheanum**

CW 347 The Knowledge of the Nature of the Human Being According to Body, Soul and Spirit. On Earlier Conditions of the Earth
CW 348 On Health and Illness. Foundations of a Spiritual-Scientific Doctrine of the Senses
CW 349 On the Life of the Human Being and of the Earth. On the Nature of Christianity
CW 350 Rhythms in the Cosmos and in the Human Being. How Does One Come To See the Spiritual World?
CW 351 The Human Being and the World. The Influence of the Spirit in Nature. On the Nature of Bees
CW 352 Nature and the Human Being Observed Spiritual-Scientifically
CW 353 The History of Humanity and the World-Views of the Folk Cultures
CW 354 The Creation of the World and the Human Being. Life on Earth and the Influence of the Stars

## C. Artistic Works

CW A 1–10; 57 The Architectural Work I: The Goetheanum and Its Predecessors
CW A 11 The Sculptural Work
CW A 12 The Goetheanum Windows. The Speech of Light. Sketches and Studies
CW A 13–16; 52–56 Painting Work
CW A 14 Sketches for the Painting of the Small Dome of the First Goetheanum
CW A 27–43 The Architectural Work II: Commercial and Residential Buildings in Dornach and Other Places [forthcoming]
CW A 45 The Graphic Work
CW A 48 The Drawing Work
CW A 51 The Art of Jewellery as a Goethean Language of Form

CW A 54.0 A Path of Training in Painting. Pastel Sketches and Watercolours
CW A 54.1 Nature Moods. Nine Training Sketches for Painters

**Eurythmy Figures**

CW A 26 Skectches of the Eurythmy Figures
CW A 26a The Eurythmy Figures of Rudolf Steiner, Artistically Executed by Annemarie Bäschlin
CW A 26b Eurythmy Figures from the Time When They Were Created

**Eurythmy Forms**

CW A 23/1 Volume I: Eurythmy Forms for Poems by Rudolf Steiner
CW A 23/2 Volume II: Eurythmy Forms for the Calendar of the Soul by Rudolf Steiner
CW A 23/3 Volume III: Euythmy Forms for Poems by J. W. von Goethe
CW A 23/4 Volume IV: Eurythmy Forms for Poems by Christian Morgenstern
CW A 23/5 Volume V: Eurythmy Forms for Poems by Albert Steffen
CW A 23/6 Volume VI: Eurythmy Forms for German Poems by Fercher von Steinwand, Hamerling, Hebbel, C. F. Meyer, Nietzsche, among others
CW A 23/7 Volume VII: Eurythmy Forms for English Poems
CW A 23/8 Volume VIII: Eurythmy Forms for French and Russian Poems
CW A 24 Volume IX: Eurythmy Forms for Tone Eurythmy

**Blackboard Drawings from Lectures**

CW A 58/1 Volume I: 20 Plates from Public Lectures 1920–1924 in CWs 73a, 74, 76, and 84
CW A 58/2 Volume II: 38 Plates from Lectures in 1919 in CWs 191 and 194
CW A 58/3 Volume III: 34 Plates from Lectures in 1920 in CWs 196 and 198
CW A 58/4 Volume IV: 33 Plates from Lectures in 1920 in CWs 199 and 200
CW A 58/5 Volume V: 31 Plates from Lectures in 1920 in CW 201
CW A 58/6 Volume VI: 46 Plates from Lectures 1920–1921 in CWs 202–204
CW A 58/7 Volume VII: 38 Plates from Lectures in 1921 in CWs 205 and 206
CW A 58/8 Volume VIII: 42 Plates from Lectures in 1921 in CWs 207–209
CW A 58/9 Volume IX: 40 Plates from Lectures in 1922 in CWs 210–212
CW A 58/10 Volume X: 35 Plates from Lectures in 1922 in CWs 213–215
CW A 58/11 Volume XI: 41 Plates from Lectures 1922–1923 in CWs 216, 218–220
CW A 58/12 Volume XII: 37 Plates from Lectures in 1923 in CWs 221–225
CW A 58/13 Volume XIII: 38 Plates from Lectures in 1923 in CWs 227–230
CW A 58/14 Volume XIV: 36 Plates from Lectures in 1923 in CWs 232 and 233
CW A 58/15 Volume XV: 37 Plates from Lectures in 1924 in CWs 233a, 234, and 243
CW A 58/16 Volume XVI: 56 Plates from the 'Karma Lectures' in CWs 235–238 and 240

CW A 58/17 Volume XVII: 21 Plates from Lectures on the History of the Anthroposophical Society in CWs 257, 258, 260, and 260a
CW A 58/18 Volume XVIII: 33 Plates from Lectures on Art in CWs 271, 276, 283, 288–290, and 291
CW A 58/19 Volume XIX: 41 Plates from Lectures on Eurythmy in CWs 278, 279, and 315
CW A 58/20 Volume XX: 27 Plates from Lectures on Speech Formation in CWs 281 and 282
CW A 58/21 Volume XXI: 42 Plates from Lectures on Education in CWs 296, 303, 304, 306, and 311
CW A 58/22 Volume XXII: 46 Plates from Lectures on Medicine in CWs 312–315
CW A 58/23 Volume XXIII: 48 Plates from Lectures in 1924 in CWs 316–318
CW A 58/24 Volume XXIV: 39 Plates from Lectures on Natural Science and the Social Question in CWs 322, 326, 327, 339, and 340
CW A 58/25 Volume XXV: 33 Plates from the 'Workers Lectures' (Volumes 1 and 2) in CWs 347 and 348
CW A 58/26 Volume XXVI: 51 Plates from the 'Workers Lectures' (Volumes 3 and 4) in CWs 349 and 350
CW A 58/27 Volume XXVII: 35 Plates from the 'Workers Lectures' (Volumes 5 and 6) in CWs 351 and 352
CW A 58/28 Volume XXVIII: 42 Plates from the 'Workers Lectures' (Volumes 7 and 8) in CWs 353 and 354
CW A 58/29 Volume XXIX: 43 Plates from Lectures and Courses on Christian Religious Activity in CWs 342–344 and 346
CW A 58/30 Volume XXX: 27 Plates from CWs 255b, 324a, 337b, and 340, Corrigenda, Plates without CW Assignment, Copies

# SIGNIFICANT EVENTS IN THE LIFE OF RUDOLF STEINER

1829: June 23: birth of Johann Steiner (1829–1910)—Rudolf Steiner's father—in Geras, Lower Austria.

1834: May 8: birth of Franciska Blie (1834–1918)—Rudolf Steiner's mother—in Horn, Lower Austria. 'My father and mother were both children of the glorious Lower Austrian forest district north of the Danube.'

1860: May 16: marriage of Johann Steiner and Franciska Blie.

1861: February 25: birth of *Rudolf Joseph Lorenz Steiner* in Kraljevec, Croatia, near the border with Hungary, where Johann Steiner works as a telegrapher for the South Austria Railroad. Rudolf Steiner is baptized two days later, February 27, the date usually given as his birthday.

1862: Summer: the family moves to Mödling, Lower Austria.

1863: The family moves to Pottschach, Lower Austria, near the Styrian border, where Johann Steiner becomes stationmaster. 'The view stretched to the mountains . . . majestic peaks in the distance and the sweet charm of nature in the immediate surroundings.'

1864: November 15: birth of Rudolf Steiner's sister, Leopoldine (d. November 1, 1927). She will become a seamstress and live with her parents for the rest of her life.

1866: July 28: birth of Rudolf Steiner's deaf-mute brother, Gustav (d. May 1, 1941).

1867: Rudolf Steiner enters the village school. Following a disagreement between his father and the schoolmaster, whose wife falsely accused the boy of causing a commotion, Rudolf Steiner is taken out of school and taught at home.

1868: A critical experience. Unknown to the family, an aunt dies in a distant town. Sitting in the station waiting room, Rudolf Steiner sees her 'form', which speaks to him, asking for help. 'Beginning with this experience, a new soul life began in the boy, one in which not only the outer trees and mountains spoke to him, but also the worlds that lay behind them. From this moment on, the boy began to live with the spirits of nature . . .'

1869: The family moves to the peaceful, rural village of Neudorfl, near Wiener Neustadt in present-day Austria. Rudolf Steiner attends the village school. Because of the 'unorthodoxy' of his writing and spelling, he has to do 'extra lessons'.

1870: Through a book lent to him by his tutor, he discovers geometry: 'To grasp something purely in the spirit brought me inner happiness. I know that I first learned happiness through geometry.' The same tutor allows him to draw, while other students still struggle with their reading and writing. 'An artistic element' thus enters his education.

1871: Though his parents are not religious, Rudolf Steiner becomes a 'church child', a favourite of the priest, who was 'an exceptional character'. 'Up to the age of ten or eleven, among those I came to know, he was far and away the most significant.' Among other things, he introduces Steiner to Copernican, heliocentric cosmology. As an altar boy, Rudolf Steiner serves at Masses, funerals, and Corpus Christi processions. At year's end, after an incident in which he escapes a thrashing, his father forbids him to go to church.

1872: Rudolf Steiner transfers to grammar school in Wiener-Neustadt, a five-mile walk from home, which must be done in all weathers.

1873–75: Through his teachers and on his own, Rudolf Steiner has many wonderful experiences with science and mathematics. Outside school, he teaches himself analytic geometry, trigonometry, differential equations, and calculus.

1876: Rudolf Steiner begins tutoring other students. He learns bookbinding from his father. He also teaches himself stenography.

1877: Rudolf Steiner discovers Kant's *Critique of Pure Reason,* which he reads and rereads. He also discovers and reads von Rotteck's *World History.*

1878: He studies extensively in contemporary psychology and philosophy.

1879: Rudolf Steiner graduates from high school with honours. His father is transferred to Inzersdorf, near Vienna. He uses his first visit to Vienna 'to purchase a great number of philosophy books'—Kant, Fichte, Schelling, and Hegel, as well as numerous histories of philosophy. His aim: to find a path from the 'I' to nature.

October 1879–1883: Rudolf Steiner attends the Technical College in Vienna—to study mathematics, chemistry, physics, mineralogy, botany, zoology, biology, geology, and mechanics—with a scholarship. He also attends lectures in history and literature, while avidly reading philosophy on his own. His two favourite professors are Karl Julius Schröer (German language and literature) and Edmund Reitlinger (physics). He also audits lectures by Robert Zimmermann on aesthetics and Franz Brentano on philosophy. During this year he begins his friendship with Moritz Zitter (1861–1921), who will help support him financially when he is in Berlin.

1880: Rudolf Steiner attends lectures on Schiller and Goethe by Karl Julius Schröer, who becomes his mentor. Also 'through a remarkable combination of circumstances', he meets Felix Koguzki, a 'herb gatherer' and healer, who could 'see deeply into the secrets of nature'. Rudolf Steiner will meet and study with this 'emissary of the Master' throughout his time in Vienna.

1881: January: '... I didn't sleep a wink. I was busy with philosophical problems until about 12:30 a.m. Then, finally, I threw myself down on my couch. All my striving during the previous year had been to research whether the following statement by Schelling was true or not: *Within everyone dwells a secret, marvellous capacity to draw back from the stream of time—out of the self clothed in all that comes to us from outside—into our innermost being and there, in the immutable form of the Eternal, to look into ourselves.* I believe, and I am still quite certain of it, that I discovered this capacity in myself; I had long had an inkling of it. Now the whole of idealist philosophy stood before me in modified form. What's a sleepless night compared to that!'

Rudolf Steiner begins communicating with leading thinkers of the day, who send him books in return, which he reads eagerly.

July: 'I am not one of those who dives into the day like an animal in human form. I pursue a quite specific goal, an idealistic aim—knowledge of the truth! This cannot be done offhandedly. It requires the greatest striving in the world, free of all egotism, and equally of all resignation.'

August: Steiner puts down on paper for the first time thoughts for a 'Philosophy of Freedom'. 'The striving for the absolute: this human yearning is freedom.' He also seeks to outline a 'peasant philosophy', describing what the worldview of a 'peasant'—one who lives close to the earth and the old ways—really is.

1881–1882: Felix Koguzki, the herb gatherer, reveals himself to be the envoy of another, higher initiatory personality, who instructs Rudolf Steiner to penetrate Fichte's philosophy and to master modern scientific thinking as a preparation for right entry into the spirit. This 'Master' also teaches him the double (evolutionary and involutionary) nature of time.

1882: Through the offices of Karl Julius Schröer, Rudolf Steiner is asked by Joseph Kürschner to edit Goethe's scientific works for the *Deutsche National-Literatur* edition. He writes 'A Possible Critique of Atomistic Concepts' and sends it to Friedrich Theodor Vischer.

1883: Rudolf Steiner completes his college studies and begins work on the Goethe project.

1884: First volume of Goethe's *Scientific Writings* (CW 1) appears (March). He lectures on Goethe and Lessing, and Goethe's approach to science. In July, he enters the household of Ladislaus and Pauline Specht as tutor to the four Specht boys. He will live there until 1890. At this time, he meets Josef Breuer (1842–1925), the co-author with Sigmund Freud of *Studies in Hysteria,* who is the Specht family doctor.

1885: While continuing to edit Goethe's writings, Rudolf Steiner reads deeply in contemporary philosophy (Eduard von Hartmann, Johannes Volkelt, and Richard Wahle, among others).

1886: May: Rudolf Steiner sends Kürschner the manuscript of *Outlines of Goethe's Theory of Knowledge* (CW 2), which appears in October, and which he sends out widely. He also meets the poet Marie Eugenie Delle Grazie and writes 'Nature and Our Ideals' for her. He attends her salon, where he meets many priests, theologians, and philosophers, who will become his friends. Meanwhile, the director of the Goethe Archive in Weimar requests his collaboration with the *Sophien* edition of Goethe's works, particularly the writings on colour.

1887: At the beginning of the year, Rudolf Steiner is very sick. As the year progresses and his health improves, he becomes increasingly 'a man of letters', lecturing, writing essays, and taking part in Austrian cultural life. In August–September, the second volume of Goethe's *Scientific Writings* appears.

1888: January–July: Rudolf Steiner assumes editorship of the 'German Weekly' *(Deutsche Wochenschrift*). He begins lecturing more intensively, giving, for example, a lecture titled 'Goethe as Father of a New Aesthetics'. He meets and becomes soul friends with Friedrich Eckstein (1861–1939), a vegetarian, philosopher of symbolism, alchemist, and musician, who will introduce him to various spiritual currents (including Theosophy) and with whom he will meditate and interpret esoteric and alchemical texts.

1889: Rudolf Steiner first reads Nietzsche *(Beyond Good and Evil).* He encounters Theosophy again and learns of Madame Blavatsky in the theosophical circle around Marie Lang (1858–1934). Here he also meets well-known figures of Austrian life, as well as esoteric figures like the occultist Franz Hartmann and Karl Leinigen-Billigen (translator of C.G. Harrison's *The Transcendental Universe).* During this period, Steiner first reads A.P. Sinnett's *Esoteric Buddhism* and Mabel Collins's *Light on the Path.* He also begins travelling, visiting Budapest, Weimar, and Berlin (where he meets philosopher Eduard von Hartmann).

1890: Rudolf Steiner finishes Volume 3 of Goethe's scientific writings. He begins his doctoral dissertation, which will become *Truth and Science* (CW 3). He also meets the poet and feminist Rosa Mayreder

(1858–1938), with whom he can exchange his most intimate thoughts. In September, Rudolf Steiner moves to Weimar to work in the Goethe-Schiller Archive.

1891: Volume 3 of the Kürschner edition of Goethe appears. Meanwhile, Rudolf Steiner edits Goethe's studies in mineralogy and scientific writings for the *Sophien* edition. He meets Ludwig Laistner of the Cotta Publishing Company, who asks for a book on the basic question of metaphysics. From this will result, ultimately, *The Philosophy of Freedom* (CW 4), which will be published not by Cotta but by Emil Felber. In October, Rudolf Steiner takes the oral exam for a doctorate in philosophy, mathematics, and mechanics at Rostock University, receiving his doctorate on the twenty-sixth. In November, he gives his first lecture on Goethe's 'Fairy Tale' in Vienna.

1892: Rudolf Steiner continues work at the Goethe-Schiller Archive and on his *Philosophy of Freedom. Truth and Science,* his doctoral dissertation, is published. Steiner undertakes to write Introductions to books on Schopenhauer and Jean Paul for Cotta. At year's end, he finds lodging with Anna Eunike, née Schulz (1853–1911), a widow with four daughters and a son. He also develops a friendship with Otto Erich Hartleben (1864–1905) with whom he shares literary interests.

1893: Rudolf Steiner begins his habit of producing many reviews and articles. In March, he gives a lecture titled 'Hypnotism, with Reference to Spiritism'. In September, volume 4 of the Kürschner edition is completed. In November, *The Philosophy of Freedom* appears. This year, too, he meets John Henry Mackay (1864–1933), the anarchist, and Max Stirner, a scholar and biographer.

1894: Rudolf Steiner meets Elisabeth Fürster Nietzsche, the philosopher's sister, and begins to read Nietzsche in earnest, beginning with the as yet unpublished *Antichrist.* He also meets Ernst Haeckel (1834–1919). In the fall, he begins to write *Nietzsche, A Fighter against His Time* (CW 5).

1895: May, *Nietzsche, A Fighter against His Time* appears.

1896: January 22: Rudolf Steiner sees Friedrich Nietzsche for the first and only time. Moves between the Nietzsche and the Goethe-Schiller Archives, where he completes his work before year's end. He falls out with Elisabeth Förster Nietzsche, thus ending his association with the Nietzsche Archive.

1897: Rudolf Steiner finishes the manuscript of *Goethe's Worldview* (CW 6). He moves to Berlin with Anna Eunike and begins editorship of the *Magazin für Literatur.* From now on, Steiner will write countless reviews, literary and philosophical articles, and so on. He begins lecturing at the 'Free Literary Society'. In September, he attends the Zionist Congress in Basel. He sides with Dreyfus in the Dreyfus affair.

1898: Rudolf Steiner is very active as an editor in the political, artistic, and theatrical life of Berlin. He becomes friendly with John Henry Mackay and poet Ludwig Jacobowski (1868–1900). He joins Jacobowski's circle of writers, artists, and scientists—'The Coming Ones' (*Die Kommenden*)—and contributes lectures to the group until 1903. He also lectures at the 'League for College Pedagogy'. He writes an article for Goethe's sesquicentennial, 'Goethe's Secret Revelation', on the 'Fairy Tale of the Green Snake and the Beautiful Lily'.

1898–99: 'This was a trying time for my soul as I looked at Christianity. . . . I was able to progress only by contemplating, by means of spiritual perception, the evolution of Christianity. . . . Conscious knowledge of real Christianity began to dawn in me around the turn of the century. This seed continued to develop. My soul trial occurred shortly before the beginning of the twentieth century. It was decisive for my soul's development that I stood spiritually before the Mystery of Golgotha in a deep and solemn celebration of knowledge.'

1899: Rudolf Steiner begins teaching and giving lectures and lecture cycles at the Workers' College, founded by Wilhelm Liebknecht (1826–1900). He will continue to do so until 1904. Writes: *Literature and Spiritual Life in the Nineteenth Century; Individualism in Philosophy; Haeckel and His Opponents; Poetry in the Present;* and begins what will become (fifteen years later) *The Riddles of Philosophy* (CW 18). He also meets many artists and writers, including Käthe Kollwitz, Stefan Zweig, and Rainer Maria Rilke. On October 31, he marries Anna Eunike.

1900: 'I thought that the turn of the century must bring humanity a new light. It seemed to me that the separation of human thinking and willing from the spirit had peaked. A turn or reversal of direction in human evolution seemed to me a necessity.' Rudolf Steiner finishes *World and Life Views in the Nineteenth Century* (the second part of what will become *The Riddles of Philosophy*) and dedicates it to Ernst Haeckel. It is published in March. He continues lecturing at *Die Kommenden,* whose leadership he assumes after the death of Jacobowski. Also, he gives the Gutenberg Jubilee lecture before 7,000 typesetters and printers. In September, Rudolf Steiner is invited by Count and Countess Brockdorff to lecture in the Theosophical Library. His first lecture is on Nietzsche. His second lecture is titled 'Goethe's Secret Revelation.' October 6, he begins a lecture cycle on the mystics that will become *Mystics after Modernism* (CW 7). November–December: 'Marie von Sivers appears in the audience. . . .' Also in November, Steiner gives his first lecture at the Giordano Bruno Bund (where he will continue to lecture until May, 1905). He speaks on Bruno and modern Rome, focusing on the importance of the philosophy of Thomas Aquinas as monism.

1901: In continual financial straits, Rudolf Steiner's early friends Moritz Zitter and Rosa Mayreder help support him. In October, he begins the lecture cycle *Christianity as Mystical Fact* (CW 8) at the Theosophical Library. In November, he gives his first 'theosophical lecture' on Goethe's 'Fairy Tale' in Hamburg at the invitation of Wilhelm Hubbe-Schleiden. He also attends a gathering to celebrate the founding of the Theosophical Society at Count and Countess Brockdorff's. He gives a lecture cycle, 'From Buddha to Christ,' for the circle of the *Kommenden*. November 17, Marie von Sivers asks Rudolf Steiner if Theosophy needs a Western–Christian spiritual movement (to complement Theosophy's Eastern emphasis). 'The question was posed. Now, following spiritual laws, I could begin to give an answer. . . .' In December, Rudolf Steiner writes his first article for a theosophical publication. At year's end, the Brockdorffs and possibly Wilhelm Hubbe-Schleiden ask Rudolf Steiner to join the Theosophical Society and undertake the leadership of the German section. Rudolf Steiner agrees, on the condition that Marie von Sivers (then in Italy) work with him.

1902: Beginning in January, Rudolf Steiner attends the opening of the Workers' School in Spandau with Rosa Luxemberg (1870–1919). January 17, Rudolf Steiner joins the Theosophical Society. In April, he is asked to become general secretary of the German Section of the Theosophical Society, and works on preparations for its founding. In July, he visits London for a theosophical congress. He meets Bertram Keightly, G.R.S. Mead, A.P. Sinnett, and Annie Besant, among others. In September, *Christianity as Mystical Fact* appears. In October, Rudolf Steiner gives his first public lecture on Theosophy ('Monism and Theosophy') to about three hundred people at the Giordano Bruno Bund. On October 19–21, the German Section of the Theosophical Society has its first meeting; Rudolf Steiner is the general secretary, and Annie Besant attends. Steiner lectures on practical karma studies. On October 23, Annie Besant inducts Rudolf Steiner into the Esoteric School of the Theosophical Society. On October 25, Steiner begins a weekly series of lectures: 'The Field of Theosophy'. During this year, Rudolf Steiner also first meets Ita Wegman (1876–1943), who will become his close collaborator in his final years.

1903: Rudolf Steiner holds about 300 lectures and seminars. In May, the first issue of the periodical *Luzifer* appears. In June, Rudolf Steiner visits London for the first meeting of the Federation of the European Sections of the Theosophical Society, where he meets Colonel Olcott. He begins to write *Theosophy* (CW 9).

1904: Rudolf Steiner continues lecturing at the Workers' College and elsewhere (about 90 lectures), while lecturing intensively all over Germany among theosophists (about 140 lectures). In February, he meets Carl Unger (1878–1929), who will become a member of the board of the Anthroposophical Society (1913). In March, he meets Michael Bauer (1871–1929), a Christian mystic, who will also be on the board. In May, *Theosophy* appears, with the dedication: 'To the spirit of Giordano Bruno'. Rudolf Steiner and Marie von Sivers visit London for meetings with Annie Besant. June: Rudolf Steiner and Marie von Sivers attend the meeting of the Federation of European Sections of the Theosophical Society in Amsterdam. In July, Steiner begins the articles in *Luzifer-Gnosis* that will become *How to Know Higher Worlds* (CW 10) and *Cosmic Memory* (CW 11). In September, Annie Besant visits Germany. In December, Steiner lectures on Freemasonry. He mentions the High Grade Masonry derived from John Yarker and represented by Theodore Reuss and Karl Kellner as a blank slate 'into which a good image could be placed'.

1905: This year, Steiner ends his non-theosophical lecturing activity. Supported by Marie von Sivers, his theosophical lecturing—both in public and in the Theosophical Society—increases significantly: 'The German Theosophical Movement is of exceptional importance.' Steiner recommends reading, among others, Fichte, Jacob Boehme, and Angelus Silesius. He begins to introduce Christian themes into Theosophy. He also begins to work with doctors (Felix Peipers and Ludwig Noll). In July, he is in London for the Federation of European Sections, where he attends a lecture by Annie Besant: 'I have seldom seen Mrs Besant speak in so inward and heartfelt a manner... Through Mrs Besant I have found the way to H.P. Blavatsky.' September to October, he gives a course of 31 lectures for a small group of esoteric students. In October, the annual meeting of the German Section of the Theosophical Society, which still remains very small, takes place. Rudolf Steiner reports membership has risen from 121 to 377 members. In November, seeking to establish esoteric 'continuity', Rudolf Steiner and Marie von Sivers participate in a 'Memphis-Misraim' Masonic ceremony. They pay 45 marks for membership. 'Yesterday, you saw how little remains of former esoteric institutions.' 'We are dealing only with a "framework" ... for the present, nothing lies behind it. The occult powers have completely withdrawn.'

1906: Expansion of theosophical work. Rudolf Steiner gives about 245 lectures, only 44 of which take place in Berlin. Cycles are given in Paris, Leipzig, Stuttgart, and Munich. Esoteric work also intensifies. Rudolf Steiner begins writing *An Outline of Esoteric Science* (CW 13).

In January, Rudolf Steiner receives permission (a patent) from the Great Orient of the Scottish A & A Thirty-Three Degree Rite of the Order of the Ancient Freemasons of the Memphis-Misraim Rite to direct a chapter under the name 'Mystica Aeterna.' This will become the 'Cognitive-Ritual Section' (also called 'Misraim Service') of the Esoteric School. (See: *Freemasonry and Ritual Work: The Misraim Service,* CW 265.) During this time, Steiner also meets Albert Schweitzer. In May, he is in Paris, where he visits Édouard Schuré. Many Russians attend his lectures (including Konstantin Balmont, Dimitri Mereszkovski, Zinaida Hippius, and Maximilian Woloshin). He attends the General Meeting of the European Federation of the Theosophical Society, at which Col Olcott is present for the last time. He spends the year's end in Venice and Rome, where he writes and works on his translation of H.P. Blavatsky's *Key to Theosophy.*

1907: Further expansion of the German Theosophical Movement according to the Rosicrucian directive to 'introduce spirit into the world'—in education, in social questions, in art, and in science. In February, Col Olcott dies in Adyar. Before he dies, Olcott indicates that 'the Masters' wish Annie Besant to succeed him: much politicking ensues. Rudolf Steiner supports Besant's candidacy. April–May: preparations for the Congress of the Federation of European Sections of the Theosophical Society—the great, watershed Whitsun 'Munich Congress,' attended by Annie Besant and others. Steiner decides to separate Eastern and Western (Christian–Rosicrucian) esoteric schools. He takes his esoteric school out of the Theosophical Society (Besant and Rudolf Steiner are 'in harmony' on this). Steiner makes his first lecture tours to Austria and Hungary. That summer, he is in Italy. In September, he visits Édouard Schuré, who will write the Introduction to the French edition of *Christianity as Mystical Fact* in Barr, Alsace. Rudolf Steiner writes the autobiographical statement known as the 'Barr Document.' In *Luzifer-Gnosis*, 'The Education of the Child' appears.

1908: The movement grows (membership: 1,150). Lecturing expands. Steiner makes his first extended lecture tour to Holland and Scandinavia, as well as visits to Naples and Sicily. Themes: St John's Gospel, the Apocalypse, Egypt, science, philosophy, and logic. *Luzifer-Gnosis* ceases publication. In Berlin, Marie von Sivers (with Johanna Mücke (1864–1949) forms the *Philosophisch-Theosophisch* (after 1915 *Philosophisch-Anthroposophisch) Verlag* to publish Steiner's work. Steiner gives lecture cycles titled *The Gospel of St John* (CW 103) and *The Apocalypse* (104).

1909: *An Outline of Esoteric Science* appears. Lecturing and travel continues. Rudolf Steiner's spiritual research expands to include the polarity of Lucifer and Ahriman; the work of great individualities in history; the Maitreya Buddha and the Bodhisattvas; spiritual economy (CW 109); the work of the spiritual hierarchies in heaven and on earth (CW 110). He also deepens and intensifies his research into the Gospels, giving lectures on the Gospel of St Luke (CW 114) with the first mention of two Jesus children. Meets and becomes friends with Christian Morgenstern (1871–1914). In April, he lays the foundation stone for the Malsch model—the building that will lead to the first Goetheanum. In May, the International Congress of the Federation of European Sections of the Theosophical Society takes place in Budapest. Rudolf Steiner receives the Subba Row medal for *How to Know Higher Worlds*. During this time, Charles W. Leadbeater discovers Jiddu Krishnamurti (1895–1986) and proclaims him the future 'world teacher,' the bearer of the Maitreya Buddha and the 'reappearing Christ.' In October, Steiner delivers seminal lectures on 'anthroposophy,' which he will try, unsuccessfully, to rework over the next years into the unfinished work, *Anthroposophy (A Fragment)* (CW 45).

1910: New themes: *The Reappearance of Christ in the Etheric* (CW 118); *The Fifth Gospel; The Mission of Folk Souls* (CW 121); *Occult History* (CW 126); the evolving development of etheric cognitive capacities. Rudolf Steiner continues his Gospel research with *The Gospel of St Matthew* (CW 123). In January, his father dies. In April, he takes a month-long trip to Italy, including Rome, Monte Cassino, and Sicily. He also visits Scandinavia again. July–August, he writes the first Mystery Drama, *The Portal of Initiation* (CW 14). In November, he gives 'psychosophy' lectures. In December, he submits 'On the Psychological Foundations and Epistemological Framework of Theosophy' to the International Philosophical Congress in Bologna.

1911: The crisis in the Theosophical Society deepens. In January, 'The Order of the Rising Sun,' which will soon become 'The Order of the Star in the East,' is founded for the coming world teacher, Krishnamurti. At the same time, Marie von Sivers, Rudolf Steiner's co-worker, falls ill. Fewer lectures are given, but important new ground is broken. In Prague, in March, Steiner meets Franz Kafka (1883–1924) and Hugo Bergmann (1883–1975). In April, he delivers his paper to the Philosophical Congress. He writes the second Mystery Drama, *The Soul's Probation* (CW 14). Also, while Marie von Sivers is convalescing, Rudolf Steiner begins work on *Calendar 1912/1913*, which will contain the 'Calendar of the Soul' meditations. On March 19, Anna (Eunike) Steiner dies. In September, Rudolf Steiner visits Einsiedeln, birthplace of Paracelsus. In December, Friedrich Rittelmeyer, future founder of The Christian Community, meets Rudolf Steiner. The *Johannes-Bauverein*, the 'building committee,' which would lead to the first Goetheanum (first planned for Munich), is also founded, and a preliminary committee for the founding of an independent association is created that, in the following year, will become the Anthroposophical Society. Important lecture cycles include *Occult Physiology* (CW 128); *Wonders of the World* (CW 129); *From Jesus to Christ* (CW 131). Other themes: esoteric Christianity; Christian Rosenkreutz; the spiritual guidance of humanity; the sense world and the world of the spirit.

1912: Despite the ongoing, now increasing crisis in the Theosophical Society, much is accomplished: *Calendar 1912/1913* is published; eurythmy is created; both the third Mystery Drama, *The Guardian of the Threshold* (CW 14) and *A Way of Self-Knowledge* (CW 16) are written. New (or renewed) themes included life between death and rebirth and karma and reincarnation. Other lecture cycles: *Spiritual Beings in the Heavenly Bodies and in the Kingdoms of Nature* (CW 136); *The Human Being in the Light of Occultism, Theosophy, and Philosophy* (CW 137); *The Gospel of St Mark* (CW 139); and *The Bhagavad Gita and the Epistles of Paul* (CW 142). On May 8, Rudolf Steiner celebrates White Lotus Day, H.P. Blavatsky's death day, which he had faithfully observed for the past decade, for the last time. In August, Rudolf Steiner suggests the 'independent association' be called the 'Anthroposophical Society.' In September, the first eurythmy course takes place. In October, Rudolf Steiner declines recognition of a Theosophical Society lodge dedicated to the Star of the East and decides to expel all Theosophical Society members belonging to the order. Also, with Marie von Sivers, he first visits Dornach, near Basel, Switzerland, and they stand on the hill where the Goetheanum will be built. In November, a Theosophical Society lodge is opened by direct mandate from Adyar (Annie Besant). In December, a meeting of the German section occurs at which it is decided that belonging to the Order of the Star of the East is incompatible with membership in the Theosophical Society. December 28: informal founding of the Anthroposophical Society in Berlin.

1913: Expulsion of the German section from the Theosophical Society. February 2–3: Foundation meeting of the Anthroposophical Society. Board members include: Marie von Sivers, Michael Bauer, and Carl Unger. September 20: Laying of the foundation stone for the *Johannes Bau* (Goetheanum) in Dornach. Building begins immediately. The fourth Mystery Drama, *The Soul's Awakening* (CW 14), is completed. Also: *The Threshold of the Spiritual World* (CW 147). Lecture cycles include: *The Bhagavad Gita and the Epistles of Paul* and *The Esoteric Meaning of the Bhagavad Gita* (CW 146), which the Russian philosopher Nikolai Berdyaev attends; *The Mysteries of the East and of Christianity* (CW 144); *The Effects of Esoteric Development* (CW 145); and *The Fifth Gospel* (CW 148). In May, Rudolf Steiner is in London and Paris, where anthroposophical work continues.

1914: Building continues on the *Johannes Bau* (Goetheanum) in Dornach, with artists and co-workers from seventeen nations. The general assembly of the Anthroposophical Society takes place. In May, Rudolf Steiner visits Paris, as well as Chartres Cathedral. June 28: assassination in Sarajevo ('Now the catastrophe has happened!'). August 1: War is declared. Rudolf Steiner returns to Germany from Dornach—he will travel back and forth. He writes the last chapter of *The Riddles of Philosophy*. Lecture cycles include: *Human and Cosmic Thought* (CW 151); *Inner Being of Humanity between Death and a New Birth* (CW 153); *Occult Reading and Occult Hearing* (CW 156). December 24: marriage of Rudolf Steiner and Marie von Sivers.

1915: Building continues. Life after death becomes a major theme, also art. Writes: *Thoughts during a Time of War* (CW 24). Lectures include: *The Secret of Death* (CW 159); *The Uniting of Humanity through the Christ Impulse* (CW 165).

1916: Rudolf Steiner begins work with Edith Maryon (1872–1924) on the sculpture 'The Representative of Humanity' ('The Group'—Christ, Lucifer, and Ahriman). He also works with the alchemist Alexander von Bernus on the quarterly *Das Reich*. He writes *The Riddle of Humanity* (CW 20). Lectures include: *Necessity and Freedom in World History and Human Action* (CW 166); *Past and Present in the Human Spirit* (CW 167); *The Karma of Vocation* (CW 172); *The Karma of Untruthfulness* (CW 173).

1917: Russian Revolution. The U.S. enters the war. Building continues. Rudolf Steiner delineates the idea of the 'threefold nature of the human being' (in a public lecture March 15) and the 'threefold nature of the social organism' (hammered out in May–June with the help of Otto von Lerchenfeld and Ludwig Polzer-Hoditz in the form of two documents titled *Memoranda,* which were distributed in high places). August–September: Rudolf Steiner writes *The Riddles of the Soul* (CW 20). Also: commentary on 'The Chymical Wedding of Christian Rosenkreutz' for Alexander Bernus (Das *Reich* ). Lectures include: *The Karma of Materialism* (CW 176); *The Spiritual Background of the Outer World: The Fall of the Spirits of Darkness* (CW 177).

1918: March 18: peace treaty of Brest-Litovsk—'Now everything will truly enter chaos! What is needed is cultural renewal.' June: Rudolf Steiner visits Karlstein (Grail) Castle outside Prague. Lecture cycle: *From Symptom to Reality in Modern History* (CW 185). In mid-November, Emil Molt, of the Waldorf-Astoria Cigarette Company, has the idea of founding a school for his workers' children.

1919: Focus on the threefold social organism: tireless travel, countless lectures, meetings, and publications. At the same time, a new public stage of Anthroposophy emerges as cultural renewal begins.

The coming years will see initiatives in pedagogy, medicine, pharmacology, and agriculture. January 27: threefold meeting: 'We must first of all, with the money we have, found free schools that can bring people what they need.' February: first public eurythmy performance in Zurich. Also: 'Appeal to the German People' (CW 24), circulated March 6 as a newspaper insert. In April, *Towards Social Renewal* (CW 23) appears—'perhaps the most widely read of all books on politics appearing since the war'. Rudolf Steiner is asked to undertake the 'direction and leadership' of the school founded by the Waldorf-Astoria Company. Rudolf Steiner begins to talk about the 'renewal' of education. May 30: a building is selected and purchased for the future Waldorf School. August–September, Rudolf Steiner gives a lecture course for Waldorf teachers, *The Foundations of Human Experience (Study of Man)* (CW 293). September 7: Opening of the first Waldorf School. December (into January): first science course, the *Light Course* (CW 320).

1920: The Waldorf School flourishes. New threefold initiatives. Founding of limited companies *Der Kommende Tag* and *Futurum A.G.* to infuse spiritual values into the economic realm. Rudolf Steiner also focuses on the sciences. Lectures: *Introducing Anthroposophical Medicine* (CW 312); *The Warmth Course* (CW 321); *The Boundaries of Natural Science* (CW 322); *The Redemption of Thinking* (CW 74). February: Johannes Werner Klein—later a co-founder of The Christian Community—asks Rudolf Steiner about the possibility of a 'religious renewal,' a 'Johannine church.' In March, Rudolf Steiner gives the first course for doctors and medical students. In April, a divinity student asks Rudolf Steiner a second time about the possibility of religious renewal. September 27–October 16: anthroposophical 'university course.' December: lectures titled *The Search for the New Isis* (CW 202).

1921: Rudolf Steiner continues his intensive work on cultural renewal, including the uphill battle for the threefold social order. 'University' arts, scientific, theological, and medical courses include: *The Astronomy Course* (CW 323); *Observation, Mathematics, and Scientific Experiment* (CW 324); the *Second Medical Course* (CW 313); *Colour*. In June and September–October, Rudolf Steiner also gives the first two 'priests' courses' (CW 342 and 343). The 'youth movement' gains momentum. Magazines are founded: *Die Drei* (January), and—under the editorship of Albert Steffen (1884–1963)—the weekly, *Das Goetheanum* (August). In February–March, Rudolf Steiner takes his first trip outside Germany since the war (Holland). On April 7, Steiner receives a letter regarding 'religious renewal,' and May 22–23, he agrees to address the question in a practical way. In June, the Klinical-Therapeutic Institute opens in Arlesheim under the direction of Dr Ita Wegman. In August, the

Chemical-Pharmaceutical Laboratory opens in Arlesheim (Oskar Schmiedel and Ita Wegman are directors). The Clinical Therapeutic Institute is inaugurated in Stuttgart (Dr Ludwig Noll is director); also the Research Laboratory in Dornach (Ehrenfried Pfeiffer and Gunther Wachsmuth are directors). In November–December, Rudolf Steiner visits Norway.

1922: The first half of the year involves very active public lecturing (thousands attend); in the second half, Rudolf Steiner begins to withdraw and turn toward the Society—'The Society is asleep.' It is 'too weak' to do what is asked of it. The businesses—*Der Kommende Tag* and *Futurum A.G.*—fail. In January, with the help of an agent, Steiner undertakes a twelve-city German lecture tour, accompanied by eurythmy performances. In two weeks he speaks to more than 2,000 people. In April, he gives a 'university course' in The Hague. He also visits England. In June, he is in Vienna for the East–West Congress. In August–September, he is back in England for the Oxford Conference on Education. Returning to Dornach, he gives the lectures *Philosophy, Cosmology, and Religion* (CW 215), and gives the third priests' course (CW 344). On September 16, The Christian Community is founded. In October–November, Steiner is in Holland and England. He also speaks to the youth: *The Youth Course* (CW 217). In December, Steiner gives lectures titled *The Origins of Natural Science* (CW 326), and *Humanity and the World of Stars: The Spiritual Communion of Humanity* (CW 219). December 31: Fire at the Goetheanum, which is destroyed.

1923: Despite the fire, Rudolf Steiner continues his work unabated. A very hard year. Internal dispersion, dissension, and apathy abound. There is conflict—between old and new visions—within the Society. A wake-up call is needed, and Rudolf Steiner responds with renewed lecturing vitality. His focus: the spiritual context of human life; initiation science; the course of the year; and community building. As a foundation for an artistic school, he creates a series of pastel sketches. Lecture cycles: *The Anthroposophical Movement; Initiation Science* (CW 227) (in Wales at the Penmaenmawr Summer School); *The Four Seasons and the Archangels* (CW 229); *Harmony of the Creative Word* (CW 230); *The Supersensible Human* (CW 231), given in Holland for the founding of the Dutch Society. On November 10, in response to the failed Hitler-Ludendorff putsch in Munich, Steiner closes his Berlin residence and moves the *Philosophisch-Anthroposophisch Verlag* (Press) to Dornach. On December 9, Steiner begins the serialization of his *Autobiography: The Course of My Life* (CW 28) in *Das Goetheanum*. It will continue to appear weekly, without a break, until his death. Late December–early January: Rudolf Steiner re-founds the Anthroposophical Society (about 12,000 members internationally) and takes over its leadership. The new board members are: Marie Steiner, Ita Wegman, Albert Steffen, Elisabeth Vreede, and Gunther Wachsmuth. (See *The Christmas Meeting for the Founding of the General Anthroposophical Society*, CW 260.) Accompanying lectures: *Mystery Knowledge and Mystery Centres* (CW 232); *World History in the Light of Anthroposophy* (CW 233). December 25: the Foundation Stone is laid (in the hearts of members) in the form of the 'Foundation Stone Meditation.'

1924: January 1: having founded the Anthroposophical Society and taken over its leadership, Rudolf Steiner has the task of 'reforming' it. The process begins with a weekly newssheet ('What's Happening in the Anthroposophical Society') in which Rudolf Steiner's 'Letters to Members' and 'Anthroposophical Leading Thoughts' appear (CW 26). The next step is the creation of a new esoteric class, the 'first class' of the 'University of Spiritual Science' (which was to have been followed, had Rudolf Steiner lived longer, by two more advanced classes). Then comes a new language for Anthroposophy—practical, phenomenological, and direct; and Rudolf Steiner creates the model for the second Goetheanum. He begins the series of extensive 'karma' lectures (CW 235–40); and finally, responding to needs, he creates two new initiatives: biodynamic agriculture and curative education. After the middle of the year, rumours begin to circulate regarding Steiner's health. Lectures: January–February, *Anthroposophy* (CW 234); February: *Tone Eurythmy* (CW 278); June: *The Agriculture Course* (CW 327); June–July: *Speech Eurythmy* (CW 279); *Curative Education* (CW 317); August: (England, 'Second International Summer School'), *Initiation Consciousness: True and False Paths in Spiritual Investigation* (CW 243); September: *Pastoral Medicine* (CW 318). On September 26, for the first time, Rudolf Steiner cancels a lecture. On September 28, he gives his last lecture. On September 29, he withdraws to his studio in the carpenter's shop; now he is definitively ill. Cared for by Ita Wegman, he continues working, however, and writing the weekly instalments of his *Autobiography* and *Letters to the Members/Leading Thoughts* (CW 26).

1925: Rudolf Steiner, while continuing to work, continues to weaken. He finishes *Extending Practical Medicine* (CW 27) with Ita Wegman. On March 30, around ten in the morning, Rudolf Steiner dies.

# Index